James Finn

Byeways in Palestine

James Finn

Byeways in Palestine

ISBN/EAN: 9783337279844

Printed in Europe, USA, Canada, Australia, Japan

Cover: Foto ©Andreas Hilbeck / pixelio.de

More available books at **www.hansebooks.com**

BYEWAYS IN PALESTINE.

BY

JAMES FINN, M.R.A.S.,
AND MEMBER OF THE ASIATIC SOCIETY OF FRANCE,
LATE HER MAJESTY'S CONSUL FOR JERUSALEM AND PALESTINE.

"The land, which we passed through to search it, is an exceeding good land."—NUMB. XIV 7.

LONDON:
JAMES NISBET & CO., 21 BERNERS STREET.
MDCCCLXXVII.

Ballantyne Press
BALLANTYNE, HANSON AND CO.
EDINBURGH AND LONDON

To His Excellency

Right Hon. Francis Lord Napier, K.T.,

&c. &c. &c.,

Governor of the Presidency of Madras,

This little Volume

is inscribed,

in grateful acknowledgment of kindness

received in

Jerusalem and elsewhere.

BY THE AUTHOR.

London, 1867.

PREFACE.

THESE papers on "Byeways in Palestine" are compiled from notes of certain journeys made during many years' residence in that country; omitting the journeys made upon beaten roads, and through the principal towns, for the mere reason that they were such.

Just what met the eye and ear was jotted down, and is now revised after a lapse of time, without indulging much in meditation or reflection; these are rather suggested by the occurrences, that they may be followed out by the reader. Inasmuch, however, as the incidents relate to out-of-the-way places, and various seasons of the year, they may be found to contain an interest peculiar to themselves, and the account of them may not interfere with any other book on Palestine.

I may state that, not being a professed investigator. I carried with me no scientific instruments, except sometimes a common thermometer: I had no leisure for making excavations, for taking angles with a theodolite, or attending to the delicate care of any kind of barometer, being employed on my proper business.

Riding by night or by day, in the heat of Syrian summer, or through snows and piercing winds of winter on the mountains, I enjoyed the pure climate for its own sake. Moreover, I lived among the people, holding intercourse with peasants in villages, with Bedaween in deserts, and with Turkish governors in towns, or dignified Druses in the Lebanon, and slept in native dwellings of all qualities, as well as in convents of different sects: in the open air at the foot of a tree, or in a village mosque—in a cavern by the highway side, or beneath cliffs near the Dead Sea: although more commonly within my own tent, accompanied by native servants with a small canteen.

Sad cogitations would arise while traversing, hour after hour, the neglected soil, or passing by desolated villages which bear names of immense antiquity, and which stand as memorials of miraculous events which took place for our instruction and for that of all succeding ages; and then, even while looking forward to a better time to come, the heart would sigh as the expression was uttered, "How long?"

These notices will show that the land is one of remarkable fertility wherever cultivated, even in a slight degree—witness the vast wheat-plains of the south; and is one of extreme beauty—witness the green hill-country of the north; although such qualities are by no means confined to those districts. Thus it is not necessary, it is not just, that believers in the Bible, in order to hold fast their confidence in its predictions for the future, should rush into the extreme of pronouncing the Holy Land to be cursed in its present capabilities. It is verily and indeed cursed in its government, and in its want of population; but still the soil is that of "a land which the Lord thy God careth for." There is a deep meaning in the words, "The earth is the Lord's," when applied to that peculiar country; for it is a reserved property, an estate in abeyance, and not even in a subordinate sense can it be the fief of the men whom it eats up. (Numb. xiii. 32, and Ezek. xxxvi. 13, 14.) I have seen enough to convince me that astonishing will be the amount of its produce, and the rapidity also, when the obstacles now existing are removed.

With respect to antiquarian researches, let me express my deep interest in the works now undertaken under the Palestine Exploration Fund. My happiness, while residing in the country, would have been much augmented had such operations been at that time, *i.e.*, between 1846 and 1863, commenced in Jerusalem or elsewhere in the Holy Land.

J. F.

CONTENTS.

	PAGE
I. OVER THE JORDAN, AND RETURN BY THE WEST,	1
II. NORTHWARDS TO BEISÁN, KADIS, ANTIPATRIS, &C.,	85
III. SOUTHWARDS ON THE PHILISTINE PLAIN AND ITS SEA COAST,	144
IV. HEBRON TO BEERSHEBA, AND HEBRON TO JAFFA,	184
V. THE LAND OF BENJAMIN,	199
VI. SEBUSTIEH TO CAIFFA,	214
VII. ESDRAELON PLAIN AND ITS VICINITY,	226
VIII. BELÂD BESHÂRAH,	253
IX. UPPER GALILEE—FOREST SCENERY,	264
X. TEMPLE OF BAAL AND SEPULCHRE OF PHŒNICIA,	283
XI. JERUSALEM TO PETRA, AND RETURN BY THE DEAD SEA,	289
XII. ACROSS THE LEBANON—(THREE PARTS,)	347
XIII. NORTH-WEST OF THE DEAD SEA,	414
XIV. SOBA,	423
XV. THE TWO BAIT SAHHOORS IDENTIFIED,	428
XVI. THE DAKOOSH COTTAGE,	435
APPENDIX A,	453
APPENDIX B,	454
INDEX OF PLACES,	461

BYEWAYS IN PALESTINE.

I.

OVER THE JORDAN AND RETURN BY THE WEST.

WE were a dozen Englishmen, including three clergymen, undertaking the above journey, accompanied by the large train of servants, interpreters, and muleteers usually required for travelling in the East. And it was on Wednesday, the 9th day of May 1855, that we started. This was considered almost late in the season for such an enterprise. The weather was hot, chiefly produced by a strong shirocco wind at the time; and, in crossing over the shoulder of the Mount of Olives, we found the country people beginning their harvest at Bethany.

We were of course escorted by a party of Arab guides, partly villagers of either *Abu Dis* or *Selwan*, (Siloam,) and partly of those Ghawârineh Arabs not deserving the appellation of Bedaween, who live around and about Jericho. These people, of both classes, form a partnership for convoy of travellers to the Jordan under arrangements made at the consulate. Without them it would be impossible either to find the way to Jericho and the river, or to pass along the deserted road, for there are always out-lookers about the tops of the hills to give notice that you are without an escort, and you would consequently still find that travellers may "fall among thieves" between Jerusalem and Jericho; besides that, on descending to the plain of Jericho you would certainly become the prey of other Arabs of real tribes, ever passing about there—including most probably the 'Adwân, to whose hospitality, however, we were now about to commit ourselves. To all this must be added, that no other Arabs dare undertake to convoy travellers upon that road; the Taámra to the south have long felt their exclusion from it to be a great grievance, as the gains derived from the employment of escorting Europeans are very alluring.

We had with us a deputed commissioner from the 'Adwân, namely, Shaikh Fendi, a brother of Shaikh 'Abdu'l 'Azeez. He was delighted with the refreshment of eating a cucumber, when we rested by the wayside to eat oranges—the delicious produce of Jaffa.

Passing the *Fountain of the Apostles*, (so called,) we jogged along a plain road till we reached a booth for selling cups of coffee, at the divergence of the road to Nebi Moosa, (the reputed sepulchre of the prophet Moses, according to the Mohammedans,) then up an ascent still named *Tela'at ed Dum*, which is certainly the ancient* Adummim, (Joshua xv. 7)—probably so called from broad bands of *red* among the strata of the rocks. Here there are also curious wavy lines of brown flint, undulating on a large scale among the limestone cliffs. This phenomenon is principally to be seen near the ruined and deserted Khan, or eastern lodging-place, situated at about half the distance of our journey. The name is *Khatroon*.

As we proceeded, our escort, mostly on foot, went on singing merrily, and occasionally bringing us tufts of scented wild plants found in crevices by the roadside. Then we came to long remains of an ancient water conduit, leading to ruins of a small convent. In a few minutes after the latter, we found ourselves looking down a fearfully deep precipice of rocks on our left hand, with a stream flowing at the bottom, apparently very narrow indeed, and the sound of it scarcely audible. This is the brook *Kelt*, by some supposed to be the *Cherith* of Elijah's history. Suddenly we were on the brow of a deep descent, with the Ghôr, or Jericho plain, and the Dead Sea spread out below. In going down, we had upon our left hand considerable fragments of ancient masonry, containing lines of Roman reticulated brickwork.

* This is one of the frequent instances of Arabic local names preserving the sound, while departing from the signification.

It was now evening; a breeze, but not a cool one, blowing; and we left aside for this time the pretty camping station of Elisha's Fountain, because we had business to transact at the village of Er-Rihha, (or Jericho.) There accordingly our tents were pitched; and in a circle at our doors were attentive listeners to a narration of the events of Lieut. Molyneux's Expedition on the Jordan and Dead Sea in 1847.

Thermometer after sunset, inside the tent, at 89° Fahrenheit. Sleep very much disturbed by small black sandflies and ants.

Thursday, 10th.--Thermometer at 76° before sunrise. The scene around us was animated and diversified; but several of us had been accustomed to Oriental affairs—some for a good many years; and some were even familiar with the particular localities and customs of this district. Others were young in age, and fresh to the country; expressing their wonderment at finding themselves so near to scenes read of from infancy—scarcely believing that they had at length approached near to

"That bituminous lake
Where Sodom stood,"

and filled with joyous expectation at the visit so soon to be made to the Jordan, and beyond it. Some were quoting Scripture; some quoting poetry; and others taking particular notice of the wild Arabs, who were by this time increasing in number about us,—their spears, their mares, their guttural language, and not less the barren desert scene before us, being objects of romantic interest.

At length all the tents and luggage were loaded on the mules, and ten men of the village were hired for helping to convey our property across the river; and we went forward over the strange plain, which is neither desert sand, as in Africa, nor wilderness of creeping plants and flowers, as on the way to Petra, but a puzzling, though monotonous, succession of low eminences,—of a nature something like rotten chalk ground, if there be such a thing in existence,—between which eminences we had to wind our way, until we reached the border of tamarisk-trees, large reeds, willow, aspen, &c., that fringes the river; invisible till one reaches close upon it.

At the bathing (or baptism) place of the Greeks, northwards from that of the Latins, to which English travellers are usually conducted, we had to cross, by swimming as we could.* King David, on his return from exile, had a ferry-boat to carry over his household, but we had none. Probably, on his escaping from Absalom, he crossed as we did.

The middle part of the river was still too deep for mere fording. Horses and men had to swim; so the gentlemen sat still on their saddles, with

* This ford was called *Ghoranêyeh.* The other is called *El Meshraa'.*

their feet put up on the necks of their horses, which were led by naked swimming Arabs in the water holding the bridles, one on each side.

Baggage was carried over mostly on the animals; but had to be previously adjusted and tightened, so as to be least liable to get wetted. Small parcels were carried over on the heads of the swimmers. These all carried their own clothes in that manner. One of the luggage mules fell with his load in the middle of the stream. It was altogether a lively scene. Our Arabs were much darker over the whole body than I had expected to find them; and the 'Adwân have long plaits of hair hanging on the shoulders when the *kefieh*, or coloured head-dress, is removed. The horses and beasts of burden were often restive in mid-current, and provoked a good deal of merriment. Some of the neighbouring camps having herds of cattle, sent them to drink and to cool themselves in the river, as the heat of the day increased. Their drivers urged them in, and then enjoyed the fun of keeping them there by swimming round and round them. One cow was very nearly lost, however, being carried away rapidly and helplessly in the direction of the Dead Sea, but she was recovered. The Jericho people returned home, several of them charged with parting letters addressed to friends in Jerusalem; and we were left reposing, literally reposing, on the eastern bank,—the English chatting happily; the Arabs smoking or sleeping under shade of trees;

pigeons cooing among the thick covert, and the Jordan nightingale soothing us occasionally, with sometimes a hawk or an eagle darting along the sky; while the world-renowned river rolled before our eyes.

"Labitur et labetur in omne volubilis ævum."

The novelty of the scenes, and the brilliancy of the atmosphere, as well the vivacity of the recent transactions in "passing over Jordan," had their duly buoyant effect upon youthful persons,—who were, however, not forgetful of past events in these places belonging to sacred history.

The baggage went on; but, as the appointed halting-place was only about two hours distant, we remained enjoying ourselves as we were during most of the day.

Among our novel friends is an Arab hero named *Gublân*, as they pronounce it here, (but it is really the Turkish word *Kaplân*, meaning *Tiger*,) and his uncle, old 'Abdu'l 'Azeez. About three years before, Gublân had been attacked by Government soldiers at Jericho. He made a feigned retreat, and, leading them into the thickets of Neb'k trees, suddenly wheeled round and killed six of them. The humbled Government force retired, and the dead were buried, by having a mound of earth piled over them. Of course, such an incident was never reported to the Sublime Invincible Porte at Constantinople; but it was a curious coincidence, that this very morning, amid our circle before the tents, after breakfast and close to that mound, we had Gublân, 'Abdu'l 'Azeez, and the Turkish Aga of the present time, all peaceably smoking pipes together in our company.

Among our gentlemen we had a man of fortune and literary attainments, who had been in Algiers, and now amused himself with dispensing with servants or interpreters—speaking some Arabic. He brought but very light luggage. This he placed upon a donkey, and drove it himself—wearing Algerine town costume. The Bedaween, however, as I need scarcely say, did not mistake him for an Oriental.

Moving forward in the afternoon, we were passing over the *Plains of Moab*, "on this [east] side Jordan by Jericho"—where Balaam, son of Beor, saw, from the heights above, all Israel encamped, and cried out, " How goodly are thy tents, O Jacob! and thy tabernacles, O Israel! As the valleys are they spread forth, as gardens by the river's side, as the trees of lign-aloes which the Lord hath planted, and as cedar-trees beside the waters. . . . Blessed is he that blesseth thee, and cursed is he that curseth thee," (Num. xxii. 1, and xxiv. 5, 6, 9.) This territory is also called the *Land of Moab*, where the second covenant was made with the people by the ministry of Moses—the one " beside the covenant which he made with them in Horeb."

Our ride was a gradual ascent; and after some

time we were met by young 'Ali, the favourite son of the principal Shaikh Dëâb, (Wolf,) with a small but chosen escort, sent on by his father to welcome us. We saw a good deal of corn land, and people reaping their harvest. This belongs to two or three scattered villages about there, under the immediate protection of the Dëâb 'Adwân. The Arabs, however, in this part of the world, do condescend to countenance and even to profit by agriculture, for they buy slaves to sow and reap for them.

In two hours and a half from the Jordan we came to our halting-place, at a spot called *Cuferain*, ("two villages")—the Kiriathaim of Jer. xlviii. 23—at the foot of the mountain, with a strong stream of water rushing past us. No sign, however, of habitations: only, at a little distance to the south, were ruins of a village called *Er Ram*, (a very common name in Palestine; but this is not Ramoth-Gilead;) and at half an hour to the north was an inhabited village called *Nimrin*, from which the stream flowed to us.—See Jer. xlviii. 34: "The waters of Nimrin shall be desolate."

We had a refreshing breeze from the north, which is justly counted a luxury in summer time. The shaikhs came and had coffee with me. They said that on the high summits we shall have cooler temperature than in Jerusalem, which is very probable.

After dinner I sat at my tent-door, by the rivulet side, looking southwards over the Dead Sea, and to the west over the line of the promised land of Canaan, which I had never before had an opportunity of seeing in that manner, although the well-known verse had been often repeated in England—

> "Oh could I stand where Moses stood,
>   And view the landscape o'er,
> Not Death's cold stream nor Jordan's flood
> Should fright me from the shore."

I then read over to myself in Arabic, the Psalms for the evening service—namely, liii., liv., and lv.

About sunset there was an alarm that a lad who had accompanied us as a servant from Jerusalem was missing ever since we left the Jordan. Horsemen were sent in every direction in search of him. It was afterwards discovered that he had returned to Jericho.

At about a hundred yards south of us was a valley called *Se'eer*, (its brook, however, comes down from the north)—abounding in fine rosy oleander shrubs.

During the night the water near us seemed alive with croaking frogs. Last night we had the sand-flies to keep us awake.

Friday, 11*th*.—Thermometer 66° before sunrise. My earliest looks were towards Canaan, "that goodly land"—"the hills, from which cometh my help." How keen must have been the feeling of his state of exile when David was driven to this side the river!

Before breakfast I bathed in the Se'eer, among bushes of oleander and the strong-scented *ghar*— a purple-spiked flower always found adjoining to or in water-beds. Then read my Arabic Psalms as usual.

Before starting, young 'Ali and his party asked us all for presents, and got none. We gave answer unanimously that we meant to give presents to his father when we should see him. Strange how depraved the Arab mind becomes on this matter of asking for gifts wherever European travellers are found!—so different from the customs of ancient times, and it is not found in districts off the common tracks of resort.

Our road lay up the hills, constantly growing more steep and precipitous, and occasionally winding between large rocks, which were often overgrown with honeysuckle in full luxuriance. The Arabs scrambled like wild animals over the rocks, and brought down very long streamers of honeysuckle, Luwâyeh, as they call it, which they wound round and round the necks of our horses, and generally got piastres for doing so. About two-thirds of the distance u· the ascent we rested, in order to relieve the animals, or to sketch views, or to enjoy the glorious scenery that lay extended below us—comprising the Dead Sea, the line of the river trees, Jericho, the woods of Elisha's Fountain, and the hills towards Jerusalem. The Bedaween have eyes like eagles; and some avouched that they could see the Mount of Olives, and the minaret upon its summit. They indicated to us the positions of Es-Salt and of Heshbân.

We had now almost attained a botanical region resembling that of the Jerusalem elevation, instead of the Indian vegetation upon the Jordan plain; only there was *ret'm* (the juniper of 1 Kings xix. 4) to be found, with pods in seed at that season; but we had also our long accustomed terebinth and arbutus, with honeysuckle and pink ground-convolvulus. The rocks were variegated with streaks of pink, purple, orange, and yellow, as at Khatroon, on the Jerusalem road. Partridges were clucking among the bushes; and the bells on the necks of our mules lulled us with their sweet chime, as the animals strolled browsing around in the gay sunshine.

When we moved forward once more, it was along paths of short zigzags between cliffs, so that our procession was constantly broken into small pieces. At length we lost sight of the Ghôr and the Dead Sea; and after some time traversing miles of red and white cistus, red everlasting, and fragrant thyme and sage, with occasional terebinth-trees festooned with honeysuckle, we came upon a district covered with millions, or billions, or probably trillions, of locusts, not fully grown, and only taking short flights; but they greatly annoyed our horses. My choice Arab, being at that time ridden by my servant, fairly bolted away with fright for a considerable distance.

At length we halted at a small spring oozing from the soil of the field. The place was called *Hheker Zaboot*—a pretty place, and cuckoos on the trees around us; only the locusts were troublesome.

'Abdu'l 'Azeez proposed that instead of going at once to Ammon, we should make a detour by Heshbon and Elealeh, on the way to his encampment. To this we all assented.

During the ride forward the old shaikh kept close to me, narrating incidents of his life,—such as his last year's losses by the Beni Sukh'r, who plundered him of all his flocks and herds, horses, tents, and even most of his clothing,—then described the march of Ibrahim Pasha's army in their disastrous attempt upon Kerak: also some of the valiant achievements of his kinsman Gublân; and then proceeding to witticism, gave me his etymological origin of the name of Hhesbân—namely, that, on the subsiding of the great deluge, the first object that Noah perceived was that castle, perched as it is upon a lofty peak; whereupon he exclaimed, *Hhus'n bân*—"a castle appears!" I wish I could recollect more of his tales.

After passing through romantic scenery of rocks and evergreen trees, at a sudden turn of the road we came to large flocks and herds drinking, or couched beside a copious stream of water gushing from near the foot of a rocky hill. This they called '*Ain Hhesbân;* and told us that the Egyptian army above alluded to, twenty thousand in number, passed the night there before arriving at Kerak. To many of them it was their last night on earth.

There were remains of large masonry lying about, and the scene was truly beautiful—to which the bells of the goats and cows added a charming musical effect.

I asked an Arab, who was bathing in a pool, where he had come from, and he sulkily answered, "From t' other end of the world!" And I suppose he was right in saying so, for what meaning could he attach to the designation, *the world*. He must have meant the world of his own experience, or that of his tribe, or his parents—probably extending to the end of the Dead Sea in one direction, to the Lake of Tiberias in another; to the Mediterranean in the west, and in the east to the wilds unknown beyond the road of the Hhâj pilgrimage. "From the other end of the world," quoth he, the companion of a shepherd boy with his flute, at a mountain spring, pitching pebbles at the sheep of his flock to keep them from wandering away over their extent of "the world."

As we proceeded, there were several other streams issuing from the hills, some of them falling in pretty cascades into thickets of oleander below. All these meeting together, formed a line of river flowing between grassy banks—near which we saw considerable remains of water-mills, not of great antiquity.

Next we reached two small forts: the one upon our side the stream they called *Shuneh*, (the usual name used for that kind of building;) the other was across the water, and they called it *Shefa 'Amer*. I should wonder if our guides knew the existence of the town called *Shefa 'Amer*, near Caiffa. They told us that both these forts had been erected by Dëâb's grandfather, but this is incredible.

Near the Shuneh I observed a very large sarcophagus, cut in the solid rock, but not so far finished as to allow of its being removed. In the court-yard there was nothing remarkable. There were, however, some ancient rabbeted stones lying near. Here I may remark, with respect to the sarcophagus, that such things are rare on the east of the Jordan, or anywhere else so far to the south. There are two lids of such lying on the plain of Sharon, alongside the Jaffa road from Jerusalem; and the next southernmost one that I know of (excepting those at Jerusalem) is an ornamented lid, near Sebustieh, the ancient Samaria; but they abound in Phœnicia.

Forward again we went, higher and higher, with wild flowers in profusion, and birds caroling all around. Then literally climbing up a mountain side, we came to a cleft in a precipice, which they called *El Buaib*, (the little gate,) with unmistakeable marks of ancient cuttings about there. Traversing a fine plain of wheat, we at length reached the ancient city of Heshbon, with its acropolis of temple and castle.

That plain would be fine exercise-ground for the cavalry of Sihon, king of the Amorites. Fresh, and almost chilly, was the mountain air; but the sky rather cloudy.

How magnificent was the prospect over to Canaan! We were all persuaded that the Mount of Olives would be visible thence on a fine day; and I have no doubt whatever that the site on which we were standing is that peak—the only peak breaking the regular outline of the Moab mountains which is seen from Jerusalem.

We scattered ourselves about in several groups among pavements and columns of temples, (the most perfect of which are in the Acropolis,) sepulchres, cisterns, and quarries, picking up fragments of pottery, with some pattern work (not highly ornamental, however) upon them, and tesseræ or the cubes of tesselated pavement, such as may be found all over Palestine. The Bedaween call them *muzzateem* or *muzzameet* indifferently. There were some good Corinthian capitals, fragments of cornices, and portions of semicircular arches, and pieces of walls that had been repaired at different periods. I entered one rock-hewn sepulchre which contained seven small chambers; six of these had been evidently broken into by main force, the seventh was still closed. This was S.W. of the Acropolis.

All the works or ornamentations above ground were of Greek or Roman construction, but we found no inscriptions or coins. Heshbon must have been at all periods a strong place for defence, but with an unduly large proportion of ornamentation to the small size of the city according to modern ideas. Before leaving this site, far inferior to 'Ammân, as we found afterwards, I got the Arabs around me upon a rising ground, and, with a compass in hand, wrote down from their dictation the names of sites visible to their sharp eyesight :—

To		To	
S.S.W.	Umm Sheggar.	S.E.S.	Kustul.
,,	Neba (Nebo?).	S.E.	Umm el 'Aamed.
,,	Main.	,,	Khan em Meshettah.
S.	Medeba.	,,	Jâwah.
S.E.S.	Ekfairat (Kephiroth ?).	,,	Kuriet es Sook.
,,	Jelool.	E.	Samek.
,,	Umm er Rumâneh.	E.E.N.	Ela'âl.
,,	Zubairah.	N.	Es-Salt.
,,	Manjah.		(The town not visible.)

These must have been the places that "stood under the shadow of Heshbon," (Jer. xlviii. 45.) One of them at least appears in Joshua xiii. 17, &c., among "the cities that are in the plain of Heshbon."*

* Tristram has since expressed (p. 535) a doubt of the verity of this name of a site, but I had it given to me both at Heshbon and Jerash, and De Saulcy has since been there.

In half an hour we came to *Ela'âl*, (Elealeh,) (Isa. xv. 4 and xvi. 9, and Jer. xlviii. 34.) Large stones were lying about, and one column standing upright, but without a capital. Fine corn-plains in every direction around. Our tents pitched at *Na'oor* were visible to the E.N.E. through an opening between two hills. Cool cloudy day; all of us enjoying the ride through wheat-fields, and over large unoccupied plains—my old friend 'Abdu'l 'Azeez still adhering to me as his willing auditor.

On coming up to his camp at Na'oor, we found that Shaikh Dëâb had already arrived.

And now I may pause in the narrative to describe the *status* of (1.) ourselves; (2.) the Arabs.

(1.) Although apparently forming one company of English travellers, we were really a combination of several small sets, of two or three persons each —every set having its own cook, muleteer, and dragoman; but all the sets on terms of pleasant intercourse, and smoking or taking tea with each other.

We calculated that our horses and mules amounted to above a hundred in number.

(2.) The whole territory from Kerak to Jerash is that of our 'Adwân tribe, but divided into three sections—the middle portion being that of the supreme chief Dëâb, the northern third that of 'Abdu'l 'Azeez, and the southern that of a third named Altchai in the south towards Kerak; but they all combine when necessary for a general object.

The 'Adwân sow corn by the labour of their purchased slaves. Gublân at Cuferain, Dëâb and his son 'Ali at Nimrin, and a portion of the tribe called "the children of Eyoob" cultivate in the same manner a tract near the Dead Sea called the *Mezraa'*. These latter attach themselves sometimes to the Dëâb section, called the *Dar 'Ali*, and sometimes to the Gublân section, called the *Dar Nim'r*.

Their district is but a comparatively narrow strip at present, as they are pressed upon by the *Beni Sukh'r* on the east, who are again pressed upon by the *'Anezeh* farther eastward; these last are allies of our people.

The Ghôr or Jordan plain is open ground for all Arabs; and a few low fellows called Abbâd Kattaleen, hold a slip of ground downwards between Es-Salt and the Jordan. Es-Salt is a populous and thriving town, the only one in all that country. Kerak, to the south, may be as large, and contain more remnants of mediæval strength, but its affairs are not so prosperous.

This station of Na'oor* is upon a long, low, green plain, lying between two lines of high ground; and on a map, it would be nearly central between the

* How often have I regretted since that we did not know of the existence of 'Arâk el Ameer, which has of late commanded so much interest. We might have so easily turned aside for that short distance.

uorthern and southern extremities of the 'Adwân country, or Belka.*

Strange and wild was the scene of the Bedawi encampment—the black tents of goats' hair, the dark and ragged population sauntering about, the flocks and the horses, the ragged or naked children; and then the women in their blue, only article of dress, long-sleeved, their uncombed hair, and lips dyed blue, all walking with dignity of step, most of them employed in hanging up washed fleeces of wool to dry. One in particular I remarked for her stately appearance, with the blue dress trailing long behind, and the sleeves covering her hands; she was giving commands to others.

As soon as we were well settled, and the first confusion over in making our several arrangements with servants, &c., Shaikh Dëâb sent a messenger asking permission for him to pay us a visit of welcome; and a serious ceremonial visit took place accordingly. The great man was arrayed in green silk, and carried a silver-handled sword and dagger; a few chosen men of the tribe formed his train; coffee, pipes, and long compliments followed. We all remarked his keen eyes, ardent like those of a hawk in pursuit of prey. On taking leave he announced his intention of presenting each gentleman with a sheep for our evening meal.

* This word signifies "a desert." It is often found in the Arabic Bible, especially in the prophetic books.

As soon as the indispensable solemnity of his visit was over, the camp became more animated; the sheep were slaughtered; various parties being formed for the feast, which was finished by the Arabs; and I invited all to my tent for tea at night, when the weather became so piercing cold that I found it necessary to have some hot brandy and water to drink.

In this place I wish to say how excellent is animal food dressed immediately after killing. The practice is found all through the Bible histories, from Abraham entertaining the angels at Mamre, to the father of the prodigal son killing the fatted calf for his reception. At that stage the meat is exceedingly tender and delicate; whereas, if left, as the European practice is, for some time after killing, it has to go through another and less wholesome process in order to become tender again. There are numerous medical opinions in favour of the Oriental method of cooking the food immediately.

Another observation will not be out of place, on the almost universal eating of mutton throughout Asia. I do not mean the anti-beef-eating Brahmins of India, but in all countries of Asia, by eating of meat is understood the eating of mutton, and horned cattle are reserved for agricultural labour. In case of exceptions being met with, they are only such few exceptions as help to prove the rule. This may perhaps be attributed to the general insecurity of animal property in the East; but that I do not think a sufficient reason to account for it. It seems, however, that the ancient Israelites were not so much limited to eating from the small cattle.

Saturday, 12th.—Thermometer 37° just before sunrise, nearly thirty degrees lower than under the same circumstances two days before. The night had been cold and damp; the grass was found wet in the places sheltered from the current of wind, which had elsewhere formed hoarfrost over the field. This reminded us of the elevation we had reached to; and we all exclaimed as to the reasonableness of Jacob's expostulation with Laban, when he asserted that "in the day the drought [or heat] consumed him, and the frost by night," (Gen. xxxi. 40.) We were upon frozen ground in the month of May, after passing through a flight of locusts on the preceding day.

A lively scene was the packing up. 'Abdu'l 'Azeez was happy at seeing us all happy, and laying hold of a couple of dirty, ragged urchins, he shook them well, and lifted them up from the ground, and offered them to me, saying, " Here, take these little imps of mine, and do what you like with them; send them to England if you will, for they are growing up like beasts here, and what can I do?" All I could do was to speak cheerfully to them, and make them some little presents. At the door of Dëâb's tent was his bay mare of high race, and his spear planted beside her. He accompanied us as far as his own encampment, two or three hours over wide plains and grassy pastures. Soon after leaving Na'oor he took us up a small hill, which was called *Setcher*, (probably *Setker* in town pronunciation,) where there were some ruins of no considerable amount, but the stones of cyclopean size. Query —Were these remains of the primeval Zamzummim? (Deut. ii. 20.)

At *Dahair el Hhumâr* (Asses' Hill) we alighted in Dëâb's own camp, not large in extent or number of people, probably only a small detachment from the main body brought with him for the occasion, but not such, or so placed, as to interfere with the camp of 'Abdu'l 'Azeez. However, the well-known emblems of the Shaikh's presence were observed— namely, his tent being placed at the west end of the line, and his spear at its entrance. Here took place the formality of returning his visit to us yesterday ; and here, after coffee and pipes, our presents were produced and given. The travellers were collected in a very long black tent, together with Dëâb, his son and friends. A screen at one end divided us from the women's apartment, *i.e.*, what would be the *Hhareem* in houses of towns; behind this curtain the women were peeping, chattering, and laughing ; of course we might expect this to be about the extraordinary-looking strangers. It has been conjectured that such a separation of the tent is implied in Gen.

xviii. 6 and 10, when "Sarah heard it in the tent-door which was behind him;" but this has no foundation in the plain narrative of Scripture, only in the Arabic translation the words seem to imply that understanding.

The presentation of offerings was a grave and solemn affair. Each donor produced his tribute with an apology for the insignificance of the gift, which was then exhibited in silence by an attendant to the populace of the tribe crowding outside.

The ceremony was concluded by shouts of welcome, and a huge meal of pilaff (rice and mutton upon a great tray of tinned copper) and léban, (curdled milk,) with more smoking. Here we took leave of the chief, who sent on a detachment of his tribe to escort us for the rest of our expedition.

Remounted, and proceeded N.E. by N.; hitherto we had come due north from Heshbon. Passed a hill called *Jehâarah*, and in a short time reached the source of the river of Ammon, rising out of the ground, with a large pavement of masonry near it. A numerous flock of sheep and goats were being watered at the spring, it being near the time of As'r—*i.e.*, mid-afternoon.

Here the antiquities of *Ammân* commenced; and remains of considerable buildings continually solicited our attention, as we passed on for quarter of an hour more to our tents, which we found already pitched and waiting for us among a crowd of ancient temples and baths and porticoes,— in a forum between a line of eight large Corinthian columns and the small river; in front too of a Roman theatre in good condition. Some of the party, who were familiar with the ruins of Rome and Athens, exclaimed aloud, "What would the modern Romans give to have so much to show as this, within a similar space!"

This was Saturday afternoon; and we had already resolved to spend our Sabbath in this wonderful and agreeable place, so remarkable in Scripture history, and so seldom visited by Europeans.

I climbed up the seats of the theatre, and rested near the top, enjoying the grand spectacle of luxurious architecture around; then descended, and walked along its proscenium; but neither reciting passages of Euripides nor of Terence, as some enthusiasts might indulge themselves in doing, before an imagined audience of tetrarchs, centurions, or legionaries, or other

"Romanos rerum dominos, gentemque togatam."

Close to this theatre was a covered and sumptuous building, which I could not but suppose to be a naumachia, from its having rising rows of seats around the central space, with a channel leading into this from the river. As the shadows of evening lengthened, the heat of the day was moderated, and I sauntered along the bank of the stream till I came to a large headless statue of a female figure lying in the water. Some men lifted it upon the green bank for me ; but it was far too heavy to be transported to Jerusalem for the Literary Society's Museum.

The swift-flowing rivulet abounded in fish, some of which the Arabs killed for us, either by throwing stones or shooting them with bullets, having no other means of getting at them ; but the latter of these methods was too costly to be often adopted. However, we had some fish for dinner in " Rabbah, the city of waters." This stream is the commencement of the Zerka, which we were to meet afterwards, after its course hence N.E. and then N.W.

I feasted a dozen Arabs at my tent-door. Shaikh 'Abdu'l 'Azeez laughed when I remarked that this place was better worth seeing than Heshbon, and said, " This is a king's city. It was the city of King *Ghedayûs;* and Jerash, which is still more splendid, was built by *Sheddâd*, of the primitive race of the *Beni 'Ad*." Beyond this, of course, it was impossible for him to imagine anything in matters of antiquity.

In my evening's Scripture reading, I was much struck with the opening of the 65th Psalm : " Praise waiteth for Thee, O God, in Zion,"—which passes over all the examples of human achievement

elsewhere, in order to celebrate the peculiar and undying honours of Jerusalem. So now the Grecian and the Roman colonies, who erected the marvels of architecture around me, are gone ; while the Jewish people, the Hebrew language, the city of Jerusalem, and the Bible revelations of mercy from God to man, continue for ever. But most particularly does this psalm, taken with the circumstances there before our eyes, point out the difference made between Ammon and Israel, and the reason for it, as predicted in Ezek. xxv., 1–7 :—
"The word of the Lord came again unto me, saying, Son of man, set thy face against the Ammonites, and prophesy against them ; and say unto the Ammonites, Hear the word of the Lord God : Thus saith the Lord God ; Because thou saidst, Aha, against my sanctuary, when it was profaned ; and against the land of Israel, when it was desolate ; and against the house of Judah, when they went into captivity ; behold, therefore I will deliver thee to the men of the east for a possession, and they shall set their palaces in thee, and make their dwellings in thee : they shall eat thy fruit, and they shall drink thy milk. And I will make Rabbah a stable for camels, and the Ammonites a couching-place for flocks ; and ye shall know that I am the Lord. For thus saith the Lord God ; Because thou hast clapped thine hands, and stamped with the feet, and rejoiced in heart with

all thy despite against the land of Israel; behold, therefore I will stretch out mine hand upon thee, and will deliver thee for a spoil to the heathen; and I will cut thee off from the people, and I will cause thee to perish out of the countries: I will destroy thee; and thou shalt know that I am the Lord."

Sunday, 13*th*.—Dew on the grass; but it was the morning dew, which, like human goodness, was soon exhaled.

After meditating on the chapters in Numbers and Deuteronomy which refer to the conduct and destinies of Ammon and Moab, and reading Jer. xlviii. and xlix. within "the flowing valley" of the 4th verse of the latter, I was summoned to divine service in a tent fitted up for the purpose,—carpets on the floor "honoris causâ;" a table covered with simple white, and a serious congregation of Englishmen before it, each with his own Bible and prayer-book. Thank God that to carry such books about in the wildest deserts is a characteristic of my countrymen!

This city of *'Ammân* is "the city in the midst of the river" of Joshua xiii. 9; and "Rabbah of the children of Ammon"—the royal city—"the city of waters" of 2 Sam. xii. 26, 27:—to the siege of which Joab invited King David, "lest he should take it, and it should be called after his name." Here was also deposited the huge iron bedstead of Og, king of Bashan.

Under the Ptolemy dynasty — successors of Alexander — it was rebuilt, with the name of Philadelphia. Several of the best edifices here, now partially ruined, belong to that period.

Under the Crusaders it was a flourishing city and district, retaining the Grecian name.

I could not but reflect on the infinite prescience that dictated the prophecies of the Bible—no tongue could speak more plainly to us than the scene around us did, the fulfilment of the denunciations that these cities of Moab and Ammon should remain *as cities* "without inhabitants" —"not a man to dwell therein"—and "driven out every man, right forth, and none shall gather up him that wandereth"—"desolate" and "most desolate."

In the afternoon we walked about to inspect the antiquities, and found several remains of Christian churches with bell-towers attached to them—certainly not originally minarets. These edifices had been afterwards, in Mohammedan times, converted into mosques, as evidenced by the niche made in the south wall of each, pointing to Mecca; and there are watch-towers for signals on all the summits of hills around. The city lies nestled in a valley between these hills.

The first building I examined was among those of the citadel placed upon a lofty eminence commanding the city, the ground-plan of which building is here shown—

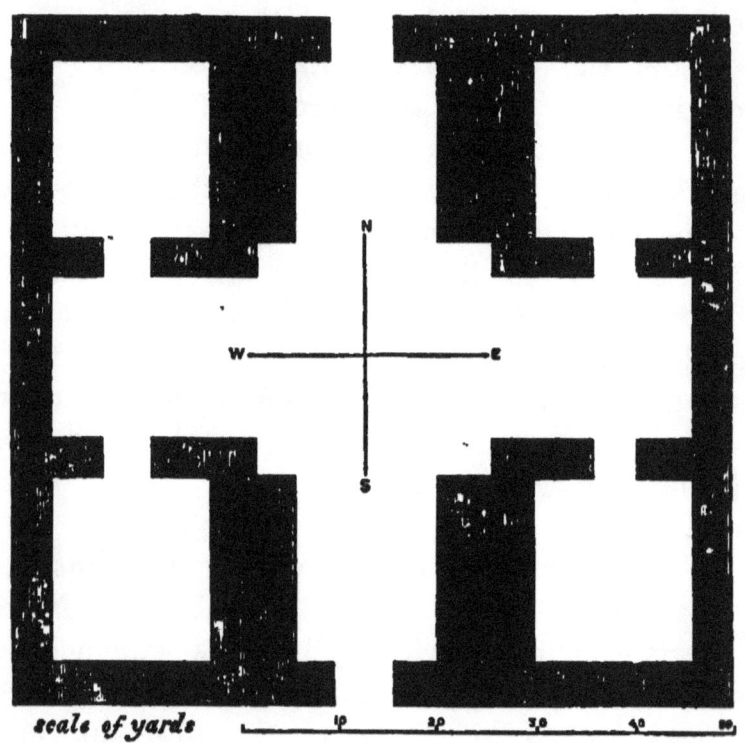

The interior of the walls was so profusely embellished with festoons of roses and vine-grapes —both sculptured in stone and wrought in stucco, and of very large size—that there was no room left for pictures or images. The roof of this building is almost all fallen in. I imagined this to have been a Christian church, of very remote antiquity, on account of the vine and the roses, which are peculiarly Christian symbols—alluding to the texts, "I am the true Vine," and "I am the Rose of Sharon;" but the chambers in each corner are difficult to account for. The east and west ends have no doors.

Near this is a square mass of masonry, upon which are standing six columns, of magnificent dimensions, which no doubt originally supported a roof. Their capitals, of chaste and correct Corinthian style, with portions of ornamental entablature, are lying near. Perhaps belonging to this, but at some distance, lies a ponderous piece of architrave, on which, between lines of moulding, is an inscription in Greek—illegible except the three letters—NΩΘ. These letters were nine inches in length.

Nigh to this, again, was a square building of rabbeted stones, equal to almost the largest in the walls of Jerusalem.

All down the hill, descending to our camp, were fragments of columns and of decorated friezes of temples, that had evidently been rolled or had slidden down from their places.

Upon various walls of dilapidated edifices I observed the curious marks, slightly scratched, which almost resemble alphabetical characters, but are not; and which have, wherever met with and wherever noticed, which is but seldom, puzzled travellers, however learned, to decipher. I copied the following:—

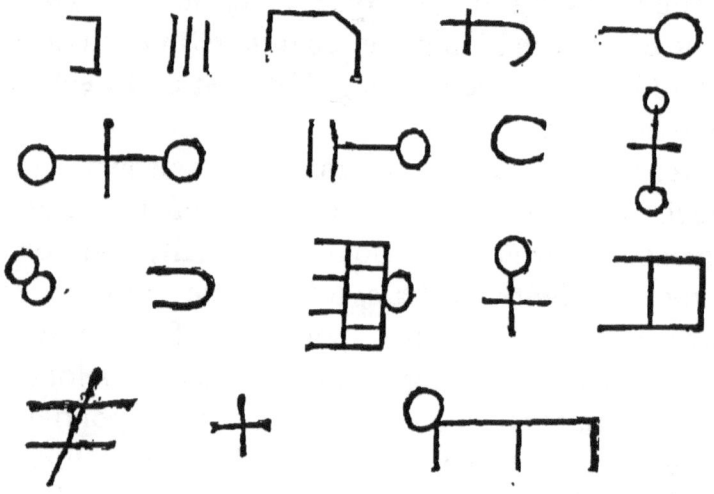

And from the shaft of a column still erect, half way down the hill, I copied the following:—

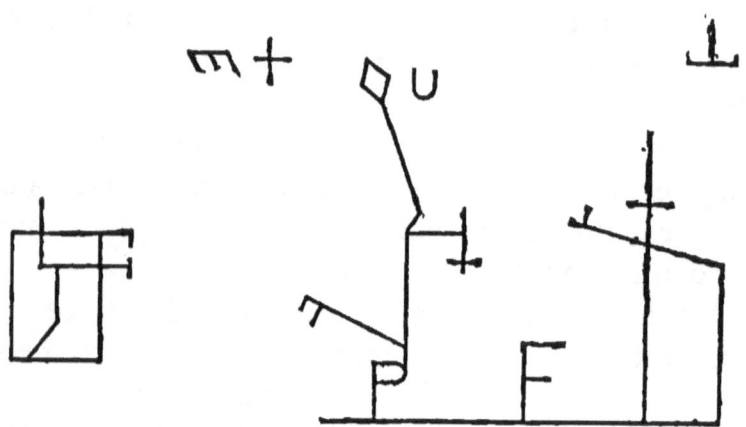

I have since learned that they are the tokens of the Bedaween Arabs, by which one tribe is distinguished from another. In common parlance they are called the *Ausam* (plural of Wasam) of the several tribes.*

In a valley to the north of us, leading westwards from the main valley, we found a beautiful mausoleum tomb,—a building, not an excavation in rock,—containing six sarcophagi, or ornamented stone coffins, ranged upon ledges of masonry, along three sides of the chamber. These were very large, and all of the same pattern—the lids remaining upon some of them, but shifted aside. Beautiful sculptured embellishments were upon the inside walls and over the portal outside, but no inscriptions to indicate the period or persons to whom they belonged. Inside, however, were rudely scratched the modern Arab tribe-signs, showing that persons of such tribes had visited there; so that Europeans are not the only travellers who help to disfigure ancient monuments by scribbling. Along this western valley were several other such mausoleums. Thence we mounted on a different side to the summit of that hill from which I have here begun my description of edifices—upon a gentle sloping road, evidently of artificial cutting, quite feasible for ascent of chariots.

Near the square (possible) church before mentioned, (though I should say that our party were not all convinced of its being a church,) is a prodigiously large cistern, of good masonry. From the top of the strong walls of the building—while

* See Appendix A.

C

some Arab boys below me were reaching birds' nests—I got from our guide the following list of sites in the neighbourhood. They were of course unable to discriminate between ancient and modern names; and I do not find one Bible name among them all:—

From north to west—
    Thuggeret el Baider.   Esh-Shemesâni.
    Kassar Waijees.   Esh-Shwaifiyeh.
    Es-Salt.   Umm Malfoof.

From west to east—
    'Abdoon.   Mesdar 'Aishah.
    Umm es Swaiweeneh.   El Mergab.

Towards the east—
    Merj Merka.   'Ain Ghazâl.
    Ursaifah (in a valley with a river).
    El Muntar el Kassar, between two artificial hills.

The people informed me of a place, a little nearer than Kerak, called *Rabbah*. This latter may be a *Rabbath-Moab*.

I have no further notes to transcribe respecting the architectural remains; but they are so numerous and so important that a week would not suffice for their thorough investigation. All our party were highly gratified at having visited this Rabbath-Ammon — *alias* Philadelphia — *alias*, at present, 'Ammân. We were not, however, so fortunate as Lord Lindsay in finding a fulfilment of the prophecy (Ezek. xxv. 5) with respect to camels, either alive or dead. Probably, when he was there, it was soon after an Egyptian military expedition to Kerak. The prodigious number of dead camels that he saw there would seem to indicate that a great Arab battle had been fought at that place shortly before. It is only in this way that we could account for a cannon-ball (about a six-pounder) which one of the boys carried about, in following us, all the afternoon, wishing us to buy it of him as a curiosity.

On returning to the tents, I found an old Jerusalem acquaintance—a Moslem named 'Abderrahhman Bek el 'Asali—and with him several people from Es-Salt; among these a Christian named Abbâs.

From conversation with them I got some fresh information on Arab affairs. These people took the opportunity of glorifying their native town; related how they are frequently at war, and that successfully, with the 'Adwân; and when acting in concert with the Abbâd, or much more so when in alliance with the Beni Sukh'r, can always repel them; only it happens that sometimes the 'Adwân get help from the more distant 'Anezeh; and this is much more than enough to turn the balance again. But even now the 'Adwân cannot come near the town; neither can they quite forget that the Saltîyeh people, during a former war, killed both the father and grandfather of Dëâb, and sent the head of the former to the tribe in a dish, with a pilaff of rice.

All the strength of the 'Adwân now lies in Shaikh Dëâb, with his son 'Ali, (who came to welcome us near the Jordan,) and Gublân the nephew. Old 'Abdu'l 'Azeez is considered childish, and unfit to lead them.

For us travellers, however, the 'Adwân are sufficient. The territory is theirs over which we are passing, and they do all they can to please us; only, of course, like all Arab guides, they take every opportunity of insinuating themselves into being fed by us, which is a condition "not in the bond."

Then came a visit of three men with good-natured countenances. These were Bedawi minstrels from Tadmor, (Palmyra,) who wander about from tribe to tribe, singing heroic poems to the accompaniment of their rebâbeh, (a very primitive sort of fiddle.) No warfare interferes with the immunity of their persons or property. They are never injured or insulted, but are always and everywhere welcome, and liberally rewarded. Of course it is for their interest to gratify the pride of their auditors by fervid appeals to their ancestral renown, or to individual prowess and generosity.

The Arabic of their chants is unintelligible to towns-people; it is the high classic language of Antar.

I had made acquaintance with these same men before at Tibneen Castle, near the Lebanon, during a season of Bairam. Being Sunday, we requested them to visit our tents in the morning. Our Arabs, however, and the dragomans kept them singing till a late hour round the fires lighted among the tents. It was a cheerful scene, in the clear starlight, and the lustrous planet Venus reflected in the running stream.

Monday, 14*th*.—After breakfast, and an entertainment of music from our troubadours, and the bestowing of our guerdon, these left us on their way to the other camp at Na'oor; and our packing up commenced.

Strange medley of costumes and languages among the grand colonnades. Our Arabs left us, having the luggage in charge, and indicating to us the camping-ground where we were to meet again at night,—thus leaving us in care of the Saltîyeh friends of ours, who were to escort us to their town and its neighbourhood, as the 'Adwân might not go there themselves.

Both the Christian and Moslem shaikhs of the town came to meet us on the way. The former was a very old man; and he could with difficulty be persuaded to mount his donkey in presence of a train so majestic, in his eyes, coming from the holy city of Jerusalem.

We passed an encampment of *Beni Hhasan*. These people are few in number, and exist under the shadow of the 'Adwân.

There were plenty of locusts about the country; but we soon came to a vast space of land covered with storks, so numerous as completely to hide the face of the earth, all of them busily employed in feeding—of course devouring the locusts. So great is the blessing derived from the visits of storks, that the natives of these countries regard it as a sin to destroy the birds. On our riding among them they rose in the air, entirely obscuring he sky and the sun from our view. One of our party attempted to fire among them with his revolver, but, by some heedlessness or accident, the bunch of barrels, being not well screwed down, flew off the stock and was lost for a time; it took more than half an hour's search by all of us to find it again, and the Arabs considered this a just punishment for wishing to kill such useful creatures.

We traversed a meadow where Shaikh Faisel, with a detachment of the 'Anezeh, had encamped for pasture, and only left it thirty-five days before. His flocks and herds were described to us as impossible to be counted; but our friends were unanimous in stating that his camels were 1500 in number.

Came to *Khirbet es Sar*, (*Jazer?*) whence the Dead Sea was again visible. Our Arabs declared that they could distinguish the Frank mountain, and see into the streets of Bethlehem. Here there is a mere heap of ruin, with cisterns, and fragments of arches, large columns, and capitals; also a very rough cyclopean square building of brown striped flint in huge masses.

This site is three hours due north of Na'oor, in

a straight line, not turning aside to Dëâb's camp or 'Ammân. Northwards hence are the well-wooded hills of *'Ajloon*. To my inquiries for any site with a name resembling Nebo, I was referred to the *Neba*, half an hour south of Heshbon, which is given in the list taken down by me at Heshbon.

Proceeding northwards, we had the hills of *Jebel Mâhas* parallel on our right hand ; and to our left, in a deep glen below, was the source of the stream Se'eer, which had flowed past us at *Cuferain*, our first encampment after crossing the Jordan.

Arrived at the ruined town (modern in appearance) of *Dabook*, from whence they say the *Dabookeh* grapes at Hebron* had their origin ; but there are none to be seen here now (see Jer. xlviii. 32, 33)— " O vine of Sibmah, I will weep for thee with the weeping of Jazer : thy plants are gone over the sea, they reach even to the sea of Jazer : the spoiler is fallen upon thy summer fruits and upon thy vintage. And joy and gladness is taken from the plentiful field, and from the land of Moab ; and I have caused wine to fail from the wine-presses," &c. : with nearly the same words in Isa. xvi. 8–10.

At a short distance upon our right was a ruined village called *Khuldah*. This was at the entrance of woods of the evergreen oak, with hawthorn, many trees of each kind twined round with honeysuckle. There Shaikh Yusuf, (the Moslem of Es-Salt,) who is a fine singer, entertained us with his

* The largest sort grown there.

performances, often bursting into extemporaneous verses suitable to the occasion and company.

On reaching an exceedingly stony and desolate place, he related the original story of Lokman the miser, connected with it:—"Formerly this was a fertile and lovely spot, abounding in gardens of fruit; and as the Apostle Mohammed (peace and blessings be upon him!) was passing by, he asked for some of the delicious produce for his refreshment on the weary way, but the churlish owner Lokman denied him the proper hospitality, and even used insulting language to the unknown traveller, (far be it from us!) Whereupon the latter, who was aware beforehand of the man's character, and knew that he was hopelessly beyond the reach of exhortation and of wise instruction, invoked upon him, by the spirit of prophecy, the curse of God, (the almighty and glorious.) And so his gardens were converted into these barren rocks before us, and the fruit into mere stones."

Such was the tale. But similar miraculous punishments for inhospitality are told at Mount Carmel, as inflicted by the Prophet Elijah; and near Bethlehem by the Virgin Mary.

From a distance we caught a distant view of the *Beka' el Basha*, or Pasha's meadow, where we were to encamp at night, but turned aside westwards in order to visit the town of Es-Salt. Upon a wide level tract we came to a small patch of ground enclosed by a ow wall, to which a space was left for entrance, with a lintel thrown across it, but still not above four feet from the ground. On this were bits of glass and beads and pebbles deposited, as votive offerings, or tokens of remembrance or respect. The place is called the Weli, or tomb, of a Persian Moslem saint named *Sardoni.* But it should be recollected that in Arabic the name '*Ajam,* or Persia, is often used to signify any unknown distant country to the east.

At '*Ain el Jadoor* we found water springing out of the rocks, among vineyards and fig and walnut trees, olives also, and pomegranates—a beautiful oasis, redeemed from the devastation of Bedaween by the strong hand of the town population. Near this the Christian Shaikh Abbâs, being in our company, was met by his venerable mother and his son Bakhi.

In every direction the town of Es-Salt is environed by fruitful gardens, the produce of which finds a market in Nabloos and Jerusalem. The scenery reminded me of the Lebanon in its green aspect of industry and wealth.

Entering the town we dismounted at the house of Shaikh Yusuf, and took our refreshment on the open terrace, on the shady side of a wall.

Some of us walked about and visited the two Christian churches: they are both named "St George," and are very poor in furniture. Of course they have over the door the universal picture in these countries of St George on his prancing gray horse. This obtains for them some respect from the Mohammedans, who also revere that martial and religious hero. Inside the churches we found some pictures with Russian writing upon the frames; the people informed us that these were presents from the Emperor Nicholas, which is worthy of notice.

The ignorance of the priests here is proverbial all over Palestine. I have heard it told of them as a common practice, that they recite the Lord's Prayer and the *Fathhah*, or opening chapter of the Koran, alternately, on the ground that these are both very sublime and beautiful; and it is said that they baptize in the name of the Father, Son, and Holy Ghost, and the Virgin Mary. There is reason to believe them very grossly ignorant; but it may be that some of these reports about them emanate from the Roman Catholic authorities in Jerusalem, who never hesitate at propagating slanders to the detriment of non-Romanists.

In a church porch I found a school of dirty ragged children reading the Psalms from the small English printed edition; not, however, learning to read by means of the alphabet or spelling, but learning to know the forms of words by rote; boys and girls together, all very slightly dressed, and one of the boys stark naked.

People came to me to be cured of ophthalmia. I got out of my portmanteau for them some sugar of lead; but it is inconceivable the difficulty I had to get a vessel for making it into a lotion—bottles or phials were totally unknown, not even cups were to be procured. At one time I thought of a gourd-shell, but there was not one *dried* in the town; so they told me. I might have lent them my drinking-cup, but then I wanted to prepare a large quantity to be left behind and to be used occasionally. I forget now what was the expedient adopted, but I think it was the last named-one, but of course only making sufficient for immediate use. I left a quantity behind me in powder, with directions to dilute it considerably whenever any vessel could be found; warning the people, however, of its poisonous nature if taken into the mouth.

One man came imploring me to cure him of deafness, but I could not undertake his case. In any of these countries a medical missionary would be of incalculable benefit to the people.

There are ancient remains about the town, but not considerable in any respect. It is often taken for granted that this is the Ramoth-Gilead of Scripture, but I believe without any other reason than that, from the copious springs of water, there must always have been an important city there. The old name, however, would rather lead us north-eastwards to the hills of *Jela'ad*, where there are also springs and ruins.

On leaving the town we experienced a good deal of annoyance from the Moslem population, one of whom stole a gun from a gentleman of the party, and when detected, for a long time refused to give it up. Of course, in the end it was returned; but

I was told afterwards that the people had a notion that we ought to pay them something for visiting their town, just as we pay the wild Arabs for visiting Jerash. What a difference from the time of the strong Egyptian Government when Lord Lindsay was there!

At a distance of perhaps half or three-quarters of an hour there is a *Weli* called *Nebi Osha;* that is to say, a sepulchre, or commemorative station of the Prophet Joshua, celebrated all over the country for the exceeding magnificence of the prospect it commands in every direction. In order to reach this, we had to pass over hills and plains newly taken into cultivation for vineyards, mile after mile, in order to supply a recent call for the peculiar grapes of the district at Jerusalem to be sent to London as raisins.

Arrived at the Weli, we found no language sufficient to express the astonishment elicited by the view before us; and here it will be safest only to indicate the salient points of the extensive landscape, without indulging in the use of epithets vainly striving to portray our feelings. We were looking over the Ghôr, with the Jordan sparkling in the sunshine upon its winding course below. In direct front was *Nabloos*, lying between Ebal and Gerizim; while at the same time we could distinguish Neby Samwil near Jerusalem, the Mount Tabor, Mount Carmel, and part of the Lebanon all at once! On our own side of Jordan we saw the extensive remains of *Kala'at Rubbâd*, and ruins of a town called *Maisĕra*. On such a spot what could we do but lie in the shade of the whitewashed Weli, under gigantic oak-trees, and gaze and ponder and wish in silence, —ay, and pray and praise too,—looking back through the vista of thirty-three centuries to the time of the longing of Moses, the "man of God," expressed in these words: "O Lord God, Thou hast begun to show Thy servant Thy greatness and Thy mighty hand: . . . I pray Thee let me go over and see the good land that is beyond Jordan, that goodly mountain, and Lebanon." The honoured leader of His people—the long-tried man "through good report and evil report,' who, during his second forty years which he spent as a shepherd in Midian, had been accustomed to the abstemious habits and keen eyesight of the desert; and, at the end of another forty years as the ruler of a whole nation, living in the desert, "his eye was not dim,"—added to which natural advantage, we are told that "the Lord showed him all the land," highly cultivated as it was then by seven nations greater and mightier than Israel,—Moses must have beheld a spectacle from Pisgah and Nebo, surpassing even the glories of this landscape viewed by us from Nebi Osha.

Turning eastwards to our evening home, we passed a ruined site called *Berga'an*, where we had one more view of the Dead Sea, and traversed large plains of ripe corn, belonging, of course, to the people of Es-Salt. The people requested me to pray to God that the locusts might not come there, since all that harvest was destined for Jerusalem.

We met some of the *'Abbâd Kattaleen* Arabs, but we were safe under the escort of the Saltîyeh instead of the 'Adwân. These 'Abbâd are the people who assaulted and plundered some seamen of H.M.S. "Spartan" in 1847, on the Jordan; for which offence they have never yet been chastised, notwithstanding the urgent applications made to the Turkish Pashas of Jerusalem, Bayroot, and Damascus. We did not arrive at the encampment till long after dark, and there was no moonlight.

The site is on a plain encircled by hills, with plenty of water intersecting the ground; the small streams are bordered by reeds and long grass. A khan, now in ruin, is situated in the midst—a locality certainly deserving its name, *Beka' el Bashà*, and is said to have been a favourite camping-station for the Pashas of Damascus in former times.

Much to our vexation, the Arabs and the muleteers had pitched our tents in a slovenly manner among the winding water-courses, so that we had wet reeds, thistles, and long grass, beetles and grasshoppers inside the tents, which again were wetted outside with heavy dew. They had done this in order to keep the cattle immediately close to us, and therefore as free from forayers as possible during the night. Such was the reason assigned, and we were all too hungry and tired to argue the matter further.

My people complained to me of the insolence of

the Saltîyeh guides that were with us; so I sent for the two shaikhs and scolded them. They persisted in it that they did not deserve the rebuke, that the complaints ought to be laid against a certain farrier who had come over from Jerusalem, &c. &c. My servant ended the affair by shouting at them, "Take my last word with you and feed upon it—'God send you a strong government.'" This at least they deserved, for they are often in arms against the Turkish government: and although so prosperous in trade and agriculture, are many years in arrear with their taxes.

Tuesday, 15th.—Early in the morning there were Saltîyeh people reaping harvest near us, chiefly in the Christian fields; for here the case is not as in Palestine, where Christians generally sow and reap in partnership with Moslems, for their own safety; but the Moslems have their fields, and the Christians have theirs apart, which shows that their influence is more considerable here; indeed, the Christians carry arms, and go out to war against the Bedaween, quite like the Moslems.

Before we left, the day was becoming exceedingly hot, and we had six hours' march before us to Jerash.

The hills abound with springs of water. We passed one called *Umm el'Egher*, another called *Safoot*, also *Abu Mus-hhaf*, and *Tâbakra*, and *'Ain Umm ed Dumaneer*, with a ruin named *Khirbet Saleekhi*.

The 'Adwân Arabs were now again our guides, the Saltîyeh having returned home; but for some distance the guides were few and without firearms, only armed with spears, and the common peasant sword called *khanjar;* perhaps this was by compact with the Saltîych, as in about an hour's time we were joined by a reinforcement with a few matchlock guns. On we went through corn-fields, which are sown in joint partnership with the Arabs and the Moslems of the town; then doubled round a long and high hill with a ruin on it, called *Jela'ad.* This I have since suspected to be Ramoth-Gilead. We descended a hill called *Tallooz;* forward again between hills and rocks, and neglected evergreen woods, upon narrow paths. A numerous caravan we were, with a hundred animals of burden, bright costumes, and cheerful conversation, till we reached a large terebinth-tree under a hill called *Shebail;* the site is called *Thuggcret el Moghâfer,* signifying a "look-out station" between two tribes. There we rested a while, till the above-mentioned reinforcement joined us. From this spot we could just discern *Jerash,* on the summit of a huge hill before us.

We now had one long and continued descent to the river Zerka. Passed through a defile, on issuing from which we observed a little stream with oleander, in pink blossom, thirty feet high, and in great abundance. Halted again at a pretty spring called *Rumân,* where the water was upon nearly a dead level, and therefore scarcely moving; then another small spring, called *Bursa*, and also '*Ain el Merubb'a'*.

Evergreen oak in all directions, but with broader leaf than in Palestine; also some terebinth-trees and wild holly-oaks. All the scenery now expanded before us in width and height and depth.

We took notice of several high hills with groves of evergreen oak on their summits; detached hills, which we could not but consider as remains of the ancient *high places* for idolatrous worship.

Still descended, till on a sudden turn of the road came the rushing of the *Zerka*, or Jabbok, water upon our ears, with a breeze sighing among juniper-bushes, and enormous and gorgeous oleanders, together with the soft zephyr feeling from the stream upon our heated faces—oh, so inexpressibly delicious! I was the first to get across, and on reaching the opposite bank we all dismounted, to drink freely from the river—a name which it deserves as at that place it is about two-thirds of the width of the Jordan at the usual visiting-place for travellers.

Some of the party went bathing. We all had our several luncheons, some smoked, all got into shady nooks by the water-side; and I, with my heart full, lay meditating on the journey we had hitherto made.

At length I had been permitted by God's good providence to traverse the territory of Moses and the chosen people antecedent to the writing of the

D

Pentateuch, when they were warring upon Ammon and Moab. How solemn are the sensations derived from pondering upon periods of such very hoar antiquity—a time when the deliverance at the Red Sea, the thunders of Sinai, the rebellion of Korah and Dathan, the erection of the tabernacle, and the death of Aaron, were still fresh in the memories of living witnesses; and the manna was still their food from heaven, notwithstanding the supplies from the cultivated country they were passing through, (Josh. v. 12.) Elisha did well in after times on the banks of Jordan, when he cried out, "Where is the Lord God of Elijah?" And we may exclaim, in contemplation of these marvellous events of the still more remote ages, "Where is the Lord God of Moses, who with a mighty hand and stretched-out arm"—"redeemed His people from their enemies; for His mercy endureth for ever!" Nations and generations may rise and pass away; phases of dominion and civilisation may vary under Assyrian, Egyptian, Hellenic, and Roman forms, or under our modern modifications; yet all this is transitory. The God of creation, providence, and grace, He lives and abides for ever. His power is still great as in the days of old, His wisdom unsearchable, and His goodness infinite. Ay, and this dispenser of kingdoms is also the guide of the humble in heart, and He cares for the smallest concerns of individual persons who rest upon Him.

Strengthened by these and similar reflections, with ardent aspirations for the future, I rose up and pursued my journey, as Bunyan's pilgrim might have done, under the heartfelt assurance that "happy is he that hath the God of *Jacob* for his help."

We were now leaving behind us much of the Old Testament country—not exclusively that of the Mosaic era, but the land which had been trodden by the patriarchs Abraham and Israel on their several removals from Padan-aram to Canaan. But, while looking back upon the grand landscape outline with an intense degree of interest, it may be well to remark that, among all our company, there was a feeling of uncertainty as to the geographical boundaries of the lands possessed by the old people of Ammon, Moab, and Bashan. Probably there had been some fluctuations of their towns and confines between the time of the exodus and the prophecies of Isaiah and Jeremiah.

One thing is certain—that we all, with one heart, were confident that God spake by Moses and the prophets; and that, with the incidents, the people and the local names we had lately passed among we might as soon believe in the non-existence of the sun and stars, as that the books called "The Law of Moses" are not in every word a record of infallible truth.

We had now a different journey, and a different

set of scenes before us, entering into the half tribe of Manasseh.

Ascending the steep mountain-sides with two of the guides, I preceded the rest of the party, and even the baggage mules. In perhaps half an hour,

(it may be more,) I came to a triumphal arch, the commencement of Jerash. One of the guides told me that they call this the Ammân Gate of the old city; for that, in ancient times, there were two brothers, one named Ammân, and the other Jerash. Each of them built a city, and gave it his own name; but called the gate nearest to his brother's city, by the name of that brother.

At this gateway I observed the anomaly of the columns on each side of the principal opening, having their capitals at the bottom of the shafts, and resting on the pediments, though in an upright position. It was very ridiculous. When could this have been done—at the original erection of the gate, or at a later rebuilding, after an earthquake had shaken the pillars? It would seem to me to be the former, as they are posted against the wall, and this is not disturbed or altered. The tops of the columns and the curve of the portal are gone, so that it cannot be seen whether originally they had capitals on the heads also of the columns. It is most probable that those remaining are not the true capitals, inasmuch as they have no volutes.

Passing by inferior monuments of antiquity,— such as a sepulchre, a single column, a sarcophagus, and then a square elevated pavement in good condition, upon which are several sarcophagi, some of them broken, and all with the lids displaced,—I came to a large circus of Ionic columns, almost all standing, and joined to each other at the top by architraves. Thence holding on the same direction forwards due north, our way was between a double row of grand Corinthian columns with their capitals, and occasional temples to the right and left. At the termination of this, but without continuing the same line, between columns of another Grecian order, I turned aside, at a vast Roman bath, to a spring of water, the commencement of a running stream, in a small meadow of tall grass and thorns, intending to pitch my tent there; but soon changed my mind, and got myself established within a wing of the Roman bath, which stood on higher ground, and had a good roof upon it.

The other gentlemen on coming up, adopted the choice of their dragomans and muleteers, near the water, after having the thorns and thistles cleared away. A fresh afternoon breeze that sprang up was peculiarly grateful to men and cattle.

After some rest, I proceeded to stroll about,— first of all to the great Temple of the Sun, on a rising ground to the west of the great colonnade, which, besides the columns along all the sides of the edifice, has a conspicuous portico in front, consisting of twelve magnificent Corinthian columns, a few of which are fallen. Thence I walked to the Naumachia, near the southern extremity of the city, (that by which we had arrived,) and found this in good condition, with the seats remaining, and the channel well defined which conveyed water for the exhibitions from the above-mentioned spring. The form is a long oval, flattened at one end.

In passing once more between the double line of Corinthian columns, I counted fifty-five of them standing, besides fragments and capitals of the missing ones lying on the ground.

From this I diverged at right angles, through a street of small public buildings, towards the bridge over the stream, (and this I called Bridge Street—part of the pavement still remains, consisting of long slabs laid across the whole width from house to house;) then upon the bridge, as far as its broken condition would allow, and returned to my home—everywhere among scattered fragments of entablature; numerous altars entire, and sculptured with garlands; also broken buildings, with niches embellished inside with sculptured ornament. In all my exploration, however, I found no statues or fragments of statues—the Mohammedan iconoclasts had long ago destroyed all these; but there were some remains of inscriptions, much defaced or worn away by the work of time.

The natural agencies by which the edifices have come to ruin seem to be—first, earthquakes; then the growth of weeds, thorns, and even trees, between the courses of stone, after the population ceased; or rain and snow detaching small pieces, which were followed by larger; also sometimes a sinking of the ground; and besides these common causes of decay, there comes the great destroyer—man.

Yet nature is always picturesque, even after the demolition of the works of human art or genius; and it is pleasing to see the tendrils, leaves, and scarlet berries of the nightshade playfully twining among the sculptured friezes which are scattered about in every position but straight lines; or other plants between the volutes, rivalling the acanthus foliage of the classic capitals.

Sunset: a beautiful landscape all around; and a pretty view of the travellers' tents, the Arabs, and the cattle below me.

After dinner I walked by starlight along the Ionic colonnade, which is a further continuation northwards of the Corinthian, and found nearly the whole length, with the intermediate pavement, remaining, consisting of squares about two feet in length, laid down in diamond pattern.

At night there were flickering lights and varieties of human voices below; the frogs croaking loud near the rivulet; and the rooks, whom I had dislodged from their home within the Roman bath, had taken refuge on the trees about us, unable to get to rest, being disturbed by our unusual sights and sounds.

Wednesday, 16th.—A visitor came early—namely, Shaikh Yusuf—with two of his people from *Soof*. The old man exhibited numerous certificates given by former travellers—all English—whom he had accompanied as guide either to Beisân or Damascus. He offered his services to take us even, if we pleased, as far as Bozrah.

Then came Shaikh Barakât el Fraikh with a large train. He is ruler over all the *Jebel 'Ajloon*, and has been residing lately on the summit of a high hill rising before us to the east, where there is a weli or tomb of a Moslem saint, the Nebi Hhood, who works miraculous cures. Barakât is in delicate health, and has twenty wives. His metropolis, when he condescends to live in a house, is at a village called *Cuf'r Enji;* but his district comprises fifteen inhabited villages, with above three hundred in ruins,—so it is said.

As for the saint himself, he has a very respectable name for antiquity, too ancient for regular chronology to meddle with—it is only known that he preached righteousness to an impious race of men previous to their sudden destruction. The circumstance of his tomb being on the summit of a high hill is perfectly consonant with the sentiments of great heroes and chiefs, as frequently expressed in poems of the old Arabs. The restoration of health which he is supposed to bestow, must be that effected by means of the fine mountain air at his place. At 'Ammân, old 'Abdu'l 'Azeez had said that Jerash was built by the Beni 'Ad, a primitive race mentioned in the Korân.

A ridiculous figure appeared of a Turkish subaltern officer, who has come into this wild desert to ask the people for tribute to the Porte. A Turkish kawwâs in attendance on him, I observed to shrug up his shoulders when he heard nothing but Arabic being spoken among us. They arrived here in the company of Shaikh Yusuf, whose son is nominally a Turkish military officer, commanding three hundred imaginary Bashi-Bozuk, or irregular cavalry. By means of such titles they tickle the vanity of the Arab leaders, and *claim* an annual tribute of 218 purses, (about £1000,) and are thus enabled to swell out the published army list, and account of revenue printed in Constantinople.*

So that next to nothing is in reality derived from these few sparse villages; and from the tent Arabs less than nothing, for the Turks have to bribe these to abstain from plundering the regular soldiers belonging to Damascus.

The 'Anezi Shaikh Faisel was encamped at only fourteen hours' distance from us.

Common Arab visitors arrived—from no one knew where: some on horseback, to see what could be picked up among us; even women and children. They must have travelled during the night. A handsomely-dressed and well-armed youth on horseback, from Soof, accosted me during one of my walks.

I bought two sheep for a feast to the Arabs that came about my tent; but they asked to have the money value instead of the feast. Alas for the degradation! What would their forefathers have said to them had they been possibly present?

Afternoon: a fine breeze sprang up, as is usual in elevated districts. I strolled again with an at-

---

* The officer deputed from the Porte lives in a pretty village called Cuf'r Yuba, and is said to have become enormously rich upon the levies which he does not transmit to Constantinople.

tendant—first outside the ancient wall on the east side of the rivulet, where it is not much dilapidated; it is all built of rabbeted stones, though not of very large size; then crossed over to the western wall, and traced out the whole periphery of the city by the eye.

In the great Corinthian colonnade, one of our party called me to him, and showed me some inscriptions about the public edifices along that line, and at the Temple of the Sun. There was one inscription in Latin, on a square pedestal; a similar one near it, broken across, had a Greek inscription. The rest were all in Greek, but so defaced or injured that seldom could a whole word be made out. However, we found, in a small temple beyond the city wall to the north, in a ploughed field, an inscription more perfect, containing the word *Nemesis* in the first line. There also I saw several mausoleums, with sarcophagi handsomely ornamented, and fragments of highly-polished red Egyptian granite columns, to our great surprise as to how they had arrived there, considering not only the distance from which they had been brought, and the variety of people through whose hands they had passed since being cut out roughly from the quarries of upper Egypt; but, moreover, the difficulty to be surmounted in bringing them to this elevation, across the deep Jordan valley, even since their disembarkation from the Mediterranean either at Jaffa or Caiffa.

The inscriptions that I had been able to collect were as follows:—

Fragments of Inscriptions found among the ruins of the Temple of the Sun at Jerash.

ΑΝΤΩΝΕΙ	2 ΚΡΑΤΟ
ΤΟΥΚΑΙΤΩΝ	ΟΤΑΛΡ
ΤΟΥΚΑΠΕΡΑ	ΠΝΑΙΑΥΙ
ΤΟΠΡΟΠΥΛ-	ΚΑΙΤΟΥΣ
ΟΡΝΗΛ . . .	-ΔΙΙΜΟ
	--ΣΤΟΛ

3 ΑΝΘΥ	4 ΣΑΡΟ-
ΗΛΙΟΥΚΑΙ	ΟΙΚΟΥΣ
ΤΠΙΑΝΤΟΥ	Ν--ΗΠ
	ΕΝ
	ΟΥΑΝ

Fragments of Inscription in the Temple oj Nemesis (?) in the ploughed field outside the wall.

ΗΝΕΜΕΣΙΣΚΑΙΤΑΠΑΡΑΚΙΜ-ΝΑΚ
ΑΙΟΚΩ . . .
. . . . ΝΕΤΟΕΚΔΙΑΘΗΚ-ΣΔΗΝ
ΗΠΙΟΙΛΠΟ . . .

Among all the hundreds of fragments of fine capitals and friezes lying about Jerash, there was not one that was not too heavy for us to carry away. I found no ornamented pottery, although we had found some even at Heshbon; neither coins, nor even bits of statues. And remarkable enough in our European ideas, so little space appeared for private common habitations—as usual among ruined cities of remote antiquity—it seemed as if almost the whole enclosure was occupied by temples or other public institutions.

Yet there must have been habitations for a numerous population. And, again, such a city implies the existence of minor towns and of numerous villages around, and a complete immunity from incursions of wild Arab tribes. These latter were unknown to a population who could build such temples, naumachia, and colonnades, and who were protected farther eastwards by the numerous cities with high roads, still discoverable in ruins beyond this —Belka and 'Ajloon. But of how different a character must have been the daily necessities of these old populations from the requirements of modern European existence. *We* should not be satisfied with the mere indulgence of gazing upon the æsthetic beauty of temples and colonnades. Climate, however, has much to do in this matter.

At night we had a general conference at the encampment respecting the future march, as we had now finished with the 'Adwân Arabs.*

* Travellers of late report that enormous sums are exacted by the 'Adwân for their escort upon this same journey as ours. It may, therefore, be acceptable to learn what was our contract, and that it was honourably acted upon—namely, three of the party to pay 1000 piastres each, and 200 each for all the rest. As there were twelve in the party, the amount was—

$$1000 \times 3 = 3000$$
$$200 \times 9 = 1800$$
$$\overline{4800}$$

This total we among ourselves divided equally, equal to 400 each.

We also agreed to make a present from each when in the terri-

The resolution was taken to proceed on the morrow to *Umm Kais*, under the guidance of Shaikh Yusuf of Soof, and proceed thence to Tiberias. He, however, would not ensure but that we might be met and mulcted by the Beni Sukh'r for leave to traverse their territory. He was to receive 500 piastres, (nearly £5,) besides 50 piastres for baksheesh; but whatever we might have to pay the Beni Sukh'r was to be deducted from the above stipulation.

Thursday, 17*th*.—Great noise of jackdaws under my vaulted roof at break of day, they having mustered up courage to return to their nests there during the night.

During the packing up of the luggage, I took a final and lonely walk along the colonnades to the Naumachia, and outside the wall S.W. of the Ammân gate, where I observed some columns, or portions of such, of twisted pattern; returned by the bridge. The thrush, the cuckoo, and the partridge were heard at no great distance, near the stream.

We left upon the meadow a parliamentary debate of Arabs gathered around the chief's spear, all the men ranting and screaming as only such people

tory, besides giving a feast at 'Ammân, and another at Jerash—the feasts were a mere trifle.

A hundred piastres came to rather less than a pound sterling.

I am glad to confirm the recent testimonies of Tristram and De Saulcy as to the honourable and noble deportment of Gublân and the other leaders of the 'Adwân people.

can, and they only at the beginning or end of a bargain.

Slowly we defiled in a long line over rising ground, higher and higher, upon a good highway, bordered on each side by numerous sarcophagi; as along the Roman Appian Way; passed the weli of *Shaikh el Bakkar*, and a sarcophagus with a long inscription in Greek, which I regretted not having discovered yesterday, so as to allow of copying it. From an eminence we took the last view of the pompous colonnades of Jerash.

Away through the green woods of broad-leaved oak, among which were to be found fine and numerous pine-trees, the air fragrant with honeysuckle, and the whole scene enlivened by sweet song of the birds, there were hills in sight all covered with pine.

Around Soof we found none of the druidical-looking remains mentioned by Irby and Mangles, but some romantic landscape and vineyards all over the hills.

Ten minutes beyond Soof we had a Roman milestone lying at our feet. Some of us set to work in clearing earth away from it, searching for an inscription, but could not spare sufficient time to do it properly. We found, however, the letters PIVS·PONTI . . . . .—indicating the period of the Antonines.

Next there met us a large party of gipsies— known, among other tokens, by the women's black hair being combed, which that of the Bedawi women would not be. What a motley meeting we formed—of Moslems, Greek-Church dragomans, Protestants, and Fire-worshippers, as the gipsies are always believed in Asia to be.

Among the oaks of gigantic size and enormously large arbutus, the effect of our party winding—appearing and disappearing, in varied costumes and brilliant colours—was very pleasing.

After a time we reached some fine meadow land, on which were large flocks of sheep belonging to the Beni Hhassan, whose tents we saw not far distant. The black and the white sheep were kept separate from each other.

And then appeared, in succession to the right and left, several of the rude erections, resembling the Celtic cromlechs, or *cist-vaens*, above alluded to, from Irby and Mangles.

Our guides told us that they abound all over the hills. All that we saw were constructed each of four huge slabs of brown flinty-looking stone, forming a chamber—two for sides, one at the back, and a cover over all, which measured eleven feet by six. Their date must be long anterior to the Roman period. They are manifestly not Jewish, and consequently are of pagan origin. Are they altars? or are they of a sepulchral character, raised over the graves of valiant warriors, whose very names and nationality are lost? or do they indeed partake of both designs — one leading easily to the other among a superstitious people, who had no light of revelation?

My persuasion is that they were altars, as they seldom reach above four feet from the ground; and if so, they would serve to show, as well as the uprights forming a square temple by the seaside, between Tyre and Sidon, that not in every place did the Israelites sufficiently regard the injunction of Deut. xii. 3, to demolish the idolatrous places of worship.*

Our road gradually ascended for a considerable time, till we attained the brow of an eminence, where our woody, close scenery suddenly expanded into a glorious extent of landscape. Straight before our eyes, apparently up in the sky, was old Hermon, capped with snow. About his base was a hazy belt; below this was the Lake of Gennesareth; and nearer still was an extent of meadow and woodland.

* Were not these the altars or other objects employed in idolatrous worship by the Geshurites and Maachathites who remained among the Israelites of Gad and Reuben?—(See Josh. xiii. 13.)

The commanding object, however, was the grand mountain,

> "That lifts its awful form,
> Swells from the vale, and midway leaves the storm.
> Though round its breast the rolling clouds be spread,
> Eternal sunshine settles on its head."

At this place we rested for a time.

All the day afterwards we kept upon high grounds, to avoid meeting any of the Beni Sukh'r —thus greatly increasing the length of the day's march, and having to scramble over rocky hills without visible paths. All this had been brought upon us by over-cleverness in bargaining with Shaikh Yusuf, our guide. We had stipulated that, in case of meeting with Bedaween Arabs, whatever should be demanded as *ghufur*, or toll for crossing their ground, should be deducted from his 500 piastres. He had informed us that the toll would be but a trifle; but after the burden of it had been once thrown upon him, he avoided the best and direct road, and we had hours of needless fatigue in consequence.

As a peasant himself, the Arabs allow him and his people to pass free, as no doubt they exact enough from the village in other forms; but they consider themselves entitled to levy tribute on European travellers. The latter, however, are always disposed to grumble at it.

We plunged again into thick green woods,—the oaks of Bashan,—with merry birds carolling all around. Oh, how cheering was the scene, after that devastated land across the river, where there is so little of forest land left in proportion to this! A friend once remarked to me, that were the two territories in the same relative conditions at the time of Joshua taking possession of Canaan, it would require a double amount of faith in God's promises, as they ascended from Jericho to Ai, to believe that they had not left the promised land behind them. Now, this might be met by several satisfactory replies; but the plainest answer for the moment is, that the countries were not then in the same conditions relatively as they now are.

We passed a rock-hewn sepulchre on the side of a hill, in good condition,—just such as may be frequently seen in Palestine proper,—then found a large herd of camels browsing; and passing through a verdant glen, which issued upon cultivated fields, we came to the village of *Mezer*, and soon after to *Tuleh*, where we got a view of Tabor, Gilboa, and Hermon,* all at the same time. Were the day clear, there could be no doubt but we should have seen also the village of Zer'een (Jezreel) and the convent on Mount Carmel.

The weather was hot, and our people suffering from thirst, as Ramadân had that day commenced.

Had a distant view of a Beni Sukh'r encamp-

* I mean Jebel esh Shaikh of the Anti-Lebanon, as I do not believe in the existence of any *little Hermon* in the Bible.

ment to our right. After a steep descent, and consequent rise again, we were upon a plain; and therefore the guide counselled us to keep close together, as a precaution against marauders.

Our tedious deviation to-day had been far to the east: we now turned westwards, as if marching right up to Tabor, over corn-fields, with the village of *Tibni* at our left, and *Dair* at our right hand.

Arrived at *Tayibeh*, and encamped there for the night. Among the first people who came up to us was an Algerine Jew, who held my horse as I dismounted. He was an itinerant working silversmith, gaining a livelihood by going from Tiberias among Arab villages and the Bedaween, repairing women's ornaments, &c.

There are plenty of wells about this place, but none with good water. Wrangling and high words among the muleteers, and fighting of the animals for approach to the water-troughs. The day had been very fatiguing; and our Moslem attendants, as they had been involuntarily deprived of water during this the first day of Ramadân, deemed it not worth while at that hour to break the fast, as evening was rapidly coming on. Upon a journey, if it be a real journey on business, they are allowed to break the fast, on condition of making up for the number of days at some time before the year expires.

Evening: beautiful colours on the western hills,

and the new moon appearing—a thin silver streak in the roseate glow which remains in the heavens after sunset. The night very hot, and no air moving.

Friday, 18*th.*—After a night of mosquito-plague, we rose at the first daybreak, with a glorious spectacle of Mount Hermon and its snowy summit to the north. Such evenings and mornings as travellers and residents enjoy in Asian climes are beyond all estimation, and can never be forgotten.

We learned that there are Christians in this village of *Tayibeh*,—as indeed there are some thinly scattered throughout the villages of *Jebel 'Ajloon*, *i.e.*, from Jerash to near Tiberias ; and in the corresponding villages on the western side of Jordan, as far as Nabloos.

I always feel deeply concerned for those " sheep without a shepherd," dispersed among an overwhelming population of Mohammedans. They are indeed ignorant,—how can they be otherwise, while deprived of Christian fellowship, or opportunities of public worship, excepting when they carry their infants a long journey for baptism, or when the men repair occasionally to the towns of Nabloos or Nazareth for trading business ; or, it may be, when rarely an itinerant priest pays them a visit ?—still they are living representatives of the Gentile Church of the country in primitive days, down through continuous ages,—their families enduring martyrdom, and to this day persecution and oppression.

for the name of Christ, in spite of every worldly inducement to renounce it. While we Europeans are reciting the Nicene Creed in our churches, they are suffering for it. They are living witnesses for the " Light of light, and very God of very God ;" and although with this they mingle sundry superstitions, they are a people who salute each other at Easter with the words, " Christ is risen," and the invariable response, " He is risen indeed ;" also in daily practice, when pronouncing the name of Jesus, they add the words, " Glory to His name."

Besides all the above, they are in many things Protestants against Papal corruption. They have no Vicar of Christ, no transubstantiation, no immaculate conception, no involuntary confession, and no hindrance to a free use of the Bible among the laity. For my part, I feel happy in sympathising much with such a people, and cannot but believe that the Divine Head of the Church regards with some proportion of love even the humblest believer in Him, who touches but the hem of His garment.

In our conversation, before resuming the journey, I mentioned the numerous villages that were to be found about that neighbourhood, utterly broken up, but where the gardens of fig, vine, and olive trees still are growing around the ruins. The people pointed out to me the direction of other such, that were out of sight from our tents; and the Jew quoted a familiar proverb of the country relating to that subject; also the Moslem shaikh, with his son, joined also in reciting it :—

> "The children of Israel built up;
> The Christians kept up;
> The Moslems have destroyed."

In saying this, however, by the second line they refer to the crusading period; and by the last line they denote the bad government of the Turks, under which the wild Bedaween are encroaching upon civilisation, and devastating the recompense of honest industry from the fertile soil.

We—starting upon our last day's journey together—passed over wide fields of wheat-stubble. On coming near the village of *Samma*, the old shaikh came out to welcome us, and inquire if his place is written in the books of the Europeans. On examining our maps, one of our party found it in his; and the rest promised the friendly old man that his village should be written down.

Proceeding through a green and rocky glen, between high hills, with a running stream, the weather was exceedingly hot. Here our party divided,— ourselves advancing towards *Umm Kais;* while the baggage and servants turned to the left, so as to cross the Jordan by the bridge *El Mejâma'a* for Tiberias. The principal intention of this was for the property to avoid the chance of falling into the hands of the Beni Sukh'r. Shaikh Yusuf now showed the relief from his mind by beginning to sing. This was all very well for him, who had nothing to lose; because, as it was said long ago—

"Cantabit vacuus coram latrone viator."

After wandering round and around, we descended into *Wadi Zahari*, "the flowering valley," where, by the water-side, were reeds and oleanders forty or fifty feet high; and near them we observed a pear-tree and a fig-tree, all alone and deserted, the remains of former cultivation. This and other previous instances attest the risk that attends rural labour in that district, being in the immediate vicinity of the Bedaween, and the utter mockery of nominal Turkish rule. Here we filled our leathern water-bottles, (called *zumzumia* in the Desert, and *máttara* by towns-people,) and climbed up a stony hill, the heat of the day increasing. No path among the rocks, and all of us angry at Shaikh Yusuf for saving himself the few piastres by conducting us among such difficulties.

Then, after some time we perceived ourselves to be near Umm Kais, by the sarcophagi, the sepulchres, and ruts of chariot-wheels upon the rocks. We rushed up to a large tree for refreshing shelter, and near it found numerous sepulchres, highly ornamented, and some of them with the stone doors remaining on the hinges, which we swung about to test the reality of their remaining so perfect, (figs. 1, 2, 3.)

Among these was the one remarked by Lord

Over the Jordan. 73

Lindsay in his Travels, bearing a Hebrew name inscribed in Greek letters, but which he has not

Fig. 1.

given quite correctly. It should be *Gaanuiph* instead of *Gaaniph*. This sepulchre is cut in black

Fig. 2.

basaltic rock, and has some broken sarcophagi remaining inside. On a round fragment of a column, near this side, is the inscription given below, (fig. 4.) The upper part is the farewell of surviving relatives

Fig. 3.

to the daughter of SEMLACHUS. The lower part, for whomsoever intended,—"*and thou also farewell,*"—carries with it a touch of nature that still affects the heart, after the lapse of many centuries.

Fig. 4.

The mausoleums and sepulchres at the opposite end of the city were even more numerous, many having Greek inscriptions upon them.

But the theatre is the most remarkable of all the objects of antiquity,—so perfect, with its rows of seats complete, surrounded by numerous public edifices and lines of columns; and then commanding from those seats a large view of the beautiful Lake of Tiberias, and of the grand mountains which enclose it, as a frame to the picture.

Here I stayed behind the rest of the party for a considerable time, charmed with the spectacle of nature, and revolving over the incidents of Herodian history, so vividly portrayed by Josephus.

Then rejoined my friends, by galloping along a Roman road, paved with blocks of dark basalt.

But before leaving this place, I must express my surprise at any person that has been there imagining for a moment that it can be the Gadara of Scripture.

The distance from the lake is so great as to be utterly incompatible with the recorded transactions in the Gospels—having valleys and high hills intervening; and even supposing the miracle of relieving the domoniac to refer not to the city but to a territory named Gadara, it is inconceivable that the territory belonging to this city (Umm Kais) could extend beyond the deep natural crevasse of the river *Yarmuk*, and then rise up a high mountain, to descend again into a plain, all before reaching the lake.

Our descent to the Yarmuk was long and steep; and upon the plain which it intersects, the heat exceeded any that I had ever encountered anywhere.

The air was like fire. Such a day I shall never forget.

The Yarmuk is so considerable a river that the Arabs call it *Sheree'a*, as they do the Jordan—only qualifying the latter as the larger one. It is called the *Sheree'a el Menâdhĕrah*, from a party of Bedaween occupying its banks in the interior.

The crevasse through which it issues is wild and romantic in the extreme. High cliffs of basalt are the confines of the water. This, on reaching the plain, is parted with several streams, (to compare great things with small,) in the fashion of the Nile or the Ganges; which the Jordan is not, either at its entrance into this lake or its entrance into the Dead Sea.

All the streams are fringed with oleander; and, in the extreme heat of the day, the horses enjoyed not only their drinking, but their wading through the rolling water.

This was the boundary between Bashan and Gilead, through the latter of which we had hitherto been travelling, and gave name to the great battle A.D. 637, where the victory obtained by the fierce *Khalid* and the mild *Abu Obeidah* decided the fate of Palestine, and opened the way of the Moslems to Jerusalem.

Over an extent of four or five miles, before reaching the Jordan, a rich harvest of wheat was being reaped upon the plain. We first attempted to cross at *Samakh*, but finding it impossible at that season, had to turn back to the ford at the broken bridge, which the natives call the 'mother of arches,' (Umm el Kanâter;) and even there the water was still deep.

Corn-fields and flocks of sheep in every direction; but all the shepherds carrying firearms. We most of us lay down on our breasts to drink greedily once more from the dear old river; and then we crossed the Jordan into the land of Canaan, going on to Tiberias, and passing on the way some Franciscan monks. What a change of associations from those of the country we had traversed exclusively for the last nine days!

How absurd the sudden and unexpected contrast from old 'Abd'ul 'Azeez and the brilliant young 'Ali Dëâb in the freedom of the desert, to the cowl and the convent of the monks—from the grand savage language of the Ishmaelite to the melifluous Italian.

At the hot baths of the lake we found our tents already pitched, and my old friend the missionary, —Thomson, from Bayroot,—who had been travelling on the eastern side of the lake, (a territory so little known,) and, as he and I believed, had discovered the true Gadara. We compared notes about affairs of the Arabs at the time.

Several of the juvenile travellers set themselves to swimming before dinner at sunset, the huge hills at the back casting long shadows across the lake.

We all had tea together, as we were to separate to our several destinations in the morning; and on

my retiring to sleep, the thermometer was at 99°
Fahrenheit inside the open tent.

Saturday, 19*th.*—Bathing before the sun rose.

Our travellers engaged the boat from Tiberias
for the day, and it came up from the town to our
camp with the sail spread. Large flights of aquatic
birds as usual flitting and diving about the lake, and
the fish abundant, rising and splashing at the surface.

For an hour or two before starting on my way
southwards, I lay on the beach contemplating the
lovely scenery, and collecting my thoughts, both
as to the past and for the future. The principal
object of meditation was of course the placid lake
itself—

"Dear with the thoughts of Him we love so well."

Then the noble old mountain of Hermon, crowned
with snow, now called *Jebel esh Shaikh ;* which the
Sidonians called Sirion ; and the Amorites called
Shenir, (Deut. iii. 9.)

Next the ever-celebrated Jordan, with its typical
resemblance to the limit dividing this life from the
purchased possession of heaven,—recalling so much
of bright images of Christian poetry employed to
cheer the weary pilgrim, in anticipation of the time
when

"We'll range the sweet fields on the banks of the river,
And sing of salvation for ever and ever!"

Gratefully acknowledging the providence which
had brought us happily so far, the present writer
then girded up his mental loins, and returned to

Jerusalem; but on the way occasionally glancing towards the eastward range of mountains,—the land of Gilead,—now called Belka and 'Ajloon, lately traversed; and with a feeling unknown since the verses were first echoed in childhood, the words would involuntarily issue from the lips:

> "Sihon, king of the Amorites,
>   For His mercy endureth for ever,
> And Og the king of Bashan,
>   For His mercy endureth for ever!"

Having learned that 'Akeeli Aga el Hhâsi was encamped on the Jordan side, at no great distance, I resolved to visit this personage, who has since then become much more famous as a French protégé, being an Arab of Algeria, but at this time only noted as having been the guide of the United States Expedition to the Dead Sea in 1848, and as being at the moment commissioned by the Turks as a Kaimakam of the district, seeing that they could not hold even nominal rule there without him.

At my starting there came up from his post a messenger, Hhasan Aga, the Bosniac officer of Bashi Bozuk, to conduct me to the tents. The Aga was dressed in a crimson silk long coat, over which was a scarlet jacket embroidered in gold, and on his legs the Albanian full kilt, or fustinella, of white calico; his saddle cloth was of pea-green silk with a white border, and yellow worsted network protected the horse's belly from flies, also a rich cloth with tassels lay over the horse's loins.

Proceeded southwards, and passed the broken bridge before mentioned. Harvest everywhere in progress, and the produce being carried home on asses to the village of *'Abadîyeh*, adjoining to the houses of which were square and flat tents made of palm-leaf matting as residences of the Ghawârineh Arabs.

Came to the ruins of a wretched little village called *Belhhamîyeh*, formerly under the patronage of the 'Adwân; and thence appeared in full view upon the hill above the great castle of the Crusaders called Belvoir, but now named *Cocab*, or *Cocab el Hawa*. Upon the plain by the river side was the encampment scattered about, and several European tents among the others denoted the presence of Turkish soldiers.

We could see the Jis'r el Mejâma'a, the bridge leading across to the land of Gilead.

Rode up to 'Akeeli's tent, and found with him the formidable Shaikh Fendi el Faiz of the Beni Sukh'r, and a musician with his rebâbeh. A slave was making coffee on a fire of dried camel's dung, although it was in the fast of Ramadân. We conversed guardedly about Deâb and the rest of the 'Adwân, and the camp at *Dahair el Hhumâr*. 'Akeeli then had brought in for his amusement a wild beast called a *fahh'd*, differing from a panther in being larger and in having black stripes down the face; it seemed wild enough, but was confined by a rope, the pulling of which, and alternately patting the creature was the amusement or occupation of the Aga. They brought me some coffee and water to drink, whereupon 'Akeeli called for some too, and said to me—" These fools of Mohammedans are keeping Ramadân, but I am a Frenchman," he then drank off the water. This man, whom Lynch, the American commander, styles a " magnificent savage," was savage enough in manners, and dirty, and half-naked. He has since, however, made his influence felt, and may perhaps do so again.

Altogether, my reception was not one in accordance with my notions of Arab hospitality. Perhaps he did not wish me to espy what was going on about him in company with Shaikh Fendi el Faiz, so I took my leave, riding towards Cocab. At an Arab encampment we got some *Leben Sheneeni*, (soured fresh milk, most delicious in hot weather,) and drank almost a pailful of it between myself, the kawwâs, and the muleteer. The heat was prodigious. In the camp were only women and children at home: the former employed in weaving and dyeing woollen trappings for horses, —serving to keep off the plague of flies,—of which articles we bought two.

'Akeeli had sent an escort to accompany us as far as the castle. One of the men was a care-worn old fellow from the far north, wearing a very heavy sheepskin coat with wide sleeves, to keep out the scorching heat of the sun, and his face covered

F

with a *mandeel*, or cotton handkerchief, to protect him from reflection from the ground; his venerable musket terminated in a rusty bayonet.

We went southwards until opposite the bridge, then turned westward to the hills, and forded the water of *Wadi Berreh*. The ascent was difficult and long, during which our escort carried on a conversation in the Arnaout language.

At the summit I sent on the servants and baggage to Jeneen, there to pitch the tents for us—the sheepskin man, the kawwâs, and I turned aside to survey the old castle at Cocab el Hawa. It has been a large and noble erection in a strong natural position; the trench and sloping walls are pretty perfect, the stone-work being still sharp-edged; the portion of the defences looking towards the Jordan consists of large stones rabbeted, equal to any work in Jerusalem or elsewhere, which must be an indication of a fortress long before the time of the Crusaders — though the stones are not of dimensions equal to those of the Jerusalem Temple wall.

All the masonry, except the rabbeted work, is constructed from the dark basalt which abounds in that district. All the space within walls, not remaining entire, and part of the trench, is occupied by miserable hovels, forming a sort of village, with patches of tobacco cultivation attached to the dwellings.

But what can one say in description of the glorious prospect from that eminence? It seemed to me to exceed the wonders of Nebi Osha: the principal objects in view being the Lake of Tiberias, the river Jordan, Tabor, Duhy, Beisân, Carmel, Hermon, a stretch of the Hauran, and the cleft of the Yarmuk. One thing surprised me, which was to see how far South Cocab is from Tabor, it had never appeared so before from the direction of Jeneen or of Nazareth. It is due east from *Duhy;* the best way of getting at it from Nabloos is across the plain of Jezreel. It is distinguishable from a great distance by means of a white-washed tower standing in the midst of the castle.

Forwards we went through a village called *Kifereh.* As usual the ride over the plain is very tedious and tiring to the limbs—a hilly country in moderation is much more comfortable. We reached *Shutta,* then the tents of the Shiûkh Arabs close under hills, and beneath a hill called *Nooris,* and at a mill called *Jalood,* we were overtaken by rain late in the year, being the 19th of May.

The sun set a good while before our arriving at Zer'een (Jezreel); the road was not straight, for a *détour* was necessary in order to ensure firm ground among the marshes; stagnated water abounds, that has been poured down from the hills of Gilboa. We passed the natural cavern from which the Jalood water issues on the side of a hill.

A large cistern is formed at the place. The inhabitants—such as we saw occasionally—were very unhealthy in appearance.

Night came on, and dew with it, to which we had been long unaccustomed. The storm cleared off, and we travelled several hours by moonlight. Then we saw abundance of fire-flies flitting across our way.

Overtaking our luggage, we all jogged on slowly together, very tired and silent, till a horseman appeared, who galloped off on our inquiry, "Who goes there?"

At length we heard the welcome sounds of frogs croaking, then dogs barking, then saw the lights of Jeneen, and being Ramadân the minaret there was illuminated with festoons of lamps.

Then we reached the appointed well-known grove of olive trees.

Our day had been very long and fatiguing—the cattle exhausted. It was Saturday night, and the week ended with the intelligence that Shaikh Barakât el Fraikh had declared war against the Beni Sukh'r, so that we had just passed through the Over-Jordan country in time to be able to do so. At Jerash I had met Barakât, and at 'Akceli's camp had met his adversary Fendi el Faiz.

II.

NORTHWARDS TO BEISÂN, KADIS, ANTIPATRIS, &c.

October 23, 1850.

LEAVING Jerusalem upon the Nabloos road, and crossing the upper portion of the valley which, lower down, after a curve becomes the valley of Jehoshaphat, we passed almost directly over the sepulchre of Simon the Just, of whom such "excellent things are spoken" in the books of the Maccabees, and in whose memory an annual festival is kept by the Jerusalem Jews on this spot on the day called ל"ג לעומר, rather more than a month after the passover. Two other saints are celebrated on the same day of the calendar—viz., R. Simeon bar Jochai, the cabbalist of Safed, author of *Zohar*, and R. Akiva of Tiberias.

Then mounting up the side of Scopus, we halted for a few minutes to survey that view of the holy city which surpasses all others, and must have done so in the palmy days of history. It was at the time of mid-afternoon, when the sun's rays pour slantingly with grand effect upon the Temple site.

I could not but recollect that this was exactly the hour appointed for the daily evening sacrifice "between the two evenings," (Hebrew of Exod. xii. 6,) and think of the choral music of Levitical services grandly reverberating among the semicircle of hills.

Meditations of this nature would lead one far away in varied directions, perhaps unsuited for the commencement of a long journey lying before us.

The next object attracting our attention was the Roman milestone lying beside the road, shortly

after passing *Sha'afât*. This I always make it a rule to examine every time of passing it. At one time I had it rolled over in order to be able to read the inscription; but I afterwards found it tossed with the writing downwards—perhaps all the better for its preservation.

The inscription I read as follows :—

IbΛOTIƁT
IMPANTONINI
IMPHADRIANI
IMPTRAIANPARTIOR
IMPNERVAE

That is to say, a register of the names of the Antonine emperors; but there must have been other names on the upper part, now broken away.

Then passed under *Er Ram* on our right hand, the Ramah of the Old Testament, but as it is not often noticed, may be found in Jeremiah xl. 1, as the place where the Babylonish captain of the guard, as a favour, released the prophet, after bringing him with the rest in chains from Jerusalem.

Slept in a house at *Ram Allah*. This is a village about three-quarters of an hour N.W. from Er Ram. The weather being cold we first lit a fire, thereby trying the utility of a chimney that was in the house—in vain, for no smoke would pass up it; it all settled in the room itself; and the people excused themselves on the ground that it had never been tried before. Probably it was a novelty imported to the place by some of the people who had been employed by Europeans in Jerusalem; and yet I have always found that the old Saracenic houses of the Effendis in Jerusalem have all of them chimneys ; and the word for *chimney* is well known in Arabic.

This being almost exclusively a Christian village, it was interesting to hear the people addressing each other as Peter, James, Elijah, John, Paul, &c., instead of Mohammed, Ali, Omar, or other such appellations. It is a little beside the purpose, but I may remark in passing, that throughout these countries there are names in use common to all religions,—some scriptural, as Abraham, Isaac, Jacob, Moses, or David ; and others mere epithets, as Assaad or Selim.

In this village are three priests, (Greek orthodox,) idle, ignorant, and coarse men ; but the peasantry are a bold set of fellows, speaking and acting very independently of clerical domination,—very indifferent as to whether they shall turn Protestants or Papists. One thing they are in earnest about, and that is to get schools for their children.

Ram Allah exhibits the same characteristic as all other Christian villages in Palestine, that of being in good condition—new houses being built, and old ones repaired ; contrary to the condition of Moslem villages, almost without one exception —that of falling to decay. There is, however, no water here ; the women bring it in jars upon their heads from *Beeri*, a considerable distance.

We made a détour from the high-road, in order to look for *Jifna*, the *Gophna* of Josephus, where Titus

Northwards to Beisân, etc. 89

and his renowned Tenth Legion (recently arrived from Britain) slept the night before reaching Jerusalem. Then the Eagles were gathered together over the doomed carcase of the city. Inquiring our way from Ram Allah to Jifna, some said there was a road without going to Beeri; some said there was none. At length we were put upon a pretty decent path.

In ten minutes we came to a sort of well with a little water, where women were thumping clothes upon stones; this is called washing in the East. Magnificent view westwards of the great plain, the Great Sea, Jaffa, Ramlah, &c.

We wandered about hills and among vineyards, and came to a small village named *Doorah*, in good condition, with water, and excellent cultivation of garden vegetables in small patches, similar to those of Selwan (Siloam) and Urtâs; then turning a corner saw Jifna at some distance, in the midst of a plain enclosed by hills; and there it must have been that the manipulus with S.P.Q.R. was posted in front of Italian tents, and the soldiers bustling about or jesting in Latin or British language, before their retiring to rest, in the spring season of the year A.D. 70.

Becoming entangled among a long belt of vineyards between us and it, and time passing away while our luggage was far on the road to Nabloos, we turned aside and regained the high-road at *'Ain Yebrood*. Reluctantly I retreated from *Jifna*, for I had wished to discover the precise road upon which Titus and his army marched towards Jerusalem. Passing *Sinjil, Lubbân,* and *Sâwîyeh,* we rested just beyond *Sâwîyeh* under the great oak, at the divergence of the valley of *Laithma.* Beneath its wide-spreading branches a flock of sheep was resting at noon (Cant. i. 7.) From these we got good draughts of fresh milk.

As evening approached, we were passing within the huge shadow of Mount Gerizim; and in Nabloos I remained till Monday morning,—this being the end of Thursday.

28th. Preparing for descent into the Jordan valley, I engaged, in addition to the usual servants, a horseman of the Bashi bozuk, recommended by the local governor, Suliman Bek Tokân. It seemed prudent to obtain this man's attendance, as he might be known and recognised by disorderly persons throughout the turbulent and unknown country before me, whatever might be his character for valour or discretion. Two of the native Protestants of Nabloos accompanied me also for about four hours on the way.

Passing Joseph's sepulchre and the village of *Asker,* (is not this Sychar? it is near the traditional Jacob's Well,) we went northwards over the plain of *Mukhneh,* equivalent to Makhaneh, " camp," in Hebrew, (the *Moreh* of Gen. xii. 6, Deut. xi. 30, and Judges vii. 1,) having left the eastern valley with *Salem* (Gen. xxxiii. 18) on our right. To my sur-

Northwards to Beisân, etc.

prise the plain was soon and abruptly terminated at the foot of a very lofty mountain, and we commenced a descent among chasms of great convulsions of nature, displaying remarkable contortions of geological strata. This brought us into the Wadi *En-Nab*, so called from the growth there of a fruit-tree, (the Jujube,) bearing that name, better in quality than anywhere else in Palestine; and, indeed, the tree is found in but few other places. At the confluence of this valley with the Wadi *Bedân* there are several fragments of ancient columns remaining, quite four feet in diameter.

Hitherto we had met many more peasants travelling with merchandise than I had expected. They were all going in one direction, namely, towards Nabloos, and therefore from Es-Salt in Gilead, beyond Jordan.

These, however, ceased after we had crossed the water of Wadi Bedân into the larger *Wadi Fara'ah,* —which is, however, the high-road to Es-Salt.

Soon afterwards we observed, by our wayside, a square of solid ancient masonry, three courses high. In England this would be certainly the pedestal of some old demolished market-cross; but it may have been the lower part of some memorial pyramid. In the previous year I had seen just such another at Ziph (Josh. xv. 55,) beyond Hebron.

Then we came upon a distinct piece of Roman paved road, which showed that we were upon the high-road between Neapolis and Scythopolis, *alias* Shechem and Bethshan, *alias* Nabloos and Beisân. —Crossed a stream richly bordered with rosy-blossomed oleander, and soon turned the head of the water. A demolished castle was on our right, commanding the entrance of Wadi Fara'ah.

Soon after noon we gained the olive-trees alongside of *Tubâs*, a prosperous village, yet inhabited by a people as rude and coarse as their neighbours. Tubâs is always liable to incursions from the eastern Bedaween, and always subject to the local wars of the Tokan and 'Abdu'l Hadi factions. I have known it to be repeatedly plundered. The natural soil here is so fertile that its wheat and its oil, together with those of *Hanoon*, fetch the highest prices in towns; and the grain is particularly sought after as seed for other districts.

The place, however, is most remarkable to us as being the *Thebez* of Judges ix. 50, where Abimelech was slain by the women hurling a millstone on his head from the wall. The more I become acquainted with the peculiar population of *Jebel Nabloos*, (*i.e.* the territory of which Nabloos is the metropolis,) a brutish people "waxing fat and kicking," the more does the history of the book of Judges, especially the first twelve chapters, read like a record of modern occurrences thereabouts. It is as truly an Arab history as any other oriental book can supply. I observed that Mount Gerizim can be

Northwards to Beisân, etc.

seen from Tubâs,—which fact seemed to give additional emphasis to the words, "And all the evil of the men of Shechem did God render upon their heads ; and upon those came the curse of Jotham, the son of Jerubbaal."

The site of Tubâs is elevated. It is still a considerable village, and possesses that decided evidence of all very ancient sites in Palestine—a large accumulation of rubbish and ashes.

I was told that here, as well as in several of the villages around, there are scattered Christians, one or two families in each among the Moslems, without churches, without clergy, without books or education of any kind ; still they are Christians, and carry their infants to the Greek Church in Nabloos for baptism. What a deplorable state of things ! Since the date of this journey the Church Missionary Society's agents have in some degree ministered to the spiritual destitution of these poor people by supplying some at least with copies of the Holy Scriptures.

Here my principal kawwâs, Hadj Mohammed es Serwân, found the fever, which had been upon him more or less for the last three days, so greatly increased, that it was not possible for him to proceed farther with me. The fever he attributed to his having, on arrival at Nabloos, indulged too freely in figs and milk together. The general experience of the country warrants this conclusion.

Poor fellow ! after several times dismounting,

and renewing his efforts to keep up with me, he was at length totally disabled; and our Protestant friends, who were now about to return home, engaged to get him into the village, and have him carefully attended to, there and at Nabloos, till he should be able to return to his family at Jerusalem. I left him under a large tree, gazing wistfully after me, and endeavouring to persuade me not to go down to that Gehennom of a place, Beisân.*

My forward journey lay through fine olive-grounds and stubble-fields of wheat. In an hour we passed *Kayaseer*, a wretched but ancient place, with exceedingly old olive-trees about it. Then going on for some time among green bushes and straggling shoots of trees, we descended to the water-bed of a valley. Once more upon a Roman road, on which at twenty minutes' distance was a prostrate Roman milestone, but with no inscription to be seen: perhaps it was on the under side, upon the ground. Then the road, paved as it was with Roman work, rose before us on a steep slope, to a plain which was succeeded by the "Robbers' Valley," (Wadi el Hharamîyeh,) in which we met two peasants driving an ass, and inquired of them, "Is the plain of the Jordan safe?"—meaning, Are there any wild Bedaween about? The reply was "It

---

* He afterwards died of fever in my service, caught by rapid travelling in the heat of July 1860, during the Lebanon insurrection, whither he accompanied my Cancelliere to rescue some of the unfortunate Christians in my district.

is safe; but the whole conversation consisted of four words in the question, and one in the answer.

Over a precipitous and broken rocky hill,—the worst piece of road I ever met with,—till we came suddenly upon the grand savage scenery of the Ghôr, with the eastern barrier of the mountains of Gilead. The river Jordan is not visible, as is the case in most parts, till one almost reaches the banks.

Here the vegetation had changed its character,— leaving all civilisation of olive-trees behind, and almost all consisting of oak and hawthorn. We had instead the *neb'k* or *dôm*-tree, and the *ret'm* or juniper of Scripture; the heat excessive.

At the junction of the Valley with the Ghôr are three Roman milestones, lying parallel and close side by side,—all of them in the shape and size stereotyped throughout the country. This, then, was probably a measured station of unusual importance; and from it the acropolis of Bethshan just comes into view. This is known in the country by the name of *El Hhus'n*.

The ground was in every direction covered with black basalt fragments, among which, however, was corn stubble remaining; and we were told that the crop belonged to the people of Tubâs.

We kept upon a straight path leading directly up to Beisân, which all the way was intersected by running streams issuing from the hills on our left, and going to the Jordan.

The water was not often good for drinking; but

at most of these rivulets our attendant, Suliman Bek's horseman, alighted to say his prayers, out of fright on account of the Arab Bedaween.

Tabor N.W. and Hermon N.E. were both prominent objects in the landscape, with the town of Beisân between the two,—the ground abounding in the kali plant and neb'k trees, with bright yellow fruit, from which we frequently saw clearly desert camels cropping the lower branches, notwithstanding the long and sharp thorns upon them.

We marched straight on, from one ancient artificial mound to another, with Beisân before us, the streams all the way increasing in width and rapidity, —some of them bordered, or even half-choked, with a jungle of oleander in flower, hemlock, gigantic canes, wild fig-trees, neb'k, and tangled masses of blackberry. Some of them we had to ford, or even leap our horses over. We were surprised at such torrents of water rushing into the Jordan at such a season of the year.

Reached Beisân at half-past six,—a wild-looking place, with magnificent mountains in every direction around, but all frowning black with volcanic basalt; and the people horribly ugly—black and ferocious in physiognomy. They were just in the busiest time of the indigo harvest; but they had herds of very fine cows brought home, as the sun in setting threw over us the shadow of the mountains of Gilboa. My companion from Jerusalem looked up with horror to these hills, and began quoting the poetic malediction of David upon them on account of the death of Saul and Jonathan : "Let there be no dew, neither rain upon you, nor fields of offerings," &c.

It was indeed a notable event in one's life to have arrived at the place where the body of the first king of Israel, with that of his son, the dear friend of David, after being beheaded, were nailed to the walls of the city. Jabesh-Gilead could not have been very far off across the Jordan; for its "valiant men arose, and went all night, and took the body of Saul, and the bodies of his sons, from the walls of Bethshan, and came to Jabesh, and burnt them there. And they took their bones and buried them under a tree at Jabesh, and fasted seven days," (1 Sam. xxxi. 12, 13). This respectful treatment was by way of grateful recompense for Saul's past kindness, as the very first act of his royalty had been to deliver them from danger when besieged by Nahash the Ammonite (1 Sam. xi.); and they kept his remains till king David removed them into the ancestral sepulchre within the tribe of Benjamin (2 Sam. xxi. 14).

To return. The people of Beisân urged upon us their advice not to sleep in our tents, for fear of Arabs, who were known to be about the neighbourhood. I however preferred to remain as I was; and many of the people slept around the tents upon heaps of indigo plant, making fires for themselves from the straw. Before retiring to sleep, I several times found the horseman at his prayers by moonlight. During the night the roaring of the water-torrents re-echoed loudly from the rocky hills.

29th.—We learned that the indigo cultivation is not very laborious. The seed is scattered over the ground, and then the people turn the streams over the surface for inundation. There is no ploughing. This is done directly after barley-harvest from the same ground. There is no produce for two years, but after that period the same stalks successively for five years produce about seventy-two-fold. I bought a timnah (measure) of the seed for curiosity, to deposit in our museum.

We finished breakfast, had the tents struck, and the mules laden, all before the sky began to look red, announcing the coming sun.

The castle of 'Ajloon was a very conspicuous object on the mountainous horizon of the east.

I then spent about three hours in exploring the Roman antiquities of the place when it bore the

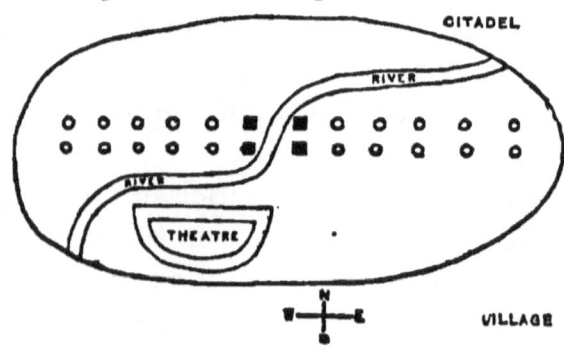

name of Scythopolis. These are all contained within or along a natural basin, of which I here give a rough map.

Northwards to Beisân, etc.

The general form is that of an oval, the centre of which has four pediments for the arch of a bridge, or a triumphal arch, over a rivulet that traverses the whole obliquely. From this central square of four pediments extends right and left one long colonnade, or dromos. Within the basin, but on the south bank of the water, is the theatre; on the north, and outside of the oval, is the lofty mound, surmounted by fortified buildings, forming the acropolis, the *Hhus'n*, which is visible for miles and miles over the country. In the S.E. corner is the modern village—a very insignificant one, but with remains of a Christian church, for I should suppose the Moslems never built so good a mosque at Beisân. Of course the present inhabitants use it for their devotions. The building is all angular, with a square tower at the south end. The principal doorway—that at the north end—is perforated into a walled-up large pointed arch.

The principal object of my curiosity was the theatre, which, like all those of the Romans and Greeks, is a building of nearly a semicircle in form, with the extremities connected by a chord or straight line; this latter was the *proscenium* or stage, and is near 200 feet in length. Upon the ground-plan, at half distance from the centre to the outer curve, the *vomitories* or passages for entrance and exit begin, leaving an open area; these are formed in concentric semicircles, divided across by radii, all coming from the one centre.

Over these passages the seats for spectators are constructed, rising higher as approaching to the outer curve—and the dens for the wild beasts, when they were to be exhibited, were under the front seats. The vomitories are of the most perfect design for utility, and still remain in complete preservation, all vaulted over with admirable workmanship.

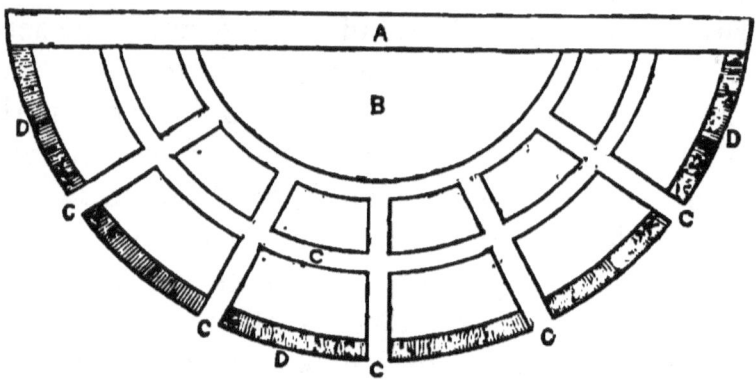

GROUND PLAN OF THE THEATRE.

A Proscenium or stage. B Vacant area. C C C Passages, above which the rows of seats are erected. D D D Outer wall.

I looked about in vain for the indentings in front of the rows of seats which had held the 'Ηχεῖα or brazen saucers, which indentings are stated to have been seen by Irby and Mangles; but we know that the 'Ηχεῖα were so placed in ancient theatres for increasing the power of voice uttered upon the stage.

The front blocks of the stage are white, and these are brought from a distance. They measure eight feet by four each. But the peculiarity of the general building lies in its being built of the black stone of the country adjacent. I afterwards saw Roman theatres at Ammân and Umm Kais, as already mentioned in the journey "Over the Jordan," but they were white; and another at Petra, but that was of rosy red. All the three—the black, the white, and the red—were each of its own one colour, without intermixture of others, except that here the stage was of another colour from the rest of the building.

I then prepared to mount to the acropolis or Hhus'n. The hill is shaped as an oblong square, sloping downwards, and rounded at the four edges. Steps have been cut into it for ascending from below.

Arriving at what appears from below to be the summit, but is not, I found a large platform, improved by art, with remains of houses and cisterns, and surrounded at the edge by a parapet wall five feet thick,—except at the eastern end, opposite to the present town, where one-third of the hill has been left rising considerably higher, and therefore a wall is not required.

In this wall, at the N.W. side, I found remains of a very massive gateway, with fragments of older columns and friezes built up into the side work. At this spot the rising hill above is particularly precipitous. I climbed to the extreme summit, but found there no remains of human labour. The view, however, as may be supposed, amply repaid the exertion. In one direction the prolonged Ghôr of the Jordan; and in another appeared the opening of the plain of Esdraelon and Tabor, with the Mediterranean far away, and Carmel almost hull down, as one might say of a ship. In the nearer distance were lines of black Arab tents, an old khan, ruins of water-mills, and rushing rivulets in abundance, the sources of which lie so high in the adjacent hills of Gilboa, that the town and the irrigation of the district are supplied from them copiously.

I picked up some tesseræ about the acropolis hill, but I saw none elsewhere near Beisân,—discovered no inscriptions, and heard of no coins.

Close to the town there were thick layers of calcareous sediment, containing petrified reeds or canes, of which I brought away specimens for our museum.

Thus ended my inspection of this really interesting place, so remarkable for being all built of black volcanic stone,—the theatre, the church, and the modern village, besides the rocks all about: add to this the vile appearance of the people, and one cannot wonder at visitors entertaining a dread and disgust at the whole.—I find that I have omitted to mention the mineral quality of the water, the most of which is undrinkable.

We left Beisân at half-past nine, after examining it more completely than the published accounts of former travellers lead us to believe they have done. Thomson's account is of later date.

Northwards to Beisân, etc.

Our journey now lay due north, along the Ghôr to Tiberias; and a very pleasing journey it proved to be.

In half an hour we had to ford a pretty wide stream, and in five minutes more were among very extensive ruins of an ancient town; upon a tumulus at its farther extremity are lying portions of three huge sarcophagi, and a portion of a thick column. This must be the "Es Soudah," (*i.e.*, *black*,) mentioned by Thomson—indeed, all ruins of that district are of black basalt, excepting the columns and sarcophagi. The name *soda* or *black* occurs in English as a synonym for *alkali*, and means the black or dark-coloured ashes of the plant *al-kali* when burnt for use—the white colour of it seen in Europe is obtained by chemical preparation.

Black tents and fires of the kali burners were visible in many directions—a delicious breeze blowing in our faces; but above everything cheerful was the green line of the Jordan banks. No snow to be seen at present at that distance upon Hermon. At half-past eleven we were beneath some castellated remains of great extent, namely, the Crusaders' *Belvoir*, now called *Cocab el Hawa*. Our ground had become gradually more undulated; then hilly, and the Ghôr narrowed: we were obliged to cross it diagonally towards the Jordan; forded a running stream abounding in oleander, where, according to his usual custom, my Egyptian servant took a handful of the flowers to wear in his waistcoat. Then the birds carolling so happily, recalling the well-known lines—

> " And Jordan, those sweet banks of thine,
> With woods so full of nightingales."

The songsters that I heard were certainly neither the linnets nor goldfinches of other parts of Palestine, but must have been the *bulbul*, the note of which, though rich and tender in expression, is not however the same with that of English nightingales.

Then we came to the bridge called *Jis'r el Mejâma'a*, which is in tolerably good condition, with one large and several smaller arches in two rows, and a dilapidated khan at the western end. I crossed over the bridge into the territory of Gilead.

The khan has been a strong edifice, but the stones of the massive gateway, especially the great keystone, are split across, as if from the effects of gunpowder.

When that bridge was erected, the country must have been in safe and prosperous circumstances; the beauty of the scenery was not found in contrast to the happiness of the people; there must have been rich commerce carried on between the far east and the towns of Palestine; and it is in reference to such a fortunate period that the wandering minstrels, even now among the Bedaween, sing the songs of the forty orphan youths who competed

Northwards to Beisân, etc.

in poetic compositions under the influence of love for an Arab maiden at the bridge of Mejâma'a.

The name is derived from the *meeting* of two branches of the Jordan in that place after having separated above. Below the bridge the bed of the river is very rocky, and the course of the water disturbed, but above the "meeting of the waters" all is beautifully smooth and tranquil; wild aquatic birds enjoying their existence on its surface, and the banks fringed with willows and oleanders. How grateful is all this to the traveller after a scorching ride of several hours.

Then the river, and with it our road, deflected back to the western hills; again the river wound in serpentine sinuosities about the middle of the plain, with little islands and shallow sands within its course. I am not sure that the delight we experienced was not enhanced by the circumstance of travelling upwards against stream. Whenever tourists find the country safe enough for the purpose, and have leisure at command, I certainly recommend to them this district of Jordan, between Beisân and Tiberias: of course this presupposes that they visit Nazareth before or afterwards.

Occasionally we came to rings of stones laid on the ground,—these mark the graves of Arabs of the vicinity; then a cattle enclosure, fenced in by a bank of earth, and thorns piled on the top. All about this were subterranean granaries for corn, having apertures like wells, but empty. Close to this was a ford to the eastern bank. The river has many interruptions certainly, but yet in two days' ride we had seen a good deal of smooth water for boating. At half-past one was reached the village of *Abadîyeh.*

Near the village we saw people cutting twigs of tamarisk and willow. At the village were large plantations of the kitchen vegetable, *Bamia,* which is a *hibiscus,* (called *ochra* in the West Indies,) the plants four feet high, with bright yellow blossom. Near the regular houses were suburb huts made of reeds. This is often seen along the Ghôr; they are tenanted by wanderers at certain seasons of the year.

There was a profusion of good wheat straw lying wasting upon the ground; it is here too plentiful to be cared for.

We saw afterwards a low wall of masonry entirely crossing the Jordan, but having now a broken aperture in the middle. In former times these artificial works were common, and served to irrigate the lands on each side. The river was never used for navigation.

At two o'clock we reached one well-known rendezvous, the old broken bridge, popularly called "Mother of Arches." The ford was now low in water. Here we rested under a neb'k tree; and on getting out the luncheon, discovered that all our stores of bread, coffee, sugar, and arrow-root had been soaked by the splashing of streams and fords that we had this day encountered.

Northwards to Beisân, etc.

The horseman fell again to his prayers. Several Arabs from the Hauran with their camels, crossed the Jordan while we were there.

Another hour took us to the baths of Tiberias; the heat very great, and by our roadside there was a whole mountain with its dry yellow grass and weeds on fire.

Near the south end of the lake are some palms growing wild. We dismounted at a quarter to four.

Next day I ascended the hills to Safed, a well-known station. The place is exceedingly healthy, enjoying the purest mountain air, as is evinced by the healthy complexion of the numerous Jews residing there; and the landscape views are both extensive and beautiful.

On the following day I undertook a few hours' excursion to *Kadis* (Kedesh Naphtali), where Barak, son of Abinoam, and Deborah, collected the forces of Zebulun and Naphtali, for marching to Mount Tabor against Sisera. It was also one of the six cities of refuge for cases of unintentional homicide, (Josh. xx. 7;) it lies to the NN.E. from Safed.

In an hour we obtained a grand view of Hermon just opposite to us, and never lost sight of it till our return. Passed between the villages of *Dilâthah* on the right, and *Taitaba* on the left; the country is all strewn with volcanic basalt. In another half-hour we had *Ras el Ahhmar* on our left. Then *Fârah* and *Salhhah* at some distance to the left, and *Alma* just before us. The volcanic brown stones had on them occasionally a thin lichen of either orange colour, or a sour pale green, like verdigris.

About this village were women and children gathering olives from the trees—first beating the boughs with poles, then picking up the fruit from the ground.

The small district around here is named "the Khait," and the people boast of its extraordinary fertility in corn-produce.

Down a steep descent of white limestone, where it is said the torrents are so strong in winter that no one attempts to pass that way. Rising again, we found near the summit of the opposite hill a spring of water, from which some Bedaween women were carrying away water in the common fashion, in goat-skins upon their backs. They were young, pretty, dirty, and ragged. Of course their rags were blue, and their lips were coloured to match.

Pleasant breeze springing up after the heat of the day. Corn stubble on the fields, and fine olive plantations, as we got near to Kadis, our place of destination; with such a wide clear road up to it, as might seem to be traditionally preserved as such from ancient times, if the Talmud be relied upon when it gives the legal width of various kinds of

Northwards to Beisân, etc. 109

roads, and prescribes twice as much for a highway towards the cities of refuge, as for any other description of road.*

The scenery around Kadis is cheerful, but the village itself consisted of only about half-a-dozen wretched houses. In passing by these, towards an orchard at the farther side, we saw some large ancient sarcophagi,—three of them lying side by side, but broken, and some capitals of columns.

After selecting our site for the tents, and setting the cook to work in his peculiar vocation, not forgetting to see that the horses were being attended, we procured a guide to conduct us down the hill to the antiquities.

There are still evidences remaining that the old city had been wealthy and celebrated—squared stones lying profusely about. At the spring of water: this was received into an embellished sar-

* According to the Talmud, private roads were made four cubits wide; public roads sixteen cubits; but the approaches to a city of refuge were thirty-two cubits in width. See Lightfoot's "Decas Chorographica," VII. Latitudo viarum Tradunt Rabini. Via. privata דרך היחיד est quatuor cubitorum—via ab urbe in urbem est octo cubitorum—via publica דרך הרבים est sedecm cubitorum—via ad civitates refugii est triginta duorum cubitorum." Bava Batra fol., 100 From Lightfoot's "Centuria Chorographica." "Synhedrio incubuit vias ad civitates hasee accommodare eas dilatando, atque omne offendiculum in quod titubare aut impingere posses amovendo. Non permissus in viâ ullus tumulus aut fluvius super quem non esset pons erat que via illuc ducens ad minimum 32 cubitorum lata atque in omni bivio, aut viarum partitione scriptum erat קלט קלט *Refugium* ne eo fugiens a viâ erraret."—Maimon in רוצה, cap. 8.

cophagus for a trough, and adjoining to it a spacious paved reservoir.

Here began a series of highly ornamental public edifices and sepulchral monuments. We went first to the farthest; and there it was greatly to be regretted that there was not with us an artist able to do justice to the exceeding beauty of the remains.

It was a large oblong building, placed east and west, an ornamental moulding running round the whole at four feet from the ground; the roof fallen in. At the eastern extremity have been three portals, of which the middle one was by far the largest; each of these decorated richly by a bead and scroll moulding. The lintel of the principal gate has fallen from its place, and now stands perpendicular, leaning against one of the uprights: this is one stone of fifteen feet in length, beautifully sculptured. Some broken pillars are lying about, and several magnificent Corinthian capitals of square pilasters, which had been alongside of the principal portal. I have never seen anywhere in Palestine any relic of so pure a Grecian taste as this temple.*

Nearer to the town is a Roman erection of large well-cut stones, which have acquired from the effects of time the fine yellow tinge which is remark-

---

* On visiting Kadis some years after, I was grieved to find all this much demolished, and the ornamentation taken away, by Ali Bek, to adorn the new works at his castle of Tibneen.

able on the relic of the Church of St John Baptist at Sebustieh.*

This was a smaller building than the other, and is nearly entire, except that the roof is fallen in. It is in a square form: at each corner is a solid square of masonry thirty feet high, and these are connected with each other by semi-circular arches, two of which are fallen, and the other two have their keystones dangling almost in the air, so slight is the hold of their voussoirs to keep them from falling. The walls rise half way up these abutments; the doorway is to the south, and has the ports and lintel richly decorated. Of the use of this erection I could form no judgment.

Between the two edifices was a mass of solid masonry, supporting a sarcophagus nearly ten feet long, with a double sarcophagus of the same dimensions at each side of it: not only the middle single one, but each double sarcophagus, was formed of one stone each. Can we doubt of the relation which the persons buried in the double ones bore to each other? The sides of these stone coffins are highly adorned with floral garlands, and the lids are lying broken across beside them.

Oh! vain expectation, to preserve the human frame from violation, by elaborate and durable monuments! There is but one safe repository for the decaying part of man, and that is what the Almighty Maker at first decreed—namely, earth

* Since fallen almost to the ground.

to earth, ashes to ashes, and dust to dust. The poorest slave, buried in a hole within the ground, is safer from man's greed and violence than the mightiest conqueror; for the massive porphyry sarcophagus of Alexander was rifled by Caligula, and after that by others, in Egypt. And the same fate has befallen the tombs of Cyrus and Darius in Persia, for the sake of the riches entombed with them.

Some copper coins were brought to us, but of no particular value: they were either corroded or broken, and of no remarkable antiquity.

As twilight faded away we returned to the tents, and had the evening meal. The wind rose considerably, so that we lighted a fire on the lee side of my tent, and gazed round upon the strange and noble scene around. There was Hermon just before us, seen indistinctly by starlight; and there was sufficient novelty and non-security in the place to keep attention awake.

The shaikh of the village came and assured us that in the Lebanon (not far distant) the Druses were up; that the convent at Maalûleh had been sacked, and twenty-two Emirs had been seized by the beastly Turks (as he denominated them); that Abu Neked was up in arms, and even the villages in the south, about Nazareth, were fighting. Of course there was considerable exaggeration in all this, but our muleteer began to pray that he might be soon safe again in Jerusalem.

The shaikh informed us that in the happy time of the Egyptian rule, under Ibrahim Pasha, his village was so populous that they cultivated fifty feddans of land, whereas now they could only work six; that then property was so safe that Arab marauders were always caught and punished, (he had himself had Bedaween kept prisoners in his house,) whereas now, under the Turks, they come into his house to steal.

While he was relating this, a man came running from the village to announce that neighbouring Arabs were just before carrying off some of their cows in the dark, but on being pursued, had made off without them.

After I got to bed, one of our people shot at a hyæna, and the villagers shouted from the roofs of their houses to know if we were attacked. In the morning they told us that they had seen the hyæna, big enough to eat a man, and that their attention had been attracted to it by the cry of an owl.

Saturday, November 2.—We returned towards Safed over the plain of *Alma.* The wheat of this district is renowned far and wide for quality and quantity of produce. The guide told us that at this place were splendid remains of antiquity; but, on arriving, we could hear of nothing but a poor cistern within a cavern. Here the black basalt recommences after the region of white limestone where we had been; and then again, at the distance of a good-sized field, we were upon common

H

brown agricultural soil. It is curious how sharply these division-lines of soil are drawn in every direction about this place.*

Thence we diverged off from yesterday's road to visit *Jish*, passing through Ras el Ahhmar. Most magnificent views of Hermon and Anti-Lebanon.

Had to go down into a valley, through which, on a former journey, we had passed on coming from *Bint Jebail*, and visited again the ancient monument in a vineyard by the roadside. It appears to have consisted of one small building The lower parts of two upright posts of its doorway remain, together with a fragment of the transverse lintel: several pieces of columns are lying about, and pediments of these *in situ*. Besides these, there is the following fragment of sculpture

ANCIENT SEPULCHRE, NEAR JISH.

* These sudden transitions are also noticed by Wetzstein in travelling over the volcanic regions east of Jordan.

nearly level with the ground, and is probably the entrance of a sepulchre, but we had no opportunity of clearing away the soil to ascertain that. The ornamentation seems to be that of laurel leaves. Near adjoining is a fragment of a round pillar, partly buried ; but on seeing Hebrew writing upon it, I cleared it away partly. Some of it was but indistinct. I could only read it thus—

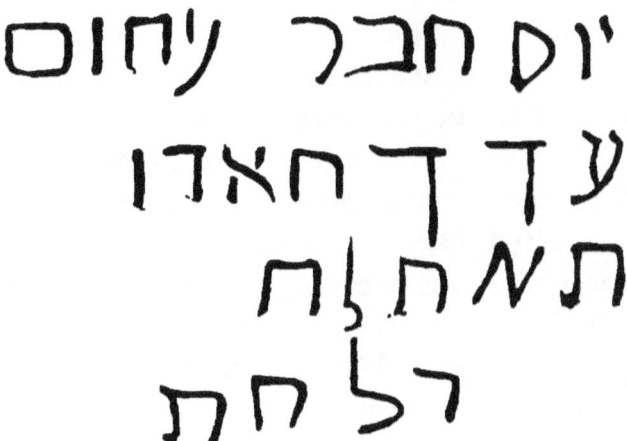

—from which not much signification can be gathered. Perhaps some cracks in the stone have disfigured the characters; but how and when did a Hebrew inscription come in such a place? The site is very agreeable, with streamlets of water tinkling among trees by the roadside.

Thence we mounted up to the village of *Jish*, the place of *John of Giscala*, the antagonist of Josephus. This seems to have been the centre-point of the dreadful earthquake in 1837, from which

Safed and Tiberias suffered so much. It occurred on the New Year's day, while the people of the village were all in church; and just as the priest held the sacramental cup in his hand, the whole village was in a moment destroyed, not one soul being left alive but the priest himself, and, humanly speaking, his preservation was owing to the arch above his head. All the villages around shared the same fate, and the greater part of the towns above mentioned. Much damage was sustained all over Palestine; and a heart-rending description of the events has since been printed, though little known in England, by a Christian Israelite, named Calman, who, together with Thomson, the American missionary, hasted from Bayroot on hearing of the calamity, and aided in saving many lives of persons buried beneath the ruins of Safed and Tiberias, during several days after the catastrophe.

This sad event serves for an era to date from; and the Jews there, when referring to past occurrences, are accustomed to say, it was so many years before (or after) the רעש (the earthquake.)

Among the ruins of Jish are no remains of antiquity, except a fragment of the thick shaft of a column and a small sarcophagus, only large enough for a child, in a field half a mile distant. The Jews appropriate this to Shemaiah Abtelin.

We passed between *Kadita* and *Taitaba*, over land strewn with volcanic stone, beginning near Jish and extending almost to those villages. The crater, of very remote times, noticed by Robinson, is about one-third of the distance from Jish to Safed; not very imposing in appearance.

The journey from Kadis to Safed is one of five hours' common travelling. We reached the olive ground encampment shortly before noon. Being the Jewish Sabbath, there was the *Eruv* suspended at the exits of the principal streets. This is an invention of the Talmudists, used in unwalled towns, being a line extended from one post to another, indicating to Jews what is the limit which they are to consider as the town-wall, and certain ordinances of the Sabbath are regulated thereby.

A strong wind from the south blew up a mist that almost concealed the huge dark ravine of *Jarmuk*, but the night became once more hot and still.

3*d*.—" And rested the Sabbath-day, according to the commandment,"—neither the principal prayer-day of the Mohammedans, which is Friday, nor the Sabbath-day of the large population of Jews about me, but that which the early Christians so beautifully named the Lord's-day, while observing it as a Sabbath. I attended divine service in the English language at the house of Mr Daniel, the missionary to the Jews : we were six in number. The rest of the day was spent in quiet reading and meditation, with visits at one time from the rabbis, and at another from the missionary.

4*th*.—An excursion to *Meroon* to visit the sepulchres of several eminent canonized rabbis. The Jews believe this place to be the Shimron-Meron of Joshua xii. 20. An odd party we formed: there were the missionary and his lady, Polish rabbis with very broad beaver hats and curled ringlets on each side of the face, a crowd of Jewish idlers walking, the Moslem attendants, and a peasant of the village we were going to. Certainly the rabbinical riding was not of a very dashing character: their reverences were all mounted on asses with mean accoutrements, for the adjustment of which they often had to dismount. Our place of destination lies at the foot of the great hill Jarmuk, and the road to it is very rough, with broken rocks fallen from the summit; but the place commands a grand prospect of Safed and the Lake of Galilee.

The first object of interest was of course the sepulchre of Rabbi Simeon bar Jochai, the patron saint of this region, and of regions beyond. He lived a miraculous life in the second Christian century; wrote the famous book (Zohar), by which, if I mistake not, the Cabbalists still work miracles; and miracles are performed in answer to prayers at his tomb—so it is believed; and his commemoration festival, in the month Iyar (see *ante*) is attended by Jewish votaries from all parts of the world, many of whom practise the heathen rite of burning precious objects, such as gold lace, Cashmere shawls, &c., upon the tomb, to propitiate his favour. On these occasions scenes of scandalous licence and riot are witnessed, and sometimes lives are lost in conflicts with Moslems begun in drunkenness. The rabbis, however, procure great gains from the annual festival or fair.

(In the town of Safed there is at least one (perhaps more) *Beth ha-Midrash*, a sort of synagogue, with perpetual endowment, for reading of the Zohar day and night for ever.)

First we entered a court-yard with a walnut-tree in the midst. At a farther corner of this court is a small clean apartment, with a lighted lamp in a frame suspended from the ceiling, which is capable of holding more lamps. In a corner of this apartment is a recess with a lamp burning before it; in this a roll of the law is kept; it is the shrine itself of the author of Zohar. One of our rabbis retired behind us for prayer. In another part of this chamber is buried Eleazar, son of the illustrious Simeon.

These sepulchres are marked out upon the roof, outside of the chamber, by a small pillar over each, with a hollow on the top of it for burning of the votive offerings as above mentioned. Near the first entrance gate is a similar pillar for lamps and offerings vowed to Rabbi Isaac, a celebrated physician.

All these three saints still perform as many miracles as ever they did; and the common people believe that any person forcing an entrance to the shrines, without express permission of the living rabbis, will be infallibly punished with sudden death. They cited instances of such visitations having occurred.

We then went to the ruin of what the Jews assert to have been a synagogue. It has been an oblong square building, one of its sides being formed by the scarped surface of a rock, and its opposite (the north) stands upon what is now the brink of a low precipice, probably from the earth having given way below at the time of the earthquake; indeed it must be so, for the one of the three portals at the east end, which was there, is now missing. The floor is solid surface of rock, and now used by the peasants for a thrashing-floor. The portals have been handsome, with bold mouldings; but no floral embellishment or inscription now remains.

The transverse lintels are each of one stone; the central one is at least fifteen feet in length.

Persons still living remember this building very much more entire than it now is. There is an abundance of large loose stones lying about, and fragments of broken columns or moulded friezes. Upon the rock by its side is a small tower that was erected by old Daher (Volney's hero of the Report on Syria) in the eighteenth century.

The village population now consists of about thirty souls, friendly to the Jews, from whom indeed they derive their principal subsistence, in consideration of guarding the sanctuaries from spoliation. Other sanctified rabbis are interred in sites about the village and the hill.*

After a temperate luncheon upon the rocks among the noble scenery in the open air, and consulting the Hebrew book of travels of R. Joseph Schwartz, (who was still living in Jerusalem,) we parted from our rabbis, and proceeded to visit Cuf'r Bera'am.

When we arrived close to *Sasa*, there was *Jish* before us on the right. We passed through a district of stones and underwood of evergreen oak; clouds and rain coming on, which overtook us sharply as we reached the village.

Some of the party being but poor riders, we were later than I had expected to be; it was quite sunset; and the people of the place, (almost all of them Maronite Christians,) headed by their priest could do no less than press us to stay through the night with them, especially as the sky threatened a continuation of rain. After deliberative counsel being taken among us, it was resolved that we could only thank the good people for their intended

---

* Strange that Benjamin of Tudela, in the twelfth century, makes no mention of R. Simeon Jochai; but does say that the great men Hillel and Shammai (of the Christian era) are interred near Safed.

hospitality, and return home. We first halted before an ancient square building, the outside of which has been much encroached upon by the alluvial earth of ages, and the simple but correct Tuscan portico, encumbered with piles of fagots for the village use during the approaching winter. The three doorways of the façade were embellished by sculptured wreaths of vine leaves and grapes. Hearing that some Hebrew inscription was to be found beneath one of the windows, we had some of the fagots removed, sufficient to enable us to read the words הבית הזה (this house, &c.); but on account of the labour required to do more with such a tangled and heavy mass of wood, besides the rain and the lateness of the hour, we were obliged to abandon the task, and go forward to the large decorated portal which is standing alone, without its edifice, in an enclosed field at about a quarter of a mile distant. This is erected upon a raised platform of masonry. Upon the transverse lintel we read the following Hebrew inscription, neatly engraved :—

יהי שלום במקום הזה ובכל מקום תושבי ... למעש
... ברכה במעשיו

(Peace be within this place, and all places of the sojourners . . . . . . to the work . . . . . . blessing in his works.) This is all written in one line, without breaks or stops, very small, and in as neat a square character as if lately copied from a printed book. The two uprights and the lintel have a

Northwards to Beisân, etc. 123

simple and chaste ornament like a bead moulding. The transverse lintel has in the middle of its length a rosette surmounted by a circular wreath, at each end of which may be seen upon close inspection, and in a slanting light, traces of a small animal, most likely a sheep, recumbent, which have been chiselled away. On a visit some years after, and on closer inspection, I remarked the same figures upon the façade of that building above mentioned, with Tuscan pillars for a portico, though pains have been taken, as in this instance, to obliterate them.

The ground all about there is strewn with moulded stones and broken columns.

We reached Safed, cold and wet, in the dark, having ridden but slowly, in order to accommodate certain individuals of the party; but it was in the month of November, at an altitude of above 2000 feet, with rain and gusts of wind coming between dark mountains.

My evening reflections alone naturally ran upon the almost unknown circumstance of Hebrew inscriptions existing upon remains of ancient and decorated edifices in this part of the country, while nothing of the sort is known elsewhere. Were the two buildings at Cuf'r Bera'am, and the sepulchre in the field below Jish, really Jewish? and if so, when were they erected?

The modern Jews, in their utter ignorance of chronology, declare these to be synagogues of the time of the second temple in Jerusalem; and affirm that, notwithstanding the destruction of Jerusalem by the Romans, this province of Upper Galilee remained without its people being led into captivity, and that many families (for instance, the Jewish agriculturists still at Bokeea', between Safed and Acre) continue now, just as they were then, in the same localities.

My good old friend Nicolayson, the late missionary to the Jews, was willing to believe a good deal about this local stability of Jews in Upper Galilee, and to give credit for a state of much prosperity among the Jews in the East during the reigns of the Antonine emperors; and his idea was the most probable one of any that I have heard advanced—namely, that these edifices (corresponding in general character with those remaining at Kadis) are really synagogues from the era of the Antonines, and that the inscriptions are of the same date; meanwhile keeping in mind that they are utterly wanting in the robust style of archaic Hebraism, and that the embellishments indicate somewhat of a low period.

For myself, after two visits to the place, and many years of consideration, I cannot bring myself to this belief; but rather conclude that they were heathen temples of the Antonine epoch, and afterwards used as synagogues by the Jews, long ago —probably during some interval of tranquillity under the early Mohammedans,—and that the Hebrew inscriptions were then put upon them.

There is some regularity and method in the

writing upon the lonely portal in the field, though even this is not so well executed as the contiguous moulding upon the same stone; but the other two inscriptions (those upon the façade of the building in the village, and that upon the broken column in the field below Jish) are put irregularly upon any vacant space that happened to be unencumbered. I am convinced that, in the latter instance, the sculpture and the writing have nothing to do with each other.

The surest demonstration, however, to my mind, lies in the evident fact of animal figures having been originally upon the same lintel where the writing now is. Although their relief-projection has been chiselled down, the outlines of the figures are unmistakable. These, I feel certain, were co-eval with the buildings, while the inscriptions are only coeval with their being defaced.

Next day we travelled southwards towards Jerusalem. On leaving the town we passed the ruins of an old church, which they call "The Church of the Forty Martyrs," (this seems to be a favourite traditional designation, as there are other such about the country;) and in half an hour reached a stream in the midst of a wood of neb'k trees, where an Arab, riding a fine mare and carrying a long spear decorated with black ostrich feathers, was driving a cow across the water—very probably plundered from some neighbouring village.

At *Yakook*—the dirtiest place in the world, I

suppose, there was a large Arab encampment, the men sitting apart from the women, and cooking going on—thence to *Hhatteen*. The volcanic stones of this region are far blacker than elsewhere; the district resembles some dismal coal district in the north of England. Thence out of the common road to *Nimrin*, by *Lubieh*, *Tura'án*, to *Cuf'r Cana*, the old and true Cana of Galilee.

At this village of peculiarly scriptural interest, the women and children were spreading cotton pods, just picked, on their house-roofs to dry. Here is a square-built cistern filled from a spring within it, and the cattle were drinking from a beautiful sarcophagus. Losing our road again we came to *Meshhad*, rather west of the usual road. Clouds lowering and frowning over Carmel. At the village of *Raineh* I noticed a man harrowing a ploughed field by dragging a bunch of prickly-pear leaves after a yoke of oxen. Arrived at Nazareth.

Next day, across the plain of Esdraelon to *Jeneen* and *Sanoor*, where we slept. Then by a new road, untraversed by Europeans. After *Jeba'*, we got into the plain of Sharon, through the large olive plantations of *Fendecomia*, (*pente*, five, and *comai*, villages—in Greek,) between *Yaero*, (a ruin,) *Adjah*, *Ramecen*, and *Attarah*, with other villages in good condition. Saw Cuf'r Ra'i very distinctly at a distance in the West, and numerous villages besides.

From an eminence we looked down upon an extensive prospect of shaded unoccupied hills, with the wide plain beyond and the Mediterranean Sea; then descended into a valley, the road winding about through immense olive groves,; the travelling was easy, and all the district bore the appearance of prosperity, such as could hardly be expected where we know that factious warfare so frequently exists. Passed *Cuf'r Rumân*. As far as *'Annâbeh* the course had been for a long time westwards; but there, at the opening of the great plain, we turned due southwards. This was four hours from *Sanoor*, at a good pace. Passed between *'Annâbeh* and *Tool el Ker'm* in changing our course. Near *Irtahh* we passed a camel-party going down to Egypt with bales of soap and tobacco for sale. We were upon the established route of trade between Damascus and Egypt, and not very far distant from Dothan, where the Midianite or Ishmaelite caravan bought Joseph from his brethren; but we had passed this on our left hand in the morning.

Soon passed *Farra'an* on our left, with a weli and a cistern below it, by the roadside. *Kalinsâwa* in sight, but far away to the right; *Ferdisia* and *Zenâbeh* on the left. The day very hot, and the peasantry observed to be, as usual in all the Philistine country, cleaner in their garments than those of the mountains.

Coasted along, parallel to the line of hills, as far as *Kalkeeleh*, where we began to turn inwards, across the fields, towards the place of our destination, namely, *Mejdal Yaba*, which was conspicuous on an eminence before us. This was at six and a half hours from *Sanoor*.

In a field we arrived at a well, where the water must have been very low down, being late in the year; for it was only obtained by jars or skins drawn up at the end of a very long rope, worked by a long line of women walking across the field, and singing at their work, while the men sat looking on and smoking.

We passed the remains of some old considerable town, where, among the fallen building stones and the lines of foundations, there was a cistern, and an ancient sarcophagus by its side; also a deep square well filled up with rubbish, and remains of quarrying work in the solid rock,—besides an unroofed building, with a semicircular arch to the doorway. Surely this must have been of Roman construction.

Arrived at *Mejdal Yaba* in nine hours from Sanoor,—a hot and tiring journey. At a short distance below us was the site of *Ras el Ain;* and farther westwards, but within sight, the tall white tower of *Ramlah*. Time—sunset.

I had a special object in coming off the common high-roads to this place, but little known, at that time not at all known, to Europeans,—namely, to visit Shaikh Sâdek, the responsible ruler of the district, and regarded by the peasantry with especial deference, out of traditional obedience to his ancient family.

We found the village and the castle in a very dilapidated condition, and the great shaikh not at home. Some of his relatives, however, received us; but both they and the peasantry were surprised, if not alarmed, at our coming. To them it seemed as if we were suddenly dropped upon them from the sky. Perhaps they had never seen Europeans before; or they might have thought us spies sent by the Turkish Government. There were plenty of idle fellows lounging about; but their supplies of food from the village were scanty, and of inferior quality.

The Sâdek family apologised for apparent want of hospitality,—explaining that the only unbroken part of the castle was but just sufficient to contain the *hareem* of the women, and there was not a single room to give me. So I was glad to have my bedding and other paraphernalia spread upon a *mustabah*, or raised stone divan, just within the gate. A narrow vaulting covered my head; but it was open at the side to the square court, into which the horses, asses, cows, and sheep were driven for the night.

After considerable delay, a rude supper was produced,—of which, however, I could not persuade the family to partake till after ourselves. They then ate up the remainder in company with my servants. They were very solemn and slow in conversation; indeed, I could not but suspect that they had some hostile schemes in preparation, which they did not wish to have ascertained or communicated to their neighbours.

I

Troubling myself very little about their local politics, I was soon on my bed, and looking up at the brilliant stars. Sleep did not come very soon, as the men kept up firing guns, and the women trilling their songs, to a late hour. They said it was on account of a wedding.

Daybreak found me up, and in full enjoyment of the exquisite luxury of open air, in a clear and pure Oriental climate, before sunrise.

The servants were all busied in various occupations, and the peasantry driving out the cattle, while I was surveying the considerable remains of an old Christian church, which now forms one side

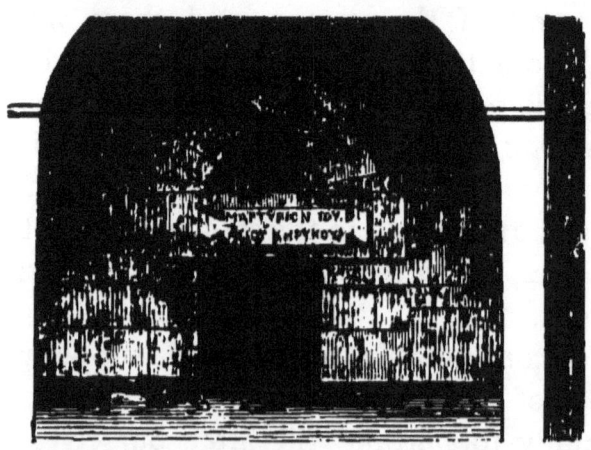

of the shaikh's mansion, and is used for a stable and a store of fodder. This vignette represents its entrance, in a corner now darkened by the arcade in which I had slept. The workmanship is massive and very rude, and the Greek of the inscription upon the lintel not less barbarous, signifying

Northwards to Beisân, etc.

"Martyr Memorial Church of the Holy Herald,"
—*i.e.*, John the Baptist.

This discovery interested me deeply, in that region so remote from any body of Christians at the present day, and among a population very like savages dwelling amid stern hill-scenery.

Not less touching was the special designation of the saint so commemorated. I believe that the Easterns pay more respect than Europeans do to the memory of him whom the Saviour himself pronounced to be greater than all the Old Testament prophets. And while we are accustomed to ascribe to him only one of his official characters,—that of the Baptizer,—they take pleasure in recalling his other scriptural offices; as, for instance, this of the *Herald*, or Preacher* of righteousness, and that of the *Forerunner*.† Indeed, individuals are not unfrequently named after him in baptism by this latter appellation, without the name John.

This building appears to have been at all times heavy and coarse in construction; indeed, one may fairly suppose that part of the frontal has at some time been taken down, and strangely put together again.

This church is the only object of curiosity that I had found along the recent novel route.

On leaving *Mejdal*, I descended to inspect once more the site so interesting to me of *Ras el 'Ain*, at half an hour's distance,—which I unhesitatingly

* Κῆρυξ.   † Ηρόδρομος.

believe to be *Antipatris*, as I conceived it to be on my first seeing the place the preceding year. I had then passed it rather late in the evening, and upon the other side.

Cuf'r Saba, to which I was then going, is a wretched village, of unburnt bricks, on the wide open plain, with no other water near it than the deposit of rain-water in an adjoining square tank of clay. Yet travelling authors have constantly pronounced this to be the locality of Antipatris. Not one of them, however, has visited the place.

What does Josephus say (Antiq. xvi. 5, 2, in Whiston)?—"After this solemnity and these festivals were over, Herod erected another city in the plain called Caphar Saba, where he chose out a fit place, both for plenty of water and goodness of soil, and proper for the production of what was there planted; where a river encompassed the city itself, and a grove of the best trees for magnitude was round about. This he named Antipatris, from his father Antipater." Πόλιν ἄλλην ἀνήγειρεν ἐν τῷ πεδίῳ τῷ λεγομενῳ Καφαρσαβᾶ .... τόπον εὔυδρον .... ἐκλεξας· κ.τ.λ. No words can be more distinctly descriptive; yet Robinson, who had not visited that district, in his positive manner lays down that the village of Cuf'r Saba is the site of Antipatris; and "doubtless" all that is said about "well watered," and "a river encompassing the city," means that some wadi or watercourse came down from the hills in that direction, and made the place watery in the winter season.

Now, what are the facts remaining at the present day? Upon the same plain with Cuf'r Saba, and within sight of it, at hardly six miles' distance, is a large mound capable of containing a small town, with foundations of ancient buildings, bits of marble, Roman bricks, and tesseræ scattered about, —but especially a large strong castle of Saracenic work, the lower courses of the walls of real Roman construction; and at the foot of the mound rises the river *Aujeh* out of the earth in several copious streams, crowded with willows, tall wild canes, and bulrushes,—the resort of numerous flocks, and of large herds of horned cattle brought from a distance, and (as I have seen there) counted by the Government inspector of the district, for the levying of agricultural taxes upon them.* This is our Ras el 'Ain.

For a considerable extent there is capital riding-ground of green grass, so rare in Palestine. Let any one familiar with that country answer, Could Herod have selected a better spot for a military station, (as Antipatris was,) just on the border, descending from the hill-country upon the plain? With this description in view, we understand all the more vividly the narrative of Felix sending St Paul to Cæsarea. To elude the machinations of

* I have been there three times, twice late in autumn, and once in July, and always found water abundant.

the conspiracy, the military party travelled by night over the hilly region; and on reaching the castle of Antipatris, the spearmen and other soldiers left him to continue the journey with cavalry upon the plain to Cæsarea, about three hours farther, (Acts xxiii. 23, and 31, 32.)

It seems impossible to avoid the conclusion that this is the true site of Antipatris; and as for Josephus calling that neighbourhood "the plain of Cuf'r Saba," that must be for the same reason as another part of the same vast extent was called the Plain of Sharon,—or as it is now very much the custom for modern travellers to call the whole Philistine plain by that name.

As for the statement that a river encompassed the city itself; I imagine that the town was not upon the elevated mound,—this was probably occupied by military works and a temple,—but upon the level of the water, among the serpentine separate streams, which soon combine into one river, the Aujeh, with its water-mills, and which was navigable for some distance inland to the north of Jaffa. In the course of ages some of these streams may have somewhat changed their direction. The mound has still a dry trench around it, which must have anciently had its current of water through it.

It cannot be that the deep trench dug by Alexander from Antipatris to the sea (Antiq. xiii. 15, 1, Whiston) can have begun at this village of Cuf'r Saba, where no water rises, and which is far away

Northwards to Beisân, etc. 135

from the hills in an open plain. Although the words are distinctly, "from Capharzaba," the trench must have originated at the river head, *i.e.*, Antipatris, where there was a fortified castle, and passed round the nearest town, viz., that of Cuf'r Saba.

I should observe, that not only Herod did well in selecting this spot for a castle, because of its situation on the verge of the mountains, commanding the road from Jerusalem to either Cæsarea or Joppa; but because it lies also upon the direct caravan track between Damascus and Egypt, nearly at right angles with the other road.

The ruined Saracenic khan which now stands on the foundations of the Roman castle, is of large size, and has a broken mosque in the centre of the enclosure.

We rested and breakfasted, from our own resources, (without taxing the Arab hospitality of Shaikh Sâdek's family at Mejdal,) at the springs of the Aujeh,—the water bubbling up warm from the ground, among stones, with aquatic birds flying over us, and the morning breeze sighing among the gigantic reeds and the willows.

We engaged a guide for what seemed likely to be a short day's journey to *Ras Kerker*, the *cursi*, or metropolis, of another dominant family—that of *Ibn Simhhan*—within the mountains; but it proved far longer than was expected.

We were conducted due south, yet so far away from the line of hills that we missed the Roman temple of *M'zeera'a*, which I do not know that, to this day, any European but myself has seen.*

To *Nebi Sari*, which is a pretty weli, two hours only from Jaffa. To *Runtieh*, which is a poor place. Then south-eastwards to *Teereh;* near which we started a gazelle across the fields.

In that part of the country the population had so greatly increased of late years that there was a scarcity of land for cultivation ; and at the end of autumn the villages contest the right of ploughing there by fights of fire-arms.

Suddenly we turned into a valley, at an acute angle with our previous road. This is named *Wadi el Kharnoob* — probably from some conspicuous karoobah-tree. In ascending the hill, I looked back, and had a beautiful prospect of Jaffa, and a white ship sailing on the sea.

We continued ascending higher and higher. Before us was a large building on a single hill, which they called *Dair Musha'al*. Passed the ruined village, *Hhanoonah*. On our right hand, among trees, was *Desrah*. Passed through *Shukbeh*. How different is the mountain air from that of the plain, so light and so pure !

Descended a little to *Shibtain*, where there was a great ancient well; and being surrounded by hills, the place was very hot. Then for some time over very dangerous paths, mounting upwards, till

---

* Since writing the above I have seen the photograph taken of this temple by the Palestine explorators in 1866.

Northwards to Beisân, etc. 137

we reached the region of a cool breeze, such as I once heard a peasant say was "worth a thousand purses" on a summer's day.

Saw *Ras Kerker*, the place of our destination, high above, in a very remarkable situation; but how to get at it was a puzzle which patient perseverance alone could solve.

We rode round and round one hill after another, till we reached *Dair'Ammâr*. Then opened upon us one of those few prospects which in a lifetime impress themselves indelibly on the mind. This was not lovely, but stern, consisting chiefly of a wild, dark alternation of lower hills, with the valleys between them.

The villages hereabouts bear an appearance of prosperity—perhaps because Turkish officials are never seen there; but the people of *Dair 'Ammâr* behaved rudely. Down, deep deep down we went, leading our horses, in order to rise afterwards to a higher elevation. At length we reached a petty spring of water, where there were some dirty, but otherwise good-looking women, who pointed out our path towards the castle at the top of the hill.

The *Ibn Simhhan* people (being the great rivals of *Abu Gosh*) had often invited me to visit them at this castle,—describing with ardour the abundance and excellence of its springs of water, and the salubrity of its atmosphere.

On arriving at the "*Ras*," after a tedious and very wearisome journey,—difficult as the place is of access,—I found it to fall far below those promises. There are no springs near it. The only water is brought up by the women from the one which we had passed far below. Only within the castle (which was begun while building forty-four years before) some old wells, with good masonry stones, were discovered. These are now put into good order, and kept full, probably in readiness at any time against a siege by the faction of Abu Gosh. Many battles and sieges take place in these remote places that the Pasha of Jerusalem never hears of.

Although of modern origin, much of the earliest part of the castle is already falling to decay—such as gates, steps, &c. It was a melancholy spectacle to walk about the place, reminding one of some small middle-aged castles that I have seen in Scotland, burnt or destroyed during old times of civil warfare; or resembling my recollection, after many long years, of Scott's description of the Baron Bradwardine's castle in its later period. And the same melancholy associations recurred yesterday at Mejdal Yaba.

The people assured us that the tortuous and rocky road that we had taken from Ras el Ain was the best and nearest that we could have taken.

We were received by a couple of relatives of Ibn Simhhan, who is now Governor of Lydd; but they conducted us to the next village, *Jâniah*, to

Northwards to Beisân, etc. 139

be entertained there by the rest of the family. On our descent to the village, we met our hosts coming to meet us.

Jâniah is a poor place; and we had glimpses of curious groups and scenes within the best one of the wretched houses. We were received in a large room, to which the access was by a steep and broken set of steps outside of the house. In the street below was a circle of the elders of the village; and at the time of sunset, one of them mounted on the corner of a garden wall to proclaim the *Adân*, or Moslem call to prayers. I did not observe that he was at all attended to.

A good number of the leading people came to visit us; and one old man quoted and recited heaps of Arabic poetry for our entertainment while awaiting the supper.

Then 'Abdu'l Lateef Ibn Simhhan, joined by another, (a humbler adherent of the family,) gave us a vivid relation of the famous battle of *Nezib* in 1838, and of his desertion from the Egyptian army to the Turkish with a hundred of his mountaineers, well armed, during the night; of how the Turkish Pasha refused to receive him or notice him till he had washed himself in a golden basin, and anointed his beard from vessels of gold; how the Turkish army was disgracefully routed; how he ('Abdu'l Lateef) was appointed to guard the Pasha's harem during the flight, etc., etc. This narrative was occasionally attested as true by a negro slave in the room, who had been with my host on that expedition.

The most lively fellow, however, of the party was one Hadj 'Abdallah of Jerusalem, who has two wives, one a daughter of Ibn Simhhan, the other a daughter of Abu Gosh!! His property in Jerusalem consists chiefly of houses let out to Jews, whom he mimicked in their Spanish and German dialects.

At length came supper; then sleep.

Saturday, 9th.—Asaad Ibn Simhhan and Hadj 'Abdallah rode with us to *Mezra'ah* to show us some ruins of an ancient city near it, called *Hharrâsheh*, where, as they told us, there are "figures of the children of men" cut in the rock. This roused our curiosity immensely, and I felt sure of success in such company; for though we were in a very wild and unknown country, we had the second greatest of the Ibn Simhhan family with us, and the Hadji was evidently popular among them all.

We sent on our luggage before us to Jerusalem by *Bait Unah* and *Bait Uksa*.

In rather less than an hour we reached *Mezra'ah*—the journey much enlivened by the drollery and songs of Hadj 'Abdallah. Both he and Asaad had capital mares and ornamented long guns. The latter was all dressed in white—the turban, abbai, etc. His face was pale, and even his mare white.

Northwards to Beisân, etc. 141

Arrived at the village, we all mounted to the roof of a house—the people paying great reverence to Asaad. Gradually we found the whole population surrounding us, and then closing nearer and nearer upon us. As the heat of the sun increased, we descended to an arcade of the same house, at the end of which there were some itinerant Christians mending shoes for the people.

A breakfast was brought to us of eggs swimming in hot butter and honey, with the usual Arab cakes of bread. The crowd could not be kept off; and the people themselves told us it was because they had never before seen Europeans.

One man asked for some gunpowder from my horn. I gave some to Asaad, and one of the villagers took a pinch of it from him; then went to a little distance, and another brought a piece of lighted charcoal to make it explode on his hand. He came to me afterwards, to show with triumph what good powder it must be, for it had left no mark on his skin.

Ibn Simhhan had to make the people move away their lighted pipes while I was giving him some of the precious powder. He then informed the assembly that I had come to see *Hharâsheh* and the sculptured figures. They refused to allow it. He insisted that I should go; and after some violent altercation and swearing the majority of the men ran to arm themselves and accompany us, so as to prevent us from carrying off the hidden treasures.

We rode away; and at every few hundred yards places were pointed out to us as sites of clan massacres, or wonderful legends, or surprising escapes, in deep glens or on high hills. At one time we passed between two cairns of stones, one covering a certain 'Ali, the other a certain Mohammed, both slain by ——. "By whom?" said I. The Hadji gave no other reply than pointing over his shoulder to Asaad. I felt as if transported a couple of centuries back to the wilds of Perthshire or Argyleshire, among the Highland clans. The local scenery was of a suitable character.

In about forty minutes we arrived at some lines of big stones, that must have belonged to some town of enormous or incalculable antiquity; and this, they told us, was *Hharrâsheh*. As for columns, the people told us to stoop into a cavern; but there we could perceive nothing but a piece of the rock remaining as a prop in the middle. "Well, now for the figures of the children of men." The people looked furious, and screamed. They gathered round us with their guns; but Asaad insisted; so a detachment of them led us down the side of a bare rocky hill, upon a mere goat-path; and at last they halted before a rough, uncut stone, whose only distinction from the many thousands lying about, was that it stands upright.

Asaad observed our disappointment, and said something—I forget the exact terms now—which led me to believe that this was not the object he had meant, and that the ignorant, superstitious people could not be coerced. He believed that this stone had been anciently set up with some meaning —probably by some one who had buried treasures ; not as indicating the exact spot, but as leading in a line connected with some other object, to the real place of concealment.

So here the matter ended ; and, when the people saw us looking disappointed, they went away satisfied to their village.

We parted from our friend Asaad Ibn Simhhan, taking one of the peasantry with us to show us the way to Ram Allah, which he did through vineyards and cheerful scenery; and we were soon again at that village after seventeen days' absence. In about two hours more we were in Jerusalem.

III.

SOUTHWARDS ON THE PHILISTINE PLAIN AND ITS SEA COAST.

THIS extensive level is the original Palestine— the Pelesheth of Exod. xv. 14, and Isa. xiv. 29. So named because it was the country of the Pelishtim or Philistines (of Genesis x. 14, and *passim*) in the Old Testament history, extending from about Cæsarea to Gaza, or farther southwards, and from the Mediterranean to the hill country of Judæa, west to east.

This district is so exclusively understood in modern times by the name Palestine or Philistia, that a deputation of Oriental Christians coming once on a friendly visit, inquired why upon my Arabic seal the English consulate was designated that of "Jerusalem and Palestine," without mention of the other territories northwards to which its jurisdiction extended, such as Galilee. I could only answer that the ancient Romans called the whole country around, nay, even that beyond Jordan, and as far as Petra, by the name of Palestine, and this fact was old enough for us now-a-days to act upon.

"Oh, the Romans!" they ejaculated, with a curious expression of countenance, as if disappointed at the mention of such comparatively modern people. So true is it that in the Holy Land, the Bible is the only book of history for Christians, and scriptural incidents are the traditions which leap over any number of centuries at a time. How little of this state of mind existing among the inhabitants of that country is comprehended in England!

But, in reference to the people Israel and the possession of it as the promised land, this allotment, shared partly by each of the tribes of Ephraim, Dan, and Judah, has a peculiar denomination—it is called the Shephêlah, (translated by the common word *vale* in Josh. x. 40, xi. 16, and elsewhere.) In Arabic authors also of Mohammedan period, this large plain bears the same name, *Siphla*, meaning the same as in Hebrew, the "low country."

Thus, as one expanse from the hills to the sea, it bears one territorial name, either Philistine or Hebraic, just as another region is called the *Negeb*, or south, (see in the verses referred to above,) or as others were designated the hill country, or the desert, or Phœnicia. And many a time have I stood on the summits of hills to the west of Bethlehem, the eye ranging over its extent from the vicinity of Carmel to Gaza, with Jaffa and Ekron in front, and have sometimes seen beyond this, ships of large size sailing past on the "great and wide sea" of the 104th Psalm.

K

The ancient Philistines were not only exceptionally, but generally, a large race of people, and the population there are to this day remarkably tall; they are, even amid disadvantages, (that especially of want of water,) much more cleanly in their persons and clothing than the peasants of the hills, and many of their habits of life are modified by their circumstances, such as the pressure of their wild Arab neighbours from the southern desert that lies between them and Egypt.

Over this plain I have made several journeys at different periods, and now proceed to put down my jottings of an excursion in the spring of 1849.

May 1st.—" Sweet May-day " in the Holy Land as well as in England.

At Rachel's sepulchre, "in the way to Ephrath, which is Bethlehem," we parted from a company of friends who had ridden with us from Jerusalem, and passed along the valley *Duhheish'mah* to the Pools of Solomon, then turned aside by the convent and village of *El Khud'r* (or St George), surrounded by flourishing vineyards. Then mounting up a stony ridge, we came in view of the wide Philistine plain, the hills falling in sucessive gradations from our feet to the level of the plain, but separate objects could scarcely be distinguished on account of the thick air of the prevailing Shirocco; green bushes, however, and abundant wild flowers,

On the Philistine Plain. 147

including the red everlasting, pheasant's eye, cistus, and some late anemones, were about us; the larks and the linnets were singing with delight.

In front was the village of *Hhusân*, and two roads led forward, that on the left to *Nahhâleen*, *Wad Fokeen*, and *Jeba'*; this was the road that I ought to have taken to *Bait Nateef*, our place for the night, but being considerably ahead of our baggage mules, I had ridden on with a kawwâs, under *Hhusân* and *Ras abu 'Ammâr;* by our wayside lay a defaced Roman milestone.

A solitary peasant youth, from whom I inquired the names of the villages about us, was so alarmed at the appearance of a European with a Turkish attendant, in a place so remote from common high-roads, that he ran off; but finding our horses keeping up with his fleet pace, he dropped behind a large stone and levelled his gun at us in sheer terror; it was difficult to get a rational reply from him.

Before us, a little to our left, was *Hhubeen*, half down a hill, at the foot of which was a valley green with waving crops of wheat and barley.

In ten minutes more there opened a fine view of *Bait 'Atâb*, in which were some good new buildings. Before arriving at this village, which is the chief one of the *'Arkoob* district, ruled by 'Othman el Lehhâm, I dismounted for rest beneath a gigantic oak, where there were last year's acorns and their cups shed around, and half a dozen saplings rising from the ground, sheltered from the sun by being all within the shadow of the parent tree; with arbutus bushes in every direction, wild thyme and other fragrant herbs serving as pasture for numerous humming bees, bright coloured bee-eaters were twittering in their swallow-like flight, and under the soothing influence of the whole, I fell into a pleasant slumber.

Some boughs of "the huge oak" were decorated with bits of dirty rags hanging upon the boughs as votive memorials of answers to prayers. Probably the site was that of a burial-place of some personage of ancient 'and local celebrity; but my attendant was positive in affirming that the people do not pray at such stations more than at any other spot whatever. There are many such venerated trees in different parts of the country. I believe that the reason as well as the amount of such veneration is vague and unsettled in the minds of the peasantry, yet the object remains a local monument from generation to generation, honoured now, as were in the Bible times—the oak of Deborah (Gen. xxxv. 8), the oak of Ophrah (Judges vi. 11), for instance, with others.

> "Multosque per annos
> Multa virûm volvens durando sæcula vincit."

By and by the groom overtook us on foot, having scoured about the neighbourhood in search of us. After another half an hour's rest, we followed him across very rocky and slippery hills towards the place of our destination—dwarf shrubs of evergreen oak, honeysuckle, a spring of water, and an old well near the village of Hhubeen, with doves cooing, and a vulture poised in the sky above. Then a ruined village called *Lesed*,* (as well as I could catch the sound from a distance,) near which, among the shrubs, the gnats troubled our horses exceedingly as evening drew on, which would imply the neighbourhood of water.

Arrived at *Bait Nateef* just at sunset, but no luggage had as yet arrived. This is *Netophah* in the lists of Ezra and Nehemiah.

The chief and elders of the village were, according to custom of the eventide, seated in a group, chattering or consulting, or calculating, probably, about taxes, or respective shares of the common harvest, or the alliances to be contracted for the next border-warfare, or marriages being planned, or the dividing of inheritances, &c. My groom was admitted into their circle, most likely welcomed as bringing the latest news from Jerusalem, or as being able to describe this strange arrival, and the road to be taken by us on the morrow.

I passed forward to select a spot for pitching the tents when they and the food should arrive. The village shaikh of course tendered all the hospitality in his power to offer, but this was

* I do not find this place in any lists or books of travels.

unnecessary beyond a supply of water, milk, and eggs.

We waited, and waited: the sun was down; the stars came out, and the moon shone over us; but at length the mule bells became audible, and our dwellings and supplies came up. Supper and sleep are needless to mention.

Wednesday 2d.—The green hills around were enlivened by the clucking of partridges among the bushes, and the olive-trees by the cooing of doves.

Leaving this position with its extensive prospect, and passing an enormous evergreen oak we crossed a noble valley, and soon reached the hill on which stands *Sh'weikeh*, (or *Shocoh* in Hebrew.) This large valley runs east to west, and is the *Elah* of Scripture, the scene of David's contest with Goliath—a wide and beautiful plain, confined within two ranges of hills, and having a brook (dry at this season) winding at half distance between them. The modern names for the vale of 'Elah are *Musurr*, from the N.E. to near Sh'weikeh; and *Sunt* after that.

The plain was waving with heavy crops of wheat and barley, and the bed of the stream, bordered by old trees of acacia, called Sunt, (in that district called Hharâz.) These are of a brilliant green in summer, but as there are no such trees elsewhere nearer than Egypt, or the Wadi 'Arabah, (for they require water,) the people relate a traditional account of their origin, and say that once upon a time the country was invaded by a king of Egypt, named Abu Zaid, bringing a prodigious army; but on the occurrence of a sudden alarm, they decamped in such haste that their tent-pegs were left in the ground, which, being made of Sunt wood, struck roots at the next rainy season, and sprung up as we see them. Can this be a confused tradition of the rout of the Philistines to Shaaraim on the fall of Goliath?

The vale or plain (for in Hebrew the word *Emek* is often applied to the latter also when lying between ranges of hills—sometimes even when they are of considerable breadth, as at Rephaim and elsewhere) is about three hours or twelve miles long, and spacious enough to allow of military occupation and action; hostile armies might of course also occupy the opposite hills. From the direction of Hebron other valleys fall into this wide plain. On another occasion I entered it by that called *Wadi'Arab* or *Shaikh*, descending from 'Ain Dirweh and *Bezur* or *Bait Soor*. Wadi'Arab is commanded at its mouth by *Kharâs* on the north and *Nuba* on the south. Near to the latter are the ruins of *'Elah*, which I have no doubt gave name to the valley, and not any remarkable terebinth-tree, as is generally guessed by commentators on the Bible, unless, indeed, some remarkable terebinth-tree at first gave name to the village. Neither Robinson nor Porter appears to have seen or heard of this site of 'Elah, neither do they mention the route by the Wadi 'Arab, which lies to the north of Wadi Soor, which they do mention.

Southwards, but further inland, lies *Keelah*, which I suppose to be the Keilah of 1 Sam. xxiii. 1, the scene of a remarkable incident in David's early career, before retiring to Ziph. The name is registered four hundred years before that in Josh. xv. 44, among the cities of Judah.

This, then, being the valley of 'Elah near to Shocoh, must have been the scene of David and Goliath's encounter. How could the Latin monks of the middle ages, and modern Roman Catholic travellers to Jerusalem, ever believe that it took place at Kalôneh near that city? The perversion can only be attributed to their ignorance concerning anything in the country beyond the immediate vicinity of their convents.

We halted at the ruined village of Shocoh (now made by a grammatical diminutive form of Arabic into Sh'weikeh) after picking each of us his five smooth stones out of the brook, as memorials for ourselves, and for friends far away, endeavouring at the same time to form a mental picture of the scene that is so vividly narrated in sacred history, and familiar to us from early childhood.

There are now no regular inhabitants at the place; only a few persons occasionally live in caves and broken houses about there. Some remnants of antiquity, however, still exist, especially the wells, of fine masonry and great depth, at the foot of the hill. This probably represents the lower Shocoh mentioned by Eusebius and Jerome in the Onomasticon, " *Soccho*, duo sunt vici ascendentibus Eleutheropoli Æliam in nono milliario, alter superior, alter inferior, qui vocantur Socchoth in tribu Judæ." Some peasants wandering about brought me to the fallen lintel of the door of a small mosque, bearing a rudely-executed Cufic-Arabic inscription, illegible because, as they said, "it had been eaten by the nights and days."

Large flocks of sheep were pasturing over the stubble, (for some of the harvest was already cut in that warm sheltered locality,) led by such shepherd boys as David the Bethlehemite may have been, and large flights of blue pigeons circling in short courses over our heads. Among the demolished houses some women were churning the milk of the flocks in the usual mode, by swinging alternately to each other a sewed up goat-skin, (the bottle of the Old Testament, Josh. ix. 4; Judges iv. 19; Ps. cxix. 83;) a hill close at hand is crowned by a Mohammedan Weli (a kind of solitary chapel) named *Salhhi*.

The view in every direction is most imposing. This rough plan will give a tolerably good idea of the Vale of 'Elah. Across the valley, opposite to Shocoh, stands a very fine terebinth-tree. Possibly in ancient days there were many such in the district, and so the valley and the village of 'Elah may have acquired this name.

'Ajoor commands a view of the great plain and the sea. From that hill, looking eastwards, the vale has a magnificent appearance as a ground for manœuvres of an army.

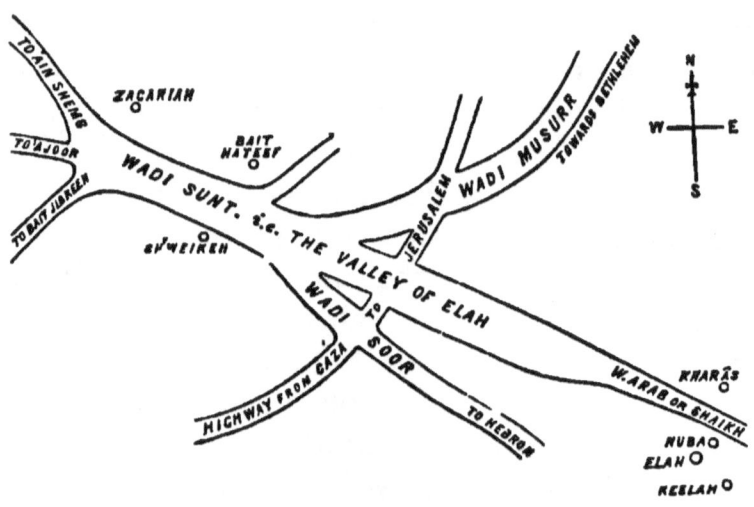

Near *Zacarîah* the Wadi es Sunt contains but few of those trees. We passed close under that prosperous-looking village with its palm-tree, mounted a rocky path, and went along a valley "covered over with corn," (Ps. cxv. 13;) here the very paths were concealed by the exuberant grain, so that we had to trample for ourselves a way through it.

Emerging on the great plain, we had to wade monotonously through an ocean of wheat. How

On the Philistine Plain. 155

I longed to have with me some of the blasphemers of the Holy Land, who tell us that it is now a blighted and cursed land, and who quote Scripture amiss to show that this is a fulfilment of prophecy.*

In many places, however, we saw how the rich produce had been trampled down and rolled upon by camels, or by Bashi-bozuk soldiers on their travels, after their horses were gorged to the full with gratuitous feeding. We met a black slave of 'Othman el Lehhâm of Bait 'Atâb, a fine fellow, well mounted and armed, and he told us that a large part of this wheat was his master's property. He had been travelling from village to village upon business. His noble bearing, and his being thus confidentially employed, reminded me of the Arabic proverb, that "Even a Shaikh's slave is a Shaikh."

In one place I remarked some hundred yards square of fine oats. This was surprising, as I knew that oats are not cultivated in Palestine. The people assured me that they were of wild growth, but they were of excellent quality; and as the name (Khafeer) seemed to be well known, it seems difficult to understand that oats have not been at some time cultivated in that part of the country. With respect to its Arabic name, it is worth notice

* Since that journey I have been told by the country people that between Gaza and Beersheba it is the practice to sow wheat very thinly indeed, and to expect every seed to produce thirty to fifty stalks, and every stalk to give forty seeds.

how near it is to the German name (Hafer) for oats. Wetzstein has since found wild oats growing on the N.E. of the Haurân.

Arrived at *'Ain Shems*, the Beth Shemesh of the Bible, (1 Sam. vi. 9, *passim*,) where, instead of the large population of ancient times, we found nothing but a weli and some fragments of peasant houses.

Due north from us as we rested, lay on the summit of a hill, *Sora'â*, which is Zorah, the birthplace of Samson, where the angel appeared to Manoah and his wife. The people told us of *Amoorîah* to the left, but we could not quite see it, and the same with respect to *Tibneh*, or *Dibneh*, the Timnath of Samson's history.

All the plain and the low hills formed one waving sheet of corn, without divisions or trees; and often, as we had no tracks for guidance, we had to take sight of some object on the horizon, and work straight forward towards it. It was amid such a wonderful profusion that Samson let loose the foxes or jackals with firebrands, taking revenge on the Philistines, and he called it "doing them a displeasure!" I have seen from Jerusalem the smoke of corn burning, which had accidentally taken fire in that very district.

On the summit of a hill, where were good square stones of old masonry, I got into a sheepfold of stone walls, looking for antiquities; but, alas! came out with my light-coloured clothes covered with fleas; fortunately the clothes were not woollen.

Further on we had *Bait Ziz*, or *Jiz*, on the right, with *Dejâjeh*, or *Edjâjeh*, and *Na'ana*, or *Ra'ana*, on the left; *Khulda* in the distance at N.W.; a vast expanse of growing grain in every direction.

The population hereabouts are a fine race for stature, and paler in complexion than our peasantry on the hills; and it ought to be the reverse, unless, as is certainly the case, they are a distinct people.

We traversed the plain to *'Akir*, which is Ekron of Scripture, one of the five principal cities of the Philistines, and chief place of the worship of Baalzebub, (2 Kings i. 3.) All our inquiries had been in vain for any name that could possibly have been Gath. The utter extinction of that city is remarkable—the very name disappearing from the Bible after Micah, B.C. 730. Amos, B.C. 787, and Zephaniah, B.C. 630, mention the four other cities of the Philistines, omitting Gath. The name never occurs in the Apocrypha or the New Testament.

'Akir is now a very miserable village of unburnt brick; indeed, all the villages of this district are of that material, owing to the extreme rarity of stone. We saw women cutting bricks out of the viscous alluvial soil, and boys swimming luxuriously in the pool of rain water settled during winter in the excavation for bricks—quarry we might style it, if the material were stone. There was plenty of ploughing in progress for the summer crops of sesamé, durrah, &c., and the people seemed rich in horned cattle.

This last feature constitutes another difference between them and the hill country. In the mountains, where the Bedaween forays are almost unknown, the cattle bred are principally sheep and goats. On the plains, flocks of sheep might be easily swept off by those marauders, oxen not so easily; the people, therefore, principally breed this species of cattle, and instead of idle shepherd boys amusing themselves with little flutes, and guiding the sheep by throwing stones at them, the herds here are driven by mounted horsemen with long poles. The flatness of the country and the frequency of oxen will serve to illustrate the exactness of Bible narratives, particularly in the matter of the wheeled carriage and the kine used for conveying the ark of God from this place, Ekron, to Bethshemesh (1 Sam. vi.)

Forward we went to *Yabneh*, (Jabneel of Josh. xv. 11, and Jabneh of 2 Chron. xxvi. 6,) where it is mentioned in connexion with Gath and Ashkelon. It was a border city of Judah, where the *Wadi Surâr*, (called here the river *Rubin*,) forms the boundary between Judah and Dan. I think we may identify it as the "Me-Jarkon and the border that is over against Japho," of Josh. xix. 46. It is the

On the Philistine Plain. 159

Jamnia, where, for a long time after the Roman overthrow of Jerusalem, was a celebrated college of the Talmudists, before, however, the traditions and speculations of the rabbis were collected into volumes of Mishna and Gemara. It is believed that the truly great and venerable Gamaliel is buried here.

Yabneh stands on a rising ground, and although a village of sun-baked bricks, it has remains of a Christian church, now used as a mosque, with a tower of stone.

While resting under a tree, awaiting the coming up of our baggage, 'Abd'errahhmân Bek el 'Asali, a companion of ours from Jerusalem, threw a stone at a young filly and cursed her, because the colours of her legs were of unlucky omen. On such matters the native Moslems entertain strong prejudices, which are based upon precise and well-known rules.

On the arrival of our mules, we pitched the tents upon a pretty green common with a row of trees; the verdure consisted of wild clover, and leaves remaining of wild flowers—chiefly of the wild pink. It is an Arab proverb that "Green is a portion of paradise."

The villages in sight were *Besheet* to the S.E., and *El Kubeibeh* to the N.E. Our day's journey from Bait Nateef had been one of only seven hours, viz., from 8 A.M. to 3 P.M.

The population seemed very industrious: they have cheerful *bayârahs*, or enclosed orchards, and the open fields were exceedingly well cultivated. The evening scene was most pleasing, comprising the return of flocks and herds from pasture, and the barley-harvest coming home upon asses and camels with bells on their necks—all enlivened by the singing or chattering of women and children.

As the day advanced I was happily employed at my tent door reading the Arabic New Testament; it should have been in Hebrew at Yamnia, as being more profitable than all the Pirké Avoth of the Talmud. At sunset our party walked out in the fields to shoot the pretty bee-eaters.

Of this village there is a tale current among the peasantry over the country, which conveys an important lesson for the conduct of human life.

An old Shaikh of Yabneh had five sons. When

very old, a complaint was brought to him that some one had stolen a cock ; so he called together his sons and ordered them all to search for the cock ; but it was not found. Some time afterwards it was represented to him that a sheep was stolen ; he then commanded his sons to go and search for the cock. They replied, " O our father, it is not a cock but a sheep that is stolen ;" but he persisted in his command, and they did what they well could, but without success. After that he was told that a cow was missing ; he again commanded his sons to look after the cock. They thinking he had lost his senses, cried, " *Sallem 'akalak ya Abuna*, (May God perfect thy understanding, O our father,) it is not a cock but a cow that is missing." " Go look for the cock," persevered the old man ; they obeyed, but this time again without success. People wondered and thought him in a state of mere dotage. Next came the news that a man was killed. The father pertinaciously adhered to his first injunctions, and ordered his sons to look for the cock. Again they returned without finding it, and in the end it came to pass that the killing of the man brought on a blood feud with his relations—the factions of several villages took up the case for revenge, and the whole town was destroyed, and lay long in a state of desolation, for want of sufficient zeal in discovering and punishing the first offence, the stealing of the cock, which thus became a root of all the rest. There is a good deal of wisdom contained in this narrative or allegory, whichever it may be considered. Offenders become emboldened by impunity, and the first beginnings should be checked.

Thursday 3*d.*—Early dew around the tents upon the green. We mounted at half-past six. I rode up to the village and got to the top of the tower in the village.

After an hour and a half, of level riding southwards, we arrived at a broad old sycamore in the middle of the road.

Another hour brought us to *Asdood* (*Ashdod*) of the Philistines, with *Atna* and *Bait Durâs* on our left. I do not know where in all the Holy Land I have seen such excellent agriculture of grain, olive-trees, and orchards of fruit, as here at Ashdod. The fields would do credit to English farming—the tall, healthy, and cleanly population wore perfectly white though coarse dresses, and carried no guns, only the short sword called the Khanjar. We rested in an orchard beneath a large mulberry-tree, the fruit of which was just setting, and the adjacent pomegranate-trees shone in their glazed foliage and bright scarlet blossoms, the hedges of prickly pear were bursting into yellow fruit, palm-trees rising beyond, the sky was of deep sapphire brilliancy, and the sun delightfully hot.

Here then had been the principal temple of the fish-god Dagon, which fell nightly in presence of the Israelitish ark. Not the only temple, however, for there is still a village near Jaffa with the name of *Bait Dajan*, and another still further north, in the same plain, but in the Nabloos district. Strange that this temple of Dagon at Ashdod should have survived and preserved its worship so late as nearly to the Christian era, when it was burnt by Jonathan the Jerusalem high priest, (Josephus Ant., xiii. 4, 4; Macc. x. 84.)

Ought not Gath to be sought between this, and Ekron, according to 1 Sam. v. ? See also 2 Chron. xxvi. 6.

Soon after remounting we arrived at the ruin of a fine old *Khan*, one of the numerous establishments of the kind upon the camel road from Damascus to Egypt, but now every one of them is broken and unfit for use. There was a noble column of granite lying across the gateway, and two Welies close adjoining.

Reached *Hhamâmeh* at 11 A.M., from which we turned aside through lanes of gardens, and over deep sand towards *'Ascalon*, leaving *Mejdal* on our left, with its lofty tower rising over an extensive plantation of olive-trees. This tower is believed to be of Moslem erection. Passing another village on our left, we at length came to *Jurah*, a wretched brick hamlet, stuck as it were against the ancient walls of Ascalon.

We were on the sea-beach at noon. Upon this beach lie stupendous masses of overthrown city wall, and numerous columns of blue-gray granite of no very imposing dimensions. A great number of these have been at some time built horizontally into those walls, from which their ends protrude like muzzles of cannon from a modern fortification. This arrangement, with the same effect, is also found at Tyre, Cæsarea, and other places along the coast.

The site or lie of the city is principally in two hollow basins, in which the detrition of houses forms now a soil for grain, for fruit gardens and good tobacco.

We were shown the ruins of what the people call "the Church," where there are several very large columns of polished granite lying prostrate, but neither there nor elsewhere could any capitals be found belonging to the columns. All over the East such objects are appropriated by townspeople as ornaments inside the houses, especially at the mouths of wells.

The people pointed out to us from a distance the spot where H. E. Zareef Pasha had lately obtained the marble slab of bas-relief, which he sent to the museum at Constantinople.

The walls of 'Ascalân are clearly distinguishable in all their circuit, and have been of great thickness.

The position of this "Bride of Syria," as the Saracens designated it, is very fine, and the prospect around must have been beautiful; but of this prize of so many sieges and neighbouring battles, the joy of Richard Cœur de Lion, where he laboured with his own hands in repairing the broken walls, only its name with the scriptural and later romantic history remain to claim our attention, and verify the prediction of the prophet Zephaniah, ii. 4–6.

I found no coins there, and none were brought to me; only some were brought to me in an after-journey at Mejdal; I therefore pass by for this time the classical allusions to the fish goddess, Deceto. A beautiful head of a female statue, but blackened by fire, brought from Ascalon, has since been sold to me, which I delivered to our museum.

We remained there an hour, then rode to *Naalcea*. The fine plain over which we galloped must have had many an English rider upon it in the Crusading times—many a man who never saw "merrie England" again, even in company with King Richard.

Naaleea, though built of brick, bears an appearance of real cleanliness; the olive plantation from Mejdal reaches thus far.

The barley reaped at *Berberah* was, I believe, the finest I have ever seen; and there were pretty roads winding among olive groves, orchards well enclosed by prickly-pear hedges, with bee-eaters skimming and twittering before us.

Bait Jirja on the left; then after a good while *Bait Hhânoon* also on the left.

Reached *Ghuzzeh* (Gaza) at 5 P.M. The very remarkable approach is by an avenue of at least a mile long, very wide like a boulevard, through an immense park of olive grounds, with the city for an object of vista at the end.

We encamped on the further side of Gaza, having the old reservoir called *Birket el Bashà* between us and the Lazaretto.

Cheerful scene of camels and asses bearing the barley-harvest home, attended by women and children; small flocks of sheep also, with their shepherd lads playing sweet and irregular airs on their *nayahs*.

Friday 4th.—I resolved to stay here over Sunday.

The morning was cool, and though our situation was entirely unsheltered, I judged even the risk of exposure to the noontide sun, when it should arrive, not to be refused, while it gave us the blessings of free air from the sea and delivery from mosquitoes, which would certainly have plagued us under the shade of the fruit-trees. There was a mean suburb in front of our position, tenanted solely by Egyptians.

The sound of the distant sea rolling on the beach (though this was out of sight,) was music to my ears. Near us was a fence of the prickly-pear, (named *Saber*, or "patience" in Arabic.) One of our party referred to its extraordinary degree of vitality, even under disadvantageous circumstances. "Yes," replied the 'Asali, "she has drunk of the water of life."

I went to visit the Lazaretto, and while conversing with the doctor (M. Espéron,) and the Turkish superintendent, four wild Arabs were brought in, their hands fettered and chains on their legs, accused of striking a soldier near *Khan Yunas.* When identified by witnesses merely uttering two or three words, they were removed, cruelly pushed about in their chains and beaten on the head by the soldiers, who enjoyed the cowardly fun which they would not dare to perpetrate had the fine tall fellows had their limbs at liberty.

The captain of the Bashi-bozuk, having called at my tents with his mounted troop, followed me to the Lazaretto.

Returning home, and after some rest, or rather a visit from some Greek Christians which gave me no rest, I went to visit the newly-arrived kaimakam, or governor, one of the celebrated 'Abdu'l-Hadi family of Nabloos. His divan room was crowded with visitors of congratulation: such as shaikhs of villages, and some dignified Arab chiefs; the latter interceding on behalf of the men recently captured by the quarantine people; the former soliciting their official investitures for their several districts. The house was exceedingly mean and shattered, but this medley of visitors formed an interesting subject of study.

I next visited the kâdi, (judge,) who was holding his court in the open air, with a canvas screen to shelter his head from the sun, in the midst of orchards and a flower garden. A cause, in which some women were vociferating and screeching in Arabic, (to which that language lends peculiar facility,) was suspended in order to receive my visit, and the litigants had to remain in silence at some distance till I left, returning to the tents.

All the people here praise the air and water of Gaza, and declare that disease of any kind is nearly unknown, except ophthalmia, which, of course, can be generally prevented. Provisions are said to be cheap; but the bread, as sold in the market, not so good as in Jerusalem or Nabloos. Probably their excellent wheat is exported to a distance.

Saturday, 5th.—Rode southwards on a day's excursion to Khan Yunas, with my people and an escort of two of the quarantine Bashi-bozuk. One of these, named Hadji Ghaneem, was a hardy old fellow, encircled by pistols and swords; his old gun, that was slung at his back, had the rusty bayonet fixed, perhaps fixed by the rust. The other, Hadji Khaleel, was an amusing companion, with plenty to tell and fond of talking.

On the Philistine Plain. 169

Started before 7 A.M., passing between cornfields, with numerous larks trilling in the air.

At some distance we came to a low hill lying on our right hand, all the ground about being mere sea sand drifted inland. This is called *Tell-ul-'Ejel*, "the Calf's Hill," so named from its being haunted by the ghost of a calf, which no one has yet laid hold of, but whenever this shall be accomplished the fortunate person will come into possession of the boundless treasures concealed within the hill. Some say that this good luck will happen to any one that is favoured with a dream of the calf three times in succession. All our party professed to believe the local tradition, especially one who had been in Europe, and from whom such credulity had been less expected; but he was sure that some tales of that nature are well founded, and if so, why not this? In my opinion, it is probably a superstition connected with some ancient form of idolatry.

Half-way along our journey we came to a village called *Ed Dair*, (the convent, perhaps the *Dair el Belahh* of the list;) but this appellation Dair is often given to any large old edifice of which the origin is unknown. Here was a loop-holed Moslem tower occupied by twenty men of the Bashibozuk. Such towers are called *Shuneh* in the singular, *Shuân* in the plural.

Khan Yunas is a hamlet of unburnt bricks, dirty and ruinous, which is not always the case with other villages of that material; the reason of this being so, I suppose to be, that most of its few houses are inhabited by Turkish soldiers. This is the last station southwards held by the sultan's forces, the next, *El Areesh*, being an Egyptian outpost. I was desirous of visiting that place had time allowed, not only for the satisfaction of curiosity on the above account, but in order to get some idea from ocular inspection whether the little winter stream or Wadi there could ever have been the divinely-appointed boundary of the land promised to Abraham and his seed for ever. My prepossession is certainly to the contrary.

However, I rode ten minutes beyond Khan Yunas, and sat to rest in a field beneath a fig-tree; the day was hot and brilliant, but there was a fine breeze coming in from the sea. The scene was picturesque enough, for there was a mosque-minaret and a broken tower rising behind a thick grove of palm-trees and orchards of fig, vine and pomegranate—a high bank of yellow sand behind the houses of the village, and the dark blue Mediterranean behind that.

With respect to the name of the place, there are many such in the country, and it is a mistake to ridicule the Moslems for believing in all of them as true sites of the large fish vomiting out Jonah, which they do not. These are, I believe, merely commemorative stations, and we are not in the habit of ridiculing Christians for having several churches under the same appellation ; also it is not quite certain that all the Welies named after Yunas (Jonas) or Moosa (Moses) do refer to the Old Testament prophets. There have been Mohammedan reputed saints bearing those names.

Near this place is a village. called *Beni Seheela*. On the return we left behind us the old Hadji Ghaneem, with his brown bayonet, and took a nearer road to Gaza, not so close to the sea as that by which we had left it. It was an easy pleasant ride, and there were barley crops almost all the way. We reached the tents in three hours from Khan Yunas.

At sunset, which is the universal dinner time in the east, I went to dine with the Governor Mohammed 'Abdu'l Hadi; it was a miserable degrading scene of gorging the pillaf with the hands and squeezing the butter of it through the fingers, without even water for drink supplied by the servants. The guests were about a dozen in number, and they were crowded so closely round the tinned tray as only to admit of their right arms being thrust between their neighbours, in order to do which the sleeves had to be tucked back; there was but little conversation beyond that of the host encouraging the guests to eat more.

Previous to eating, the governor and his younger brother performed their prayers in brief, after experiencing some difficulty in finding the true Kebleh direction for prayer, the rest of the company gossiping around them all the time. Above our heads was suspended a rude copper lamp, and the terrace just outside the door was occupied by slaves and other attendants; boughs of adjoining palms and other trees were softly stirred by an evening breeze, and the imperial moon shone over all.

After washing of hands and a short repose, (the other guests smoking of course their chibooks and narghilehs, and chatting upon topics of local interest,) I asked leave, according to Oriental etiquette, to take my departure.

Sunday, 6th.—Read the eighth chapter of Acts in Arabic, and some of our English liturgy in that noble language, with one of my companions. I feel certain, concerning the dispute whether the word ἔρημος (desert) in the twenty-sixth verse of the above chapter, refers to the city or to the road, that the true sense of the passage is this, " Go toward the south unto the way that goeth down from Jerusalem unto Gaza "—*i.e.*, the way which is desert or free from towns and villages—as in Matt. iii. 1, and other places where the word in question does not imply the common European idea of any desolate wilderness.

I enjoyed a Sabbath stillness during most of the day, the people having been instructed that English Christians observe the Lord's-day with more serious composure than it is the habit of native Christians to do.

In the afternoon, however, the governor came on a visit with a long train of attendants mounted on beautiful horses, for which, indeed, this district is famed—there were specimens of Mânaki, Jilfi, K'baishân, Mukhladîyeh, &c., &c. Mohammed, of course, discoursed as well as he could on European politics, and stayed long.

After his departure I strolled to look at some short columns of marble standing on a slight swell of ground; they are now inscribed to the memory of certain Moslem martyrs in battle of our fourteenth century, *i.e.*, about seven centuries after the Hej'ra. These columns look very much as if they had been taken from some old Christian church, then each sawn into halves, and each of the halves partly sliced on one side to receive the inscription.

After sunset I dined with old Ibrahim Jahhshân, and his numerous household, (the principal one of the Christian families,) and a troop of friends. It was not a better entertainment than that of the kaimakam yesterday; perhaps, it would not be desirable for him to surpass the constituted authority of the city in such matters.

Among the company was the Nâzir el Aukâf, (the superintendent of mosque-endowment property,) also a Durweesh from Lahore, consequently a British subject,—he was full of fun, and wanted me to make him a present of some fulminating balls and crackers; he assured me that in the Hharam (sanctuary, commonly called the Mosque of Omar,) at Jerusalem, there were at least thirty such British subjects as himself residing, including his own brother. A Turkish soldier present drank wine, as soon as the commissioner for inquiring into the delinquencies of the late governor had turned his back upon the table.

Before dinner I had accompanied the family to the church, (Greek rite,) where the priest was waiting to receive me. It was a poverty-stricken edifice, purposely kept so, in order to obviate the envy and malice of the Mohammedans; and all the Christians that I saw in Gaza were a stupid-looking people; they are few in number, and grievously oppressed by their numerous Moslem fellow-townsmen, being far away from the notice of consuls. One cannot but regard with compassion a people who have for ages endured suffering for the name of Christ, while facilities are offered for acquiring wealth and honour by apostasy. Generaation after generation remains still as firm in their Christian creed as those before them, and now perhaps more so than ever.

I was surprised to learn that it is only about two generations since the Samaritans ceased to be a sect in Gaza, with their place of worship—they are now found nowhere but in Nabloos.

There is a slave-traffic in Gaza; but it only consists in the consignment of articles already commissioned for in Egypt, on behalf of private purchasers in Syria—at least, so the world is given to understand. The boundary of the two countries is so near that the Arabic dialect spoken here nearly approaches the Egyptian.

I made some inquiries as to the popular ideas on the achievements of Samson at Gaza, but only obtained such uncertain and even contradictory answers, that on this journey it did not seem worth while to take any great trouble on the subject; but I certainly had not expected to get better information from either the Mohammedans or from the poor ignorant Christians there.

The night was most beautiful, with full moonlight streaming, and stars peering between the swaying fronds of the lofty palm-trees, which grow more luxuriantly in Gaza then I had seen elsewhere.

The muleteers singing around their watch-fire.

Monday, 7th. — Tents struck and march commenced at 7 A.M. We returned through the great avenue by which we had arrived, but soon diverged upon the road to Hebron.

Alongside of *Bait Hhanoon* by half-past eight, where there was abundance of bee-eaters, and these imply fruit-trees. 'Abd' errahhmân tried to shoot some, but failed, having no small shot, but only bullets for his gun.

At nine we left *Timrah* a little on our left. The people everywhere busied in reaping barley—a very lively scene; the reapers, as usual all over Palestine, wearing large leather aprons exactly like those used by blacksmiths in England, only unblackened by the forge; the women had face veils of the Egyptian pattern. Cows, goats, and sheep were feeding at liberty in the fields upon the new stubble.

In thirty-five minutes more we arrived at *Semsem*, leaving *Bait Nejed* on the right.

At five minutes past ten we reached *B'rair*, near which we rested for an hour, the day being very sultry, under an old tamarisk-tree, which on the plains instead of *Turfa* is called *Itil*.

An intelligent old man named 'Ali came up to me from the reaping and conversed much on the sad condition of agricultural affairs, complaining of the cruel oppression suffered by the peasantry from their petty local tyrants, and entreated me if I had any means of letting the Sultan of Constantinople know of it, that I would do so. He particularly described the exactions they had to endure from Muslehh el 'Az'zi of Bait Jibreen, and all his family.

Thence passing over an extensive plain, we had in sight for a long time a distant Dair (so-called convent) and village of *Karâteen*, also at one time a village called *Hhata*.

At twenty minutes to one we reached *Falooja;* the heat had become intense, and incessant swarms of black stinging flies annoyed our horses beyond patience. In fact the Philistine plain (which, however, we were now soon to leave) was always noted for the plague of flies, and this gave rise to the ancient deprecatory worship of Baal-zebub, "the lord of flies," by that people; there is still a village upon the plain named *Dair ed Dubân*, "the convent (or temple) of flies." Later in the summer this plague is said to be so intolerable to horses and animals of burden that travelling is only attempted there by night-time.

At length came a rustling noise along the fields and rain fell slowly in drops large as good teaspoonfuls, yet the heat was so great that my coat of nearly white linen did not for some time show marks of wetness; a black cloud from which the water fell accompanied us along the line of route, and the rain from it increased.

Over the plain going eastwards we had for a long time in view a rocky hill with a Weli crowning its summit; on our right, *i.e.* southwards, a conspicuous object, and called *'Arâk Munshîyah* (the rock of Munshîyah.) This is not to be confounded with the similar cliff cropping out of the plain, but upon our left, and called *Tell es Sâfieh*.

We noticed several deserted villages with small breastworks and turrets of loose construction remaining where the peasantry had of late resisted the raids of the southern Bedaween, but unsuccessfully. We were told by a solitary foot-passenger of such incursions having taken place only a day or two before, whereupon our muleteers took fright and hurried on apace. We all examined the state of our firearms, while the storm was driving furiously in our faces.

The rain was over as we reached *Bait Jibreen*, just after 3 P.M. This important place was our station for the day. We pitched in an eligible situation under a line of olive-trees at some distance from the houses, in view of the principal antique buildings. The principal people came out to welcome us, especially 'Abdu'l 'Azeez, the brother of the Nâzir Shaikh Muslehh, for whom I had brought a letter of recommendation from the governor of Gaza.

We were fatigued as much as anything from the effect of the shirocco wind. Then dark clouds from a distance with thunder surrounded us. As the time of sunset approached, the preparations for dinner were interrupted by the driving of a heavy shirocco, low, near the ground, which soon became so strong that the tents began to tumble over, and we took refuge in the house of 'Abdu'l 'Azeez ; there was, however, no rain.

Here then I was lodged in a house of sun-baked bricks plastered inside with mud, but as clean as such a house could possibly be. There were cupboard recesses in the walls, a fireplace and chimney, wooden nails driven into " sure places " in the walls, (see Isa. xxii. 23,) strange scratches of blue and red painting in fancy scrolls, &c. ; a raised Mastabah or dais, and a lower part of course near the door, for guests to leave their shoes there ; the

On the Philistine Plain. 179

whole being roofed by a few strong beams wattled between with faggot-wood. A piece of ancient marble lay across the doorway.

The very rudely fabricated lamp was lighted from a huge clump of wood taken burning from the hearth. Dinner as uncivilised but as hospitable as could be expected at half-past nine. I should have had my own long before but for the tempest outside.

News arrived that eighty people from *Kuriet el 'Aneb* (the well-known village of Abu Gosh on the Jerusalem road from Jaffa) were escaping to us across the hills on account of troubles at their home.

Then we very soon lay down to sleep.

Tuesday 8th.—'Abdu'l 'Azeez and his two young sons escorted us in looking over the ruins of old Eleutheropolis, as their town was called in the period of early Christianity. These consist of a church near the great well, another on a hill farther eastwards called St Anna, or, as the Arabs pronounce it, *Sandanna*, and numerous extensive caverns, probably enlargements by art from nature.

The former church has a roof remaining only over one of the aisles; the ground plan of the whole edifice is, however, sufficiently marked out by the fragments of columns *in situ.*

St Anna is larger and more perfect than this; the semicircular apse is entire, and there are remains of other buildings attached to the church

It stands on high ground, and commands a very fine prospect.

The caverns are formed in the substance of chalk hills, often in a circular form, with a rounded roof, through which an aperture admits both air and daylight. Antiquarians are puzzled to account for the origin of these, as they are too numerous and capacious to be needed for supply of water; besides that in common times the large well and aqueducts that bring water from a distance would suffice for that purpose. They are likewise too extensive and deep to be required for magazines of grain, such as the villages on the open plains cut into the underground rocks for preservation of their food from the raids of the Bedaween; perhaps, however, some were used for one of these purposes and some for the other.

Near the entrance of one of these excavations, in which there are passages or corridors with running ornament sculptured along each side, we found figures (now headless, of course, since the Moslem conquest) resembling church saints in Europe— one, indeed, had its head remaining, though disfigured, and the arms posed in the manner of the Virgin Mary when holding the infant Saviour. These were sculptured in the chalk rock itself, and standing in niches hollowed behind them. If these were really what they seemed to be, they must have been made in the era of the Latin

On the Philistine Plain. 181

kingdom, for the Oriental Christians have never made *images* of the saints.

In two other of these caverns, high up on their sides or within the cupola, we saw short inscriptions of black paint, (if I remember rightly,) the large characters of which had very much the general forms of Cufic-Arabic, but not the Cufic of the old coins. There was also an ornamented cross in this cupola, and other crosses in other chambers. We were totally unable to satisfy ourselves as to how the inscriptions could have been written at such inaccessible heights. Certainly the present race of people are unable even to deface them, were they disposed to do so.

One excavation we entered with some trouble near the top, and out of some labyrinthine passages we descended a spiral staircase, with a low wall to hold by in descending, all cut into the solid but soft rock; there were also small channels for conducting water from above to the bottom—these demonstrate the use of the whole elaborate work in this instance, namely for holding water.

Returning to rest awhile in the house, 'Abdu'l 'Azeez assured me that immensely tall as he is, he had had eight brothers, all at least equal to himself; most of them had been killed in their faction battles, and his father, taller than himself, had died at the age of thirty-one. His sons could neither read nor write; they at one time made a beginning, but the teacher did not stay long enough to finish the job. "However," said he, pointing to the one sitting by us, perhaps ten years of age, "he can ride a mare so that none of our enemies can possibly overtake him."

We left Bait Jibreen soon after 9 A.M., riding through a grove of olives, and soon arrived alongside of *Dair Nahhâz*,* and afterwards *Senâbrah*. By noon we were quite off the plain, and entering a beautiful green valley bounded by cliffs of rock sprinkled with dwarf evergreen oak and pines, the spaces between them being filled up with purple cistus, yellow salvia, and other flowers. This con-

* In a journey to Gaza from Hebron, in the spring season of 1853, I was proceeding from the great oak down a long valley —but I was induced to deviate from the direct line by the tidings of *Bait Jibreen* being infested or taken by the Tiyâhah Arabs.

We everywhere found the peasantry armed, and on arriving before *Dair Nahhâz*, almost within sight of that town, and communicating with the village for water to drink, as I rested under a tree, Mohammed 'Abd en Nebi sent me word that Bait Jibreen was recovered from the Arabs, and now occupied by themselves; that thirty-five corpses of Arabs were lying round Bait Jibreen, and one of the two Arab chiefs (Amer) was slain—he himself was wounded in the knee.

From hence to Gaza we passed *Zeita*, where a breastwork had been hastily thrown up by the peasantry, and into which a number of armed men rushed from a concealment, and parleyed before they would allow us to pass on. Then to *Falooja*, and between *Idsaid* and *Karatiyah* on our right, and the Arâk Munshîyah on the left. Halted at Brair for the night.

The return from Gaza was by Ascalân, Mejdal, Julis, the two Sawafeers, Kasteeneh, Mesmiyeh, and Latron, on the Jaffa road to Jerusalem.

tinued for an hour, by which time we had gradually attained a considerable elevation, where we had our last survey for that journey of the Philistine plain and its glorious long limit, the Mediterranean Sea.

In another quarter of an hour we rested among the wreck of *Khirbet en Nasâra*, (ruins of the Christians,) not far from Hebron. Thence I despatched a messenger to my old friend the Pakeed (agent in temporal affairs) of the Sephardim Jews in the city, and he sent out provisions to my halting-place under the great oak, above a mile distant from Hebron.

In regard to the researches after the lost site of Gath, I may mention that on a later visit to Bait Jibreen, I got Shaikh Muslehh (the government Nâzir, and the head of his family) to tell me all the names of deserted places he could recollect in his neighbourhood. I wrote from his dictation as follows, but it does not seem that the object of inquiry is among them. In Arabic the name would most probably be *Jett* or *Jatt*.

Merâsh.	Munsoorah.	Umm Saidet.
Sagheefah.	Shemanîyeh.	'Arâk Hala.
Lahh'm.	Shaikh Amân.	'Attar.
Kobaibeh.	Obêyah.	St Anna.
Fort.	Ghutt.	Judaidah.
Martosîyah.	Ahhsanîych.	Ilmah.

CHAPTER IV.

HEBRON TO BEERSHEBA, AND HEBRON TO JAFFA.

IN August 1849 I left my large family encampment under the branches of the great oak of Sibta, commonly called Abraham's oak by most people except the Jews, who do not believe in any Abraham's oak there. The great patriarch planted, indeed, a grove at Beersheba; but the "*Eloné Mamre*" they declare to have been "plains," not "oaks," (which would be *Alloné Mamre*,) and to have been situated northwards instead of westwards from the present Hebron. With a couple of attendants I was bound for Beersheba. The chief of the quarantine, not having a soldier at home, gave us a peasant to walk with us as far as the *Boorj*, (Tower,) with a letter of *our own* handwriting in his name, addressed to the guard there, directing them to escort us further.

Scrambling up a steep rough lane, due south from the tree, with vineyards on either side richly laden with fruit, and occasional sumach-trees bearing bright red berries, we were rewarded on the summit by a vast prospect of country, hilly before us in the south, Moab and Edom mountains to the left, and Philistia plains with the Mediterranean on the right.

All nature was revived by the evening sea-breeze, and the sun in undiminished grandeur was retiring towards his rest.

On a summit like this, with a wide expanse laid out for survey, there are large and lively ideas to be conceived in matters of Scriptural geography. Consider, for instance, on that spot Psalm cviii., with its detail of territories one after another. That "psalm of David" declares that God in His holiness had decreed the future dispensations of *Shechem*, (there is its position, Nabloos, in the north of the circular landscape;) then the *valley of Succoth*, (there it is, the Ghôr, or vale of the Jordan,) coasting between *Gilead*, *Manasseh*, and *Ephraim;* also *Moab*, with its springs of water, where He would (speaking in human poetic language) wash His feet, at the period of treading with His shoe over *Edom:* that remarkable event paralleled in the Prophecy of Isaiah lxiii., when, in apparel dyed red from Bozrah, the conqueror tramples down the people in his anger. The Psalmist then has to triumph over *Philistia*, that large Shephêlah stretched between us and the sea—concluding with the exclamation, "Who will bring me into the strong city (Petra)? who will lead me into Edom?"

All this was accomplished by the providence of God in the history of David, that shepherd boy of Bethlehem, at whose coronation all Israel was gathered together at Hebron, just behind the spectator on this eminence.

To return, however, from the solemnity of these historical meditations to the commonplace transactions of the journey, we had to carry on a considerable amount of wrangling with the muleteers, who were continually allowing their animals to stumble, and the ropes of the luggage to come loose, so that the things fell to the ground; I sent them back, and we proceeded without tents or bedding, only two blankets and our cloaks. The true reason of the men's behaviour lay in their dread of being attacked by wild Arabs, and having their animals carried off.

It was about sunset, and our track lay over plains of arable land, between hills clothed with the usual dwarf evergreens, of baloot, arbutus, &c., then over eminences with tall fragrant pines, and the evening breeze sighing among their branches, such as I had only once heard since leaving Scotland, and that was in the Lebanon. Old stumps and half trunks of large trees standing among myriads of infantile sprouts of pines attested the devastation that was going on, by means of the peasantry, for making of charcoal, and for supplying logs to the furnaces of Hebron, where very rude manufactures of glass are carried on.

Hebron to Beersheba.   187

Along a glen which opened into an arable plain with stubble of millet (durrah) remaining, but no village near. There we met a party of Arab women, and after them a boy mounted on a camel, who informed us that he was coming from *Merj-ed-Dôm*, lying between us and *Samua'*, where there are remains of antiquity, such as large doorways, cisterns, &c.

The country was all level enough for carriages; and it is probable that all the way in the south is practicable in like manner, for we know that Joseph sent carriages from Egypt to his father at Beersheba.

The *Boorj* is simply a look-out tower, now used for quarantine purposes, ridiculous as they may be in the pure air of the desert.

There are relics of a village about it; but as the people are living in caverns rather than taking pains to rebuild their houses, we may infer that they do not feel secure on the very last remnant of fixed habitations towards the great southern wilderness, although under Turkish government.

They are, however, kept in considerable awe of the petty officers stationed there; for when one of our party was impatient at the intrusion of a cat near our supper cloth, the people besought us not to injure the animal, seeing that it was the property of the *Dowleh* (Government.) They furnished us with eggs and milk; and, after our meal, we lay down on the leeward side of the town, to await the rising of the moon. We had a fire burning near us, its red light flickering over the wild scene ; the sky with its milky-way over our heads, and the polar star in the direction of England, fixed in its well-known place.

The villagers had their own chatting round the watchfire, discussing local politics, chiefly as to whether 'Abderrahhman the governor of Hebron was likely to accept the Pasha's invitation to meet 'Abdallah Wafa Effendi, who was sent with overtures of reconciliation between the brothers of the Amer family. This being a question that bore very nearly on their personal interests.

I awoke just as the moon gleamed in the east, but did not arouse the youths for another half hour, till I became apprehensive of evil effects from their sleeping in the moonlight.

After coffee we mounted and went forward, escorted by two of the quarantine guardians. There were no more hills, but the remaining country was all of hard untilled ground, with sprinklings of tamarisk and kali bushes, which showed we were entering on a new botanical region.

Arrived at an Arab encampment, where our escort were obliged to hire the shaikh for showing us the way, as they either did not know it, or, which I believe the more probable, did not dare to take travellers over his land without his sharing in the profits, even though they were officials of quarantine. He soon came up, riding a fine mare of the

Hebron to Beersheba. 189

Saklâwi race, and his spear over the shoulder, glittering in the moonlight. His name was *Ayân*, and his people were a small offset from the great *Tiyâhah* tribe. We passed several other such stations, of which we were always made aware beforehand by the barking of their dogs, and by seeing the camels browsing or reposing at a little distance from the tents.

As the night advanced, the mist rose and increased till the stars were obscured and the moon scarcely perceptible; our clothes also became nearly wet through.

We reached Beersheba (now called *Beer-es-Seba*) perhaps a couple of hours before daylight, and after sharing some food, wrapt the blankets over our heads, and lay down with our heads against the parapet stones of the great well, and fell asleep, notwithstanding the cold wet mist.

I rose before the sun, and wrote two letters to friends in England by morning twilight.

The mist disappeared as the glorious sun came forth; and we walked about to survey the place. The wide plain around was disused arable land, showing in some places some stubble from a recent harvest, but only in small patches, which in the early spring must have been cheerful to the sight.

Near us was a pretty water-course of a winter torrent, shallow and comparatively wide, but then quite dry.

The great well has an internal diameter at the

mouth of twelve feet six inches, or a circumference of nearly forty feet. The shaft is formed of excellent masonry to a great depth until it reaches the rock, and at this juncture a spring trickles perpetually. Around the mouth of the well is a circular course of masonry, topped by a circular parapet of about a foot high. And at a distance of ten or twelve feet are stone troughs placed in a concentric circle with the well, the sides of which have deep indentions made by the wear of ropes on the upper edges.

The second well, about 200 yards farther south, is not more than five feet in diameter, but is formed of equally good masonry, and furnishes equally good water. This is the most common size of ancient wells throughout Palestine.

Two other wells of proportions about equal to the first well were shown us, but they are filled to the brim with earth and stones; and Shaikh Ayân told us of two others. The barbarous practice of filling up wells from motives of hostility was adopted at this place very soon after Abraham had dug them. (Gen. xxvi. 15, &c.) Who can tell how often these have been opened, closed and opened again?

All Arab-speaking people wish to count neither more nor less than seven wells here, and so create the name *Seba;* but even in this way the etymology would not hold good, for the term *seven wells* would be *Seba Beâr*, not *Beer-es-Seba*. From the

Hebron to Beersheba.

Hebrew history, however, we know how the designation was first given. Gen. xxi. 31, "Wherefore he called that place Beersheba, because there they *sware* both of them," *i.e.*, Abraham and Abimelech. Yet it deserves notice that the verb *to swear* is identical with the numeral *seven;* and in the three preceding verses we find Abraham ratifying the oath by a sacrifice of *seven* ewe-lambs as a public guarantee for the fulfilment of the conditions; the killing of lambs with this view is a usage which still obtains in the country.

On a rising ground near the wells are scattered lines of houses, covering a considerable space; but all that now appears is of inferior construction, and of no importance.

Soon after sunrise the Arabs of the vicinity came to water their flocks and camels at the troughs. Young men stripping themselves nearly naked, two at each well, pulled up goat-skins of water by the same rope, hand over hand, and singing in loud merriment, with most uncivilised screams between the verse lines. These men were of very dark complexion—not quite black, but nearly so.

There were linnets singing also, but in far more agreeable melody; but where they could be was more than I could discover—not a tree or a shrub was within sight-distance.

After an hour we commenced our return by a different route from that of our arrival. Shaikh Ayân and Hadj 'Othman, of the quarantine, amusing themselves with jereed-playing and other mimic manœuvres of warfare, which they performed very cleverly.

The shaikh being dismissed with sufficient compliments on each side, we proceeded upon the main track from Egypt across the plain towards *Doherîyeh*, passing occasional parcels of durrah stubble rising out of mere scratches of the soil, varied by the wilderness plants of tamarisk, &c. When one remembers the fact of that same land in the days of Abraham and Isaac producing a hundredfold of corn, (Gen. xxvi. 12,) how deplorable it is to see it lying untilled for want of population, and serving only as so much space for wild tribes to roam over it! Surely it will not always remain so.

Crossing a good road at right angles with ours, we met a large caravan of camels going eastwards. The people told us they were going to *Ma'ân*, (beyond Petra,) one of the Hadj stations between Damascus and Mecca, where stores of provisions are always laid up by the Government for supply of the pilgrims at the appointed season of the year.

Approaching the hills, we rested from the heat, which had become considerable, beneath a neb'k-tree, where all the roads between Egypt and Hebron meet at a point.

At the entrance of a valley between the hills the quails were very numerous, and so tame as to come almost under the horses' feet. Unfortunately, just at the time when wanted, my fowling-piece was found to be unloaded, that is to say, not reloaded after having gone off yesterday by an accident.

It was a relief from the great heat to mount the hills to Doherîyeh, although the road was tiresome, winding round and among the bases of almost circular hills in succession. At the village all the population was cheerfully employed in threshing or winnowing the harvest, and their flocks crouched in the shade of the trees. It was early in the afternoon, and we lay down to rest under the branches of a fig-tree growing out of a cavern, which cavern was so large that we placed all our horses in it.

We parted from the quarantine soldiers, and took a guide for Hebron. The road was good and direct, through a pleasant country, so that we made quick progress. At an hour and three-quarters from Doherîyeh we arrived at a pretty glen of evergreen oak and pine; and at the entrance of this glen is a fountain, called *Afceri*, of beautiful water issuing from a rock.

Shortly after we joined the route by which we had left our encampment yesterday, near the fountain of *Dilbeh*, where we had drawn water when outward bound. Then came to an ancient well of good masonry, hexagonal in shape, but without water. A cistern for rain-water was close adjoining.

Reached the oak of Sibta in twenty-eight hours after leaving it, well pleased with having been able to visit Beersheba, the scene of many ancient and holy transactions, in the days when the great patriarchs, Abraham, Isaac, and Jacob, walked humbly with their God, and God gave them a faith capable of overthrowing mountains.

In conclusion, I may express my regret that, although residing in the country many years afterwards, I could not get an opportunity of visiting either Beer-la-hai-roi or Isaac's well of Esek. (Gen. xxvi. 20.) Concerning the former we find some indications in an appendix to Williams' *Holy City*; and I have been assured personally that the latter is still held in estimation by the Bedaween tribes, under the name of *Esâk*, and frequented as a rendezvous for making truces and covenants.

On breaking up our camp at Abraham's oak, the family took the direct road for Jerusalem, while I struck across the Philistine plain for Jaffa.

With one horseman and a kawwâs, I diverged westwards from the common road just before the descent to 'Ain Dirweh, between it and the ruined town of Bait Soor, (Bethzur of Joshua xv. 58,) leaving Hhalhhool of the same verse on my right hand. Advanced gradually down a woody glen of the usual evergreen oak and pine. The higher part of the valley is in excellent cultivation, with careful walls, and drains to keep off the winter rains that descend from the hills, although no villages were in sight except in one place on an

Hebron to Beersheba. 195

eminence to the left, where an apparently well-built village was entirely abandoned. It is called *Ma'naeen;* and the history of it, as I have since learned, is that it was only a few years before built by a colony of refugees from oppression in sundry villages, who concerted to set up on their own account, without regard to the authority of their family connexions, or of the hereditary shaikhs. So daring an innovation upon national customs was resented by a coalition of all the country round, who made war upon them, and dispersed the people once more to their miserable homes. The Turkish Government allowed of this proceeding, on the ground that to suffer the establishment of new villages (which of course implies new shaikhs to rule them) would derange the account-books of the taxes, which had been definitely fixed years before under the Egyptian Government.

Lower down, where the glen became narrow and stony, a large rock has been hewn into a chamber for some ancient hermit, not unlike the one in the Wadi Ahhmed between Rachel's sepulchre and Batteer (Bether) near Jerusalem, only in this case the entrance is shaded by venerable karoobah-trees, so large as to cover the road also with their branches.

We were met by various camel-parties carrying kali for the glass-works of Hebron during the approaching winter, also fine mats and other goods from Damietta, which, after being landed at Jaffa, are thus conveyed by reliefs of camels to their destination of Hebron, Bethlehem, and Jerusalem.

On emerging from the valley (Wadi Arab or Shaikh) into the open Vale of 'Elah, we had *Kharâs* perched on an eminence close at our right, and *Nuba* similarly posted to our left.

Also the ruins of *'Elah* were on our left, and far behind our left hand, in among the hills, on a commanding height, was Keelah.

We were now traversing the Valley of 'Elah, which runs north-westwards, and which I have described in my former journey. Now, as on that visit, I saw young shepherd lads pasturing large flocks as David may have done over the same ground.

This time, however, I had entered the valley from a different point—viz., from its eastern end at Kharâs, and not where Shocoh and Bait Nateef lie opposite to each other.

We then traversed the same country as then as far as the village of *Khuldah*, which is a very thriving place, and where, as usual, on the wide plains there are not many flocks of sheep, but herds of horned cattle instead, driven by men on horseback. This is an indication of insecurity, on account of forays of Bedaween Arabs, from whom on their approach they have to scamper as fast as they can.

The same insecurity is attested by each of these villages having its *Shuneh*, or little rude tower-with a breast-work, in which the peasants may defend themselves when in sufficient force to do so.

Next came *Saidoon*, where we obtained a distant prospect of Ramlah and Lydd, with Gimzo at the mouth of the Bethhoron Pass, (2 Chron. xxviii. 18,) and Ras-el-Ain still beyond, with its fountains and rich lands conspicuous on the Great Plain, backed by the hills of Ephraim. Then we passed the poor clay-built village of *Deâneh*, where the people were winnowing a large harvest of millet, and the Government tax-farmers with their soldiers, lent by the authorities, measuring the heaps.

Lastly, we entered the vast olive grounds belonging to Ramlah, and found our tents (which had been sent on by another road) just as the Moeddin in the minaret was calling to sunset prayers.

I am never weary of the scenery about Ramlah; we have there the most picturesque Orientalism of all Palestine—a warm climate, numerous waving palm-trees, with the large reservoir for cattle drinking, all gilded in brilliant sunlight, together with the busy voices of a considerable population.

A burly fellow of a wandering durweesh or sorcerer, with rows of large black beads round his neck, came up to us, and bellowed out one of the ninety-nine attributes of God, according to the Moslems: "Ya Daeem," (O thou everlasting!) This was by way of asking alms. My companion gave him some, which I would not have done.

In the morning we ascended to the top of the great White Tower, called "the Tower of the Forty," meaning forty martyrs. This is a favourite appellation of ancient ruins in Palestine. I do not know what it alludes to. And from among the Comandalune windows I copied the following vignette.

V.

THE LAND OF BENJAMIN.

WHO has ever stood upon the Scopus hill, north of Jerusalem, (his mind first prepared by biblical reading and biblical feeling,) facing northwards, and seeing at one glance, as upon a map, the land of the tribe of Benjamin, without desiring to wander about there, were it only to experience the reality of standing and breathing upon the sites of 'Anathoth, Michmash, Gibea of Saul, and Gibeon? It can be most of it performed in one day, and sometimes a line through it is traversed in that time by English residents of Jerusalem, namely, from Jerusalem to Michmash and Bethel, and the return.

There is also a pleasant spot above Lifta, in a grove of olives, figs, and pomegranates, where Europeans have sometimes established summer camps for their families. At that spot it is delightful to repose in the evening shadows cast by the trees, and gaze over the landscape of Benjamin, with a deep valley sinking in immediate front, only to rise again to the greater height of Nebi Samwil and a landscape view extending as far as the rock

Rimmon, which stands in pyramidal form upon the horizon.

There are, however, several ancient and biblical sites known to exist within that circuit that are not visible from either of those stations, and only to be perceived on reaching the places themselves. For instance, Bait Hhaneena of Nehemiah xi. 32.

There is '*Adâsa*, the scene of a great victory gained by Judas Maccabæus over the mighty host of Nicanor; this I discovered from the peasants ploughing one day, while resting after a gazelle chase. It is not far from Gibeon. "So Nicanor went out of Jerusalem, and pitched his tents in Bethhoron, where an host of Syrians met him. But Judas pitched in Adasa with three thousand men. . . . . So the thirteenth day of the month Adar [*i.e.* on the eve of Purim] the hosts joined battle: but Nicanor's host was discomfited, and he himself was first slain in the battle. . . . . Then they pursued after them a day's journey, from Adasa unto Gazera, sounding an alarm after them with their trumpets," (Macc. vii. 39–45,) *i.e.* a day's journey for an army, perhaps, that day's journey after fighting; for it is a pleasant ride with respect to distance, as I proved by riding to *Jadeerah*, passing through Beer Nebâla.

And on another day's expedition alone, I was riding near 'Anâta (Anathoth) eastwards from the village, thinking over the faith of the prophet Jeremiah, in purchasing a family estate, the future occupation of which was contrary to all human probability, and after recounting to myself the cities of Benjamin allotted to the priests, as Anathoth, (to which the treasonable priest Abiathar belonged, 1 Kings ii. 26,) Gibeon, and Geba, wondering what had become of the fourth city Almon, (Josh. xxi. 17, 18,) I came up to a hill on which appeared some remains of an ancient town; there my horse carried me up the steep side, and while passing among the lines of foundations on the summit, a peasant who joined me said the place was called *'Almân*. Some time afterwards, I was riding on the other side of the same hill, in the direction of *Hhizmeh*, (the Az-maveth of Neh. vii. 28, as I suppose,) when a peasant informed me that the place on the hill was named *Almeet*. This corresponds to the other name of the town as given in 1 Chron. vi. 60, and vii. 8, where it is Alemeth. So remarkable a preservation of both names by another people than the Jews, after long or perhaps repeated desolations, appears to me almost miraculous, and is a fresh illustration of the exact verbal inspiration of Holy Scripture.

I once visited the rock Rimmon of Judges xx. 47. The first part of the journey was made in company with Lieutenant Vandevelde, going from Jericho to Bethel, a totally-unknown road; it must have been the same as that taken by Joshua after the fall of Jericho.

This was in 1852. The Arabs were unwilling to take us in that direction, probably on account of some local hostilities to which they might be exposed. At first they denied there was any road that way, then said it was so difficult that we could not reach Bethel in less than two days, which was ridiculous, considering the shortness of the distance. At length we resolved to find a road without them, and ordered the luggage to go round by Khatroon, or if necessary by Jerusalem, but to meet us at Bethel that night.

Shaikh Mohammed el Hejjâz then sent with us his slave Sulimân. By his having that Moslem name, I should suppose this to be a freed-man, inasmuch as it is not the custom to give Moslem or Christian names to slaves; they may be only called Jewel, Diamond, Cornelian, Thursday, Friday, &c. It is not uncommon for a freed-man to be still called in popular speech *a slave;* but not in serious earnest or in matters of business, and not unless they are blacks from Africa.

It is not unusual in the East for a slave, even though still in bondage, to be educated in reading and writing, to be trained in military accomplishments, and so to be employed as confidential agent of property, or trainer of children in the family, riding the best horses and carrying weapons of best quality. And this Sulimân was a bright specimen of that class of men,—of good bodily presence, merry-humoured, and well-accoutred.

The first part of the journey in crossing the Quarantana mountain was precipitous, and even

The Land of Benjamin.   203

dangerous for strangers; but the summit being attained, the whole of the remaining distance was a level plain. We were upon remains of an ancient road, with wells frequently occurring by the wayside; many of them, however, choked up with stones and earth.

Plodded quietly along, when, about two hours from Jericho, we were surprised by hearing human wailing and cries for mercy near us. This was discovered to come from a boy of about twelve years of age, who had concealed himself behind a bush of *ret'm*, (juniper of Scripture.) He had never seen Europeans before, and, on perceiving the Hejjâz slave at our head, was apprehensive that we should plunder him of his ass and her foal. He was a peasant of *Dair Dewân*,* a village on the way before us.

In half an hour more we came up to a cleanly-dressed and pleasant-looking shepherd lad, who was not at all afraid of us. He conducted us to a well of good water, named *Beer Mustafa*, a little off the road, at the heading of the small wadi *Krishneh;* there we rested half an hour.

In another hour we reached the ruins of *Abu Sabbâkh*, from which we had *Remmoon* visible on our right.

During all the day's journey we passed through a good deal of wheat and barley cultivation, the crops ripening fast, it being at the beginning of May.

* Pronounced sometimes *Dewân*, sometimes *Debwan*.

In another half hour we arrived at Dair Dewân, the Beth-aven of Scripture,* a flourishing village,— remarkably so, as evinced by its buildings, its fruit orchards, and corn fields all around. Progress in such affairs is a sure token of a village being peopled by Christians. In the well-kept cemetery belonging to the place, it was pleasant to see an enormous quantity of large blue iris flowers growing between the graves, and often concealing them from view till nearly approached.

Turning abruptly westward, in twenty minutes we came to the hill of stones called Tell-el-hajjar, which I had on a former occasion identified as the site of Ai, lying as it does between Beth-aven and Bethel, (Josh. viii.,) and having the deep valley alongside northwards. Here Vandevelde took bearings, with his theodolite, of points within sight; and in a quarter of an hour from this we reached Bethel, (now called Bait-een,) that is in less than five hours, including an hour's stoppage at the Tell from the 'Ain-es-Sultân by Jericho, where the Arabs had, for their own reasons, tried to persuade us that the journey was impossible, or would at least occupy two days.

Our tents and luggage arrived soon after we did. Bait-een has been so often described, and its biblical events so often quoted by travellers, that it is not necessary to do so while professedly dealing only

Beth is represented by the modern word *Dair*, and *Aven* has become *Ewân*, with the Syriac *d'* signifying *of*.

The Land of Benjamin. 205

with byeways in Palestine ; yet this may be said, that no distance of time can entirely efface the exquisite pleasure of exploring ground and sites so accurately corresponding as this did to the topography of the Bible, and belonging to events of such antiquity as the acts of Abraham and Joshua.

In the morning I separated from my friends, who were preceding towards Damascus, and, accompanied by Sulimân and a kawwâs, went on my way to *Remmoon*, (the rock Rimmon.) Started at half-past seven in a thick shirocco atmosphere, keeping on the northern high road for about a quarter of an hour in the direction of *Yebrood*, then turned sharply eastwards over corn-fields, and descended into a deep hot valley. The flowers of the field were chiefly cistus, red or white, and hollyhocks four feet high. Then ascended to at least a corresponding height into terraces of fruit-trees well-cultivated ; and still mounting, to a fine plain of wheat, at the end of which was Remmoon, one hour and a quarter from Bait-een.

The village is built upon a mass of calcareous rock, commanding magnificent views towards the south, including the Dead Sea and the line of the Jordan ; higher hills bounded the north, on which was conspicuous the town of *Tayibeh*, near which is a *weli* or *mezâr* (pilgrimage station) named after St George, who is an object of veneration to both Moslems and Christians. The people of Tayibeh are all or mostly Christians, and have a church with a resident priest.

We rode up the street of Remmoon, and found the shaikh and principal men of the town lazily smoking in the shadow of a house.

My object was of course to inquire for a cavern that might be capable of containing six hundred men during four months. The people all denied the existence of such a cavern, but after some parley I was conducted to two separate caverns on the west side of the hill, then to two others on the eastern side which are larger, and to each of which we had to arrive through a house built at its opening. They told me of two others upon the hill, but of much inferior size. Those that I entered were not remarkable for dimensions above the many that are to be found over the country. It is probable that the whole of the refugees might sleep in these several places, if there were no village there at the time, which seems probable; but it was merely my own preconceived notion that they all lived in one vast cavern. The text of Judg. xx. 47 does not say so.

The village is in good condition, and the cultivation excellent in every direction around it. On leaving it for the return to Jerusalem I proceeded due southwards. In the fields the people were industriously clearing away stones—a sure symptom of peace, and consequent improvement.

Crossed a valley named *Ma'kook*, and arrived at

The Land of Benjamin. 207

Mukhmâs (Michmash) in less than two hours from Remmoon. Rested in the fine grove of olive-trees in the valley on the north of the town for an hour. The birds were singing delightfully, though the time was high noon, and our horses enjoyed some respite from the sanguinary green flies which had plagued them all the way from Remmoon; their bellies and fetlocks were red with bleeding. In this matter I particularly admired the benevolence of the slave Sulimân. Yesterday, after a sharp run across a field, perhaps in the vain hope of escaping the tormentors, he dismounted, and the mare followed him, walking like a lamb. He then sat down to switch away the flies, and rub her legs inwards and outwards. To-day he had taken off his Bedawi kefieh, or bright-coloured small shawl, from around his head, and suspended it between her legs, then, as he rode along, was continually switching between her ears with a long bunch of the wild mustard-plant.

On leaving Mukhmâs in the hottest part of the day, we had to cross the Wadi *Sûaineet*, along which to our left appeared the northern extremity of the Dead Sea. At a short distance down the valley there are remarkable precipices on each side, which must be the Bozez and Seneh,* renowned for the bold adventure of Jonathan and his armour-bearer,

---

* It is worthy of notice that Suwân (in Arabic) (diminutive, *Suwaineet*) signifies "flint." These rocks being flinty, it is possible that *Seneh* in Hebrew may have had the same meaning.

and near these projections are some large old karoobah-trees.

Emerging upwards from this wadi one comes to *Jeba'*, (the Gibeah of Saul, so often mentioned,) upon a table-land extending due east, in which direction I visited, five years before, an ancient ruin, which the people of Jeba' call *El Kharjeh;* it consisted of one principal building of contiguous chambers, built of nicely squared stones, put together without cement, like several of the remains at Bethel.

These stones are gray with weather stains, but seldom more than three courses in height remain in their places, though in one place five.

From this site, as well as from Jeba', there is a very striking view of the northern extremity of the Dead Sea.

The guide told us of a vast cavern in the Wadi Sûaineet capable of holding many hundred men, near to the above-mentioned karoobah-trees, and therefore just the suitable refuge for the Israelites, (1 Sam. xiv. 11,) besides the Bozez and Seneh; and he told us that half-way down the precipice there is a course of water running towards the Ghôr.

Few incidents in the Bible are so real to the eye and feelings as the narrative of Jonathan and his office-bearers when read upon the spot of the occurrence, or near it at Jeba'.

We passed *Jeba'* at about a quarter of a mile to

The Land of Benjamin.

our right, and in another quarter of an hour were at the strange old stone parallelograms under *Hhizmeh*, which had been often before visited in afternoon rides from Jerusalem.

These are piles of large squared stones of great antiquity, carefully built into long parallel forms, and now deeply weather-eaten. No use of them can be imagined. I have visited them at all seasons of the year, and at different hours of the day, but they still remain unintelligible. They are disposed in different directions, as will be seen in the following drawing of them, carefully taken by

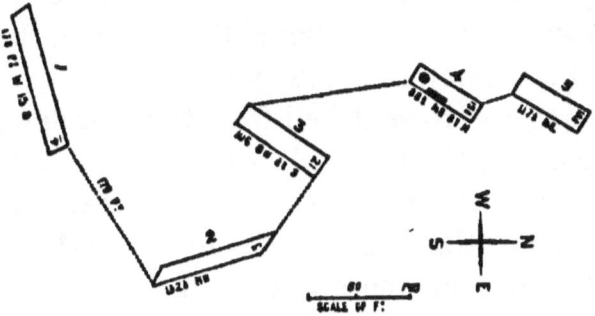

measurement in my presence, and given me by a friend now in England, the Rev. G. W. Dalton of Wolverhampton. On one face of No. 4 is a kind of entrance, and on the top surface a round hole about two feet in depth, but they lead to nothing, and are probably the work of modern peasantry, removing stones from the entire block; in the former case for the mere object of shade from the sun, and the latter for the charitable purpose common among

Moslems, who often cut basins into solid rocks, to collect rain or dew for birds of the air or beasts of the field.

Corroded monuments like these, in so pure and dry an atmosphere, bespeak a far more hoary antiquity than the same amount of decay would do in an English climate.

I know of a spot on the side of a wild hill upon the way between Ai (as I believe the place called the *Tell* to be) and Mukhmâs, where there are several huge slabs of stone, rather exceeding human size, laid upon the ground side by side exactly parallel. These can be nothing else than gravestones of early Israelitish period, but of which the memorial is now gone for ever.

Crossing the torrent-bed from the parallelogram, and mounting the next hill, we were at Hhizmeh; then leaving 'Anâta on the left, we traversed the Scopus near the Mount of Olives, and reached Jerusalem in four hours and a half of easy riding from Remmoon.

One ought not to quit the mention of this land of Benjamin by omitting the *Wadi Farah.*

This is a most delightsome valley, with a good stream of water, at a distance of rather more than two hours from Jerusalem to the N.E.

The way to it is through 'Anâta, already described, from which most of the stones were quarried for the English church in the Holy City, and then alongside the hill on which stands the ruins with the double name of 'Almân and 'Almeet, discovered by me as above-described.

Once, in the autumn season, a party of us went to Wadi Farah, and arriving on its precipitous brink found the descent too difficult for the horses; these, therefore, were left in charge of the servants, while we skipped or slid from rock to rock, carying the luncheon with us.

The copious stream was much choked near its source, which rises from the ground, by a thick growth of reeds, oleanders in blossom, and gigantic peppermint with strong smell. There were small fish in the stream, which was flowing rapidly; wild pigeons were numerous, and a shepherd boy playing his reed pipe, brought his flock to the water. Need it be said, how refreshing all this was to us all after the long summer of Jerusalem.

There were remains of a bridge, and considerable fragments of old aqueducts, *i.e.*, good-sized tubes of pottery encased in masonry, but now so broken as to be quite useless; these lead from the springhead towards the Jordan at different levels, one above another. There was also a cistern of masonry, with indications of water-machinery having been at one time employed there; but all these evidences of population and industry are abandoned to savages and the action of the elements.

Dr James Barclay of Virginia, author of "The City of the Great King," believes this site to be that of "Ænon, near to Salim," where John was baptizing, "because there was much water there," (John iii. 23.)

There can scarcely be a doubt that it is the *Parah*, belonging to the tribe of Benjamin, in Josh. xviii. 23, and that therefore it was a settled and cultivated place before the children of Israel took possession of the land.

The district around,—indeed, all eastwards of 'Anâta,—is now unappropriated; parts of it, however, are sown—not always the same patches in successive years—by the people of the nearest villages in a compulsory partnership with the petty Arabs of the Jordan plain. The peasantry are forced to find the seed and the labour, and yet are often defrauded of their share of the produce by the so-called partners bringing up friends and auxiliaries from the plain, just as the grain is ripening, and carrying off the produce by night, or setting fire to whatever they cannot seize in this hasty operation; and this takes place about two hours from the citadel and garrison of Jerusalem. Do not ask where is the Turkish government!

The people are driven to sow the grain upon these conditions, under risk of having their own crops destroyed or devastated near their homesteads, and in no case dare they offer any resistance.

I was once unwillingly present at a grievous scene near Elisha's fountain. Nâs'r Abu' N'sair, shaikh of the Ehteimât, one of the parties at all times in the above-described partnerships, was seated smoking his chibook beneath an old neb'k tree when some Christian peasants from *Tayibeh* approached him with deep humility, begging permission to sow grain upon that marvellously fertile plain of Jericho. For some reason which did not appear, it suited him to refuse the favour. In vain the suppliants raised their bidding of the proportion to be given him from the proceeds; they then endeavoured to get me to intercede in their behalf, frequently making the sign of the cross upon themselves, thereby invoking my sympathy as a fellow-Christian on their side; but on several accounts it seemed most prudent for me to leave the parties to their own negotiations, only speaking on their behalf afterwards by sending a kawwâs to recommend kindness in general to the Christian villages. It may be that this step met with success, but I could not but be sincerely desirous to have such Arab vermin as these mongrel tribes swept off the land.

VI.

SEBUSTIEH TO CAIFFA.

IN October, 1848, I found myself at Sebustieh, the ancient Samaria, having come thither from Jerusalem by the common route through Nabloos, *i.e.*, Shechem. Since that time I have often been there, but never without a feeling of very deep interest, not only in the beauty of its site, worthy of a royal city, or in the Roman remains still subsisting, but also in the remarkable fulfilments of Biblical prophecy which the place exhibits. The stones of the ancient buildings are literally poured down into the valley, and the foundations thereof discovered, (Micah i. 6.)

We left the hill and its miserable village by the usual track through a gateway at its eastern side. Down in the valley lay fragments of large mouldings of public buildings, and the lid of a sarcophagus reversed, measuring eight feet in length.

At first we took the common road northwards, and ascending the hill above *Burka*, from the summit had a glorious prospect of the sea on one side, and of the populous village country, well cultivated, stretched before us; we left the common road to *Sanoor* and *Jeneen*, turning aside under *Seeleh*, a double village nearest to us, with *A târa* further west.

The muleteers had preceded us during our survey of Sebustieh, on the way to 'Arâbeh, and we could see nothing of them before us—the road was unknown to us, and no population could be seen, all keeping out of sight of us and of each other on account of the alarm of cholera then raging in the country.

At Nabloos that morning, two hours before noon, we had been told of twenty having been already buried that day, and we saw some funerals taking place. At Sebustieh, the people had refused for any money to be our guides; one youth said, "he was afraid of the death that there was in the world."

So my companion and I, with a kawwâs, paced on till arriving near sunset at a deserted village standing on a precipice which rose above a tolerably high hill, and which from a distance we had been incorrectly told was 'Arâbeh; at that distance it had not the appearance of being depopulated, as we found it to be on reaching it. Numerous villages were in view, but no people visible to tell us their names. The district was utterly unknown to maps, as it lies out of the common travellers' route. This village, we afterwards learned, is *Rami*, and antique stones and wells are found there. Though our horses were much fatigued, it was necessary to go on in search of our people and property, for the sun was falling rapidly.

Observing a good looking village far before us to the N.W., and a path leading in that direction, we followed it through a wood of low shrubs, and arrived at the village, a place strong by nature for military defence, and its name is *Cuf'r Ra'i.* There was a view of the sea and the sun setting grandly into it.

For high pay, we obtained a youth to guide us to 'Arâbeh; shouldering his gun, he preceded us. "Do you know," said he, "why we are called Cuf'r Ra'i?—It is because the word Cuf'r means blaspheming infidels, and so we are—we care for nothing." Of course, his derivation was grammatically wrong; for the word, which is common enough out of the Jerusalem district and the south, is the Hebrew word for a village, still traditionally in use, and this place is literally, "the shepherd's village."

We passed an ancient sepulchre cut in the rock by our wayside, with small niches in it to the right and left; the material was coarse, and so was the workmanship, compared to ours about Jerusalem.

The moon rose—a jackal crossed a field within a few yards of us. We passed through a large village called *Fahh'mah, i.e.,* charcoal, with fragments of old buildings and one palm-tree. Forwards over wild green hills, along precipices that required extreme caution. The villages around were discernible by their lights in the houses. At length 'Arâbeh appeared, with numerous and large lights, and we could hear the ring of blacksmiths' hammers and anvils—we seemed almost to be approaching a manufacturing town in "the black country of England."*

Arrived on a smooth meadow at the foot of the long hill on which the place is built, I fired pistols as a signal to our people should they be there to hear it, and one was fired in answer. To that spot we went, and found the tents and our people, but neither tents set up nor preparations for supper. Village people stood around, but refused to give or sell us anything, and using defiant language to all the consuls and pashas in the world.

Till that moment I had not been aware that this was the citadel of the 'Abdu'l Hadi's factions, and a semi-fortification. [Since that time, I have had opportunities of seeing much more of the people and the place.]

Sending a kawwâs to the castle, with my compliments to the Bek, I requested guards for the night, and loading my pistols afresh, stood with them in my hand, as did my second kawwâs with his gun, and we commenced erecting the tents.

* 'Arâbeh does not appear in any map before Vandevelde in 1854.

Down came the kawwâs in haste to announce that the Bek was coming himself to us, attended by his sons and a large train.

First came his nephew from his part, to announce the advent; then a deputation of twenty; and then himself, robed in scarlet and sable fur, on a splendid black horse of high breed. I invited him to sit with me on my bed within the tent, widely open. The twenty squatted in a circle around us, and others stood behind them; and a present was laid before me of a fine water-melon and a dozen of pomegranates.

Never was a friendship got up on shorter notice. We talked politics and history, which I would rather have adjourned to another time, being very tired and very hungry.

He assured me that when my pistols were heard at the arrival, between 700 and 800 men rushed to arms, supposing there was an invasion of their foes, the Tokân and Jerrâr, or perhaps an assault by the Pasha's regulars from Jerusalem, under the pretext of cholera quarantine—in either case they got themselves ready.

He stayed long, and then went to chat with my Arab secretary in his tent, leaving me to eat my supper. He gave orders for a strong guard to be about us for the night, and a party to guide us in the morning on our way to Carmel.

This personage (as he himself told me) had been the civil governor inside of Acre during the English bombardment of 1840; and his brother had first introduced the Egyptians into the country eleven years before that termination of their government.

In 1852 I had arrived at 'Arâbeh from Nabloos by a different route, and turned from this place not seawards as now, but inland to Jeneen : whence I again visited it on my return. It seems worth while to give the details of this route.

Starting from Nabloos at half-past ten we passed *Zuwâtah* close on our right, and *Bait Uzan* high up on the left. Here the aqueduct conveying water from the springs under Gerizim to gardens far westwards, was close to the high-road. Arriving at *Sebustieh* and going on to *Burka* we quitted the Jeba' road, and turned to *Seeleh* which lay on our left, and *Fendecomia* high up on the right, *Jeba'* being in sight.

Soon after this we turned sharply north-west to *'Ajjeh*, and thence arrived at 'Arâbeh in five and a half hours from Nabloos.

After leaving 'Arâbeh for Jeneen we got upon a fine plain, namely, that of Dothan. On this, near to another road leading to Kabâtiyeh, is a beautiful low hill, upon which stands Dothan, the only building left to represent the ancient name being a cow-shed; however, at the foot of the hill is a space of bright green sward, whence issues a plentiful stream of sparkling water, and here among some trees is a rude stone building. This spot is now called *Hafeereh*, but the whole site was anciently Dothân, this name having been given me by one peasant, and Dotân by another.

On my return hither a few days later I found a large herd of cattle, and many asses going to drink at the spring. Dothan is well known to shepherds now as a place of resort, and must have been so in ancient times. Here then, in the very best part of the fertile country of Ephraim, is the pasture-ground to which Joseph's brethren had removed their flocks from the paternal estate at Shechem, and where they sold their brother to the Arab traders on their way to Egypt. This may help to mark the season of the year at which Joseph was bought and sold. It could only be at the end of the summer that the brethren would need to remove their flocks from exhausted pasture-ground at Shechem to the perennial spring and green watered land at Dothan; this would also be naturally the season for the Ishmaelite caravan to carry produce into Egypt after the harvest was ended. Be it remembered that the articles they were conveying were produce from the district of Gilead—(" balm of Gilead" is mentioned later in Scripture)—and it is specially interesting to notice that Jacob's present, sent by his brethren to the unknown ruler in Egypt, consisted of these same best fruits, " Take of the best fruits of the land, balm, honey, spices and myrrh, nuts and almonds."

Dothan is about half an hour distant from 'Arâbeh, and therefore six hours or a morning's walk for a peasant from Shechem.

More solemn, however, than the above interesting recollection, was that of the horses and chariots of fire which had encircled the very hill upon which I stood, when Elisha "the man of God," lived in Dothan, and smote the Syrian army at the foot with blindness, and led them away to Sebustieh, (Samaria,) 2 Kings vi.

After leaving Dothan, at the falling in of this road to Jeneen with that from Kabâtieh, stands a broken tower on an eminence above the well *Belâmeh*, which Dr Schultz has identified with the Belmen, Belmaim, and Balamo of the Book of Judith, (chap. iv. 4; vii. 3; viii. 3.)

To resume—Away early in the morning. Paid the night-guard and sent a present of white loaf bread and some tea to the Bek.

It was promised that we should reach Carmel in nine hours, across an unknown but pretty country in a different direction from Lejjoon and Ta'annuk (Taanach of Judges i. 27,) which I had designed for my route, and towards the sea-coast.

Our guides were gigantic men, beside whom my tall peasant servant Khaleel appeared to disadvantage, and their guns were of a superior description to what one commonly sees in Palestine. The peasantry also were large men with good guns.

First, due west for quarter of an hour towards *Kubrus*, situated upon a hill, but before reaching it, turned sharply northwards, through a rocky defile of ten minutes, when we fell in with a better road which, they said, came also from 'Arâbeh, and on towards a fine village named *Yaabad* in a lovely plain richly cultivated; there were after the earlier crops young plantations of cotton rising, the fields cleared of stones and fenced in by the most regular and orderly of stone dykes.

Before reaching *Yaabad*, we turned due west, our guides alone being able to judge which of the many footpaths could be the right one.

Reached the poor village *Zebdeh*, then over a green hill with a prospect of the sea. Cæsarea visible at a distance, and in the middle distance *Jit* and *Zeita*. Near us were ruins of a strong place called *Burtaa*, said to have a supply of delicious water. Our journey was all over short evergreens rising from stony ground. So lonely—none in sight but ourselves for hours after hours. "Green is the portion of Paradise" exclaimed our people.

At *Cuf'r Kara*, a clean mud village in the fragments of columns lying about, we rested beneath some huge fig-trees while the luggage, guarded by some of the escort, jogged forwards; for muleteers never like resting their animals, or at least do not like unpacking them before the end of the day's march; the trouble is too great in reloading them. The riding horses were tied up under the trees, and we got some melons and eggs from the village.

After an hour we remounted and went on steadily north-west. Soon reached *Kaneer*, where was a cistern with wide circular opening of large masonry, bespeaking high antiquity.

Then to *Subâriyeh* on a small rise from a hollow with one palm-tree. The well was at a distance from the village, and the women washing there. One man asked one of them to move away while he filled our matara (leathern bottle.) She said she would not even for Ibrahim Pasha, whereupon he roared out, " One sees that the world is changed, for if you had spoken in that manner to one of Ibrahim's meanest of grooms, he would have burned down your town for you." The matara was then filled.

In another quarter of an hour we were pacing through a wide Riding (as we use the term in the old English Forests for a broad avenue between woods.) This opened into a plain of rich park scenery, with timbered low hills all about, only of course no grass: in the centre of this stands *Zumâreen*, perched on a bold piece of rock. Many of the trees were entirely unknown to us Southerners; some of the evergreens were named to us as Maloch, &c., and there were bushes of Saris with red berries.

Out of this we emerged upon the plain of the sea-coast, at a wretched village bearing the attractive name of *Furadees* (Paradise.) Here the people were sifting their corn after its thrashing, and we got a boy to refresh us with milk from his flock of goats. Only those experiencing similar circumstances of hot travelling, can conceive the pleasure of this draught, especially after having had to gallop round the boy, and coax and threaten him to sell the milk for our money.

The way lay due north, hugging to the hills parallel to the sea, but at a distance from it: numerous wadis run inland, and at the mouth of each is a village. The first was *Suâmeh*, the next *'Ain el Ghazâl*, (Gazelles fountain,) wretched like the rest, but in a pretty situation—then *Modzha*, and *Mazaal*, and *'Ain Hhood*, (a prosperous looking place,) and *Teeri*.

The sun set in the blue water, and we were still far from Carmel—our animals could scarcely move: sometimes we dismounted and led them—passed the notable ruins of Tantoorah, (Dora of the Bible,) and Athleet on our left—moonlight and fatigue. There was a nearer way from Zumâreen, but it would have been hilly and wearisome. After a long while we overtook our muleteers without the baggage, for the Kawwâs Salim, they said, had been so cruel to them that they had allowed him to go on with the charge towards Carmel.

At length we climbed up the steep to the convent. Being very late we experienced great difficulty in gaining admission. There was no food allowed to the servants, no barley for the horses, and for a long time no water supplied.

In the morning we found great changes had taken place since 1846. The kind president had gone on to India—the apothecary Fra Angelo was removed to a distance—John-Baptist was at Caiffa and unwell. The whole place bore the appearance of gloom, bigotry, dirtiness, and bad management.

In the afternoon I left the convent, in order to enjoy a perfect Sabbath on the morrow in tents at the foot of the hill, open to the sea breeze of the north, and with a grand panorama stretched out before us.

And a blessed day that was. We were all in need of bodily rest, ourselves, the servants and the cattle—and it was enjoyed to the full—my young friend and I derived blessing and refreshment also from the word of God. The words, "Come unto me, all ye that labour and are heavy laden, and I will give you rest," seemed to have a reviving significance, as well as those of "Whosoever drinketh of the water that I shall give him shall never thirst; but the water that I shall give him, shall be in him a well of water springing up into everlasting life."

Such a Sabbath in the Holy Land is true enjoyment.

VII.

ESDRAELON PLAIN AND ITS VICINITY.

May 1851.

FROM Jeneen, (En-gannim, Josh. xxi. 29,) to Acre, *i.e.*, towards the north-west, and skirting the great plain under the line of the hills of Samaria,—thus following the western coast of Zebulon to the south of Asher.

The road was enlivened by numerous companies of native people travelling from village to village.

In an hour and a half from Jeneen we were at *Seeleh*, a cheerful and prosperous-looking place; and in three-quarters of an hour more we were abreast of both *Ta'annuk* and *Salim*, at equal distances of quarter of an hour from the highway; the former on our left hand, and the latter on the right. These places were at that time tolerably well peopled.

Here we gained the first view of Mount Tabor from a westerly direction, and indeed it was curious all along this line to see in unusual aspects the well-remembered sites that lie eastwards or northwards from Jeneen, such as Zera'een (Jezreel,)

Jilboon (Gilboa,) Solam (Shunem,) or Fooleh and Afooleh. In fact, we overlooked the tribe or inheritance of Zebulon from Carmel to Tabor.

With respect to the circumstance of numerous passengers, whom we met this morning, it was a pleasant exception to the common experience of that district, where it is often as true now as in the days of Shamgar the son of Anath (see Judges v. 6), that the population fluctuates according to the invasions or retiring of tyrannical strangers. That vast plain affords a tempting camping-ground for remote Arabs to visit in huge swarms coming from the East with their flocks for pasture; and in the ancient times this very site between Ta'annuk and Lejjoon, being the opening southwards, gave access to the Philistines or Egyptians arriving in their chariots from the long plain of Sharon, or a passage over this plain to that of the great hosts of Syria under the Ptolemies, with their elephants.

In all ages the poor peasantry here have been the victims of similar incursions, "the highways were unoccupied, and the travellers walked through byeways." Yet though chased away from their homes, the populations returned, whenever possible, with pertinacious attachment to their devastated dwellings, and hence we have still the very names of the towns and villages perpetuated by a resident people after a lapse of almost thirty-three hundred years since the allotment made by Joshua, (xiii.–xxi., &c.,) and the names were not then new.

I have myself known villages on the Plain of Esdraelon to be alternately inhabited or abandoned. At one time Fooleh was a heap of ruins, while its neighbour Afooleh had its residents; on my next visit it was Fooleh rebuilt, and the other a heap of overthrown stones, or next time both of them lying in utter silence and desertion. The same with *Mekebleh*, sometimes inhabited, but more frequently a pile of broken-down houses, with some remains of antique sculpture lying on the surface of its hill; and the same occasionally, though not so frequent in vicissitude, with *Iksal.*

From this exposure to invasion of royal armies or of nomade tribes, ("children of the East," Judges vi. 33,) it has always been the case that no towns were built in the central parts of this plain; and even when the kings of Israel had their country residence at Jezreel, that situation was selected because it was nestled close to the hills, and had ravines on two sides of it, serving as fortifying trenches made by nature.

At the present time there are no trees upon that broad expanse, not even olives, to furnish lights for dwelling, either of villages or tents. The wretched people grow castor-oil plants instead for that purpose, sown afresh every year, because these afford no temptation to the hostile Arabs.

That year, however, of 1851, and probably for some time previous, the plain (Merj ibn Amer is its Arabic name,) had been at peace, unmolested by

Esdraelon Plain and its Vicinity. 229

strangers; consequently I saw large crops of wheat there, and fields of barley waving in the breeze. These were mostly the property of a Turkomân tribe, who, like the Kenites of old, reside there in tents, neither building houses nor planting vineyards, though to some extent they sow seed. They have been long upon that ground, but move their tents about, according to the exigences of pasture for their flocks and herds. I believe, however, that they pay "khooweh" (brotherhood,) *i.e.* tribute and military aid, to the Sukoor Arabs for protection and peace under common circumstances.

We had frequently to cross small streams issuing from the ranges of hills, along the base of which our road lay; but they accomplished only short courses, for they were soon absorbed into the ground or settled into morasses, which emitted strong miasma under the influence of the sun. Some petty springs were seen rising from the ground itself, and near each of these were sure to be met some relics of antiquity, such as good squared building stones, or door-posts, or broken olive presses, or fragments of sarcophagi, while the adjacent hills exhibited the hewn lines in the form of steps, remaining from ancient quarrying. The deep alluvium of the plain furnishes no stone whatever for such purposes.

In forty minutes from Ta'annuk, we came to the small mills of *Lejjoon*, (the Roman *Legio*, named from a military station there.) At that time of the year the body of water was not considerable, and there is no village there.

In fifty minutes more we crossed a rivulet named *Menzel el Basha*, (the Pasha's halting-place,) and in twenty minutes more, the *'Ain Kaimoon* with abundance of water. This is at the foot of a hill which has on its summit the vestiges of the large ancient town *Kaimoon*.

This hill is long, narrow, and curved like a cucumber, lying at the south-east end of Mount Carmel, and having the Kishon river on its outer or north-eastern side. Here, therefore, we come distinctly upon the western geography of the Zebulon tribe. In Joshua xix. 11, the border of Zebulon is given as reaching "to the river that is before Jokneam." I do not doubt that this river is the Kishon, or that Jokneam is the "Jokneam of Carmel," in chapter xii. 22, which was given to the Levites "out of the tribe of Zebulon, Jokneam with her suburbs," (chap. xxi. 34.) This place, Kaimoon or Yokneam, must have been one of particular value in a military point of view, commanding as it did the pass of the Kishon valley on one side, and the *Wadi Mel'hh* on the other. Such a post would be in good hands, when intrusted to the bold and warlike tribe of Levi. In the same way several other defensible posts were committed to their charge all over the country.*

* As Hebron, Bethshemesh, Gibeon, Shechem, Beth-horon, Ta'annuk, Jeneen, &c., besides the cities of refuge.

Esdraelon Plain and its Vicinity. 231

On my present journey I passed round the outer line of Tell Kaimoon, having Kishon on the right. In so doing we crossed various tributary streams—the first one, in quarter of an hour from 'Ain Kaimoon, was in *Wadi el Kasab*, (valley of reeds or canes)—the stream was bordered by reeds and a profusion of tall oleander in gorgeous pink flower.

In this neighbourhood, the Turkomâns had commenced reaping their grain. They are a race of people not to be mistaken for Arabs, men of strong build, and with a smiling expression on their clear, ruddy countenances. Besides Arabic, they speak their own coarse dialect of Turkish—several of them came running to us with handfuls of wheat from their harvest. They possess large herds of oxen with good horses.

In another half hour we were at *'Ain el Sufsâfeh*, (the "fountain of the willow-tree,") where the water issues from a rock, and in its bed are two willow-trees; upon the bank were plenty of blackberry bushes.

Just before this we had by the roadside a common looking Arab burial-place, named *Shaikh Sâd;* probably from some Mohammedan devotee of that name interred there; and among the stones about the graves is a fragment of an ancient cornice, deeply sculptured in the pattern here shown.

In a quarter of an hour further we passed *Wadi*

Fragment of Sculpture at Shaikh Sâd, near Lejjoon, on the Plain of Esdraelon.

Keereh, with its full stream of water, and plenty of oleander for adornment.

Thence in about half an hour we arrived at *Wadi Mel'hh* ("Salt valley,") with its rivulet and wild holly-oaks, in which is a great highway leading southwards. This separates the Samaria ridge and Kaimoon from the extremity of the long Mount Carmel.

Having thus passed from one end to the other along the side of the hill of Kaimoon, we turned aside from the road, for taking refreshment under a large oak halfway up that hill, where wild holly-oaks were springing from the ground to mingle with the sombre yet shining boughs of the tree. This was at the sudden contraction of the country into a narrow neck leading to the Plain of Acre.

Esdraelon Plain and its Vicinity. 233

This strait is bounded on one side by Carmel, and on the other by the Galilean hills, both sides clothed with abundance of growing timber; and through its midst is the channel of the Kishon, deeply cut into soft alluvial soil, and this channel also is bordered with oleander and trees that were enlivened with doves, thrushes, linnets, and goldfinches. The modern name of the river is the *Mokatta* (the ford,) and that of the valley *El Kasab*, derived from the spring and valley before-mentioned.

At the narrowest part of this "Kasab" stands a hill, forming a serious impediment to the progress of armies, named *Tell el Kasees* (Hill of the Priest,) which name may be a traditional remembrance of Elijah slaying the priests of Baal; but inasmuch as the word "Kasees" is in the singular number, the appellation may be more likely derived from some hermit residing there in a later age. At any rate, this Tell lies immediately below the site of that memorable sacrifice, and at the point where the Kishon sweeps round to the foot of the mountain a path descends from the "Mohhrakah," *i.e.*, the place of the burnt-offering, to the river. It must, therefore, have been the spot where the priests of Baal were slain, whether the hill be named from the fact or not; and nothing can be more exact than the words of the Bible in 1 Kings xviii. 40.

We were preparing to remount for continuing the journey when our guide espied four wild-looking

Arabs walking with long strides up the hill, so as to pass behind and above us; they were well armed, and made no reply to our challenge. As our horses and the guide's spear would have benefited us little on the steep hill-side, but on the contrary were tempting prizes, and as our fire-arms were not so numerous as theirs, we thought fit to pace away before they should obtain any further advantage of situation over us.

In another quarter of an hour we left the straight road to Caiffa, and struck out northwards, crossing the Kishon at a fort opposite a village on a hill called *El Hharatheeyeh*, just before we should otherwise have come to a low hill covered with a ripe crop of barley, which, from its formation and other circumstances, bore the appearance of an ancient fortified place. This hill was named '*Asfi*, as I wrote it from pronunciation. This, with the *Hharatheeyeh*, one assisting the other, would prove a good military defence at this end of the valley, as Kaimoon and the Kasees were at the other.

Dr Thomson, in his "Land and the Book," chap. xxxi., considers this site to be that of "Harosheth of the Gentiles," (Judges iv. 13,) and I have no doubt that his supposition is correct; the topography agrees, and the etymology in both Hebrew and Arabic is one, viz., "ploughed land." This author, however, makes no mention of '*Asfi*, though he speaks of "the double Tell."

Whether 'Asfi was an aboriginal home of the

Esdraelon Plain and its Vicinity. 235

people in the modern *Esfia* on the summit of Carmel, I have no means of knowing; but that a population, when emigrating to a new settlement, sometimes carried their name with them, appears in Scripture in the instance of Luz, (Judges i. 26,) and of Dan in the 19th chapter.

Previous to this day's journey I had no adequate idea of the quantity of water that could be poured into the Kishon channel by the affluents above-mentioned, (since our passing the Lejjoon stream which runs in an opposite direction,) namely, the Menzel el Basha, the 'Ain Sufsâfeh, Wadi Keereh, and Wadi Mel'hh, all these on the Carmel side of the river, and omitting the more important spring called *Sa'adeh*, near *Beled esh Shaikh*, on the way to Caiffa.

Still portions of the channel are liable to be dried up in that direction, although the bed extending to Jeneen if not to Gilboa contains springs from the ground at intervals, but the level character of the country and the softness of the ground are unfavourable to the existence of a free river course. There was but little water at Hharatheeyeh when we crossed in the month of May. The 'Ain Sa'adeh, however, which I did not then visit, never fails, and in full season, the Kishon near the sea becomes a formidable river, as I have more than once found.

To return to the valley "El Kasab," we were assured that in winter time the whole breadth is sometimes inundated, and even after this has subsided, the alluvial soil is dangerous for attempting to travel in, it becomes a bog for animals of burden. Thus it is quite conceivable that at the occurrence of a mighty storm, divinely and specially commissioned to destroy, the host of Sisera and his chariots would be irretrievably discomfited.

Where the scene opened upon the plain of Acre there was extensive cultivation visible, and the town of Caiffa appeared with the grove of palm-trees in its vicinity.

The view hence of the Caiffa bay reminds us of the prophetic blessing pronounced by the patriarch Jacob. "Zebulon shall dwell at the *haven* of the sea, and he shall be for a haven of ships." I am convinced that this Hebrew root חוֹף (English *haven* and the German *hafen*) is perpetuated not only in those words but in the modern appellation, Caiffa, or as it may be more properly written *Hhaifa*. The Arabic letter ح is the real equivalent for ח in Hebrew; by grammatical permutation the letter ו rightly becomes ف in Arabic, and thus we have حيفا Hhaifa, which Europeans turn into Caiffa.

We then reached a low natural mound on which are ruined walls of great thickness, the levelled surface on the summit had been probably all occupied by one castle with its outworks, but we saw it yellow with a ripe crop of barley. This place is *Hurbaj*, and the neighbourhood abounds with destroyed villages, the natural consequence of being so near to Acre, and being the *palæstra* or wrestling ground of great nations in successive ages.

We arrived at Acre in exactly twelve hours from Jeneen, and pitched the tents outside upon a bank between two trenches of the fortification, commanding extensive views in every direction, and were fanned by sea breezes from the bay.

In conclusion, I may observe that the plain called by the Greeks *Esdraelon*, as a corruption of Jezreel, is that named "Megiddo" in Old Testament Scripture. In the New Testament it bears the prefix of the Hebrew word *Har* (mountain) minus the aspirate, being written in Greek, and so becomes "Armageddon" in the book of Revelation.

For topographical reasons it is very likely that the city of Megiddo was at Lejjoon. There is a village of *Mujaidel* on the north side of the plain, not far from Nazareth, but this is a diminutive of the Arabic *Mejdal*, so common in Palestine as a variation from the Hebrew Migdol.

Besides the above journey I made an excursion in 1859 on the summit of Carmel itself.

Leaving the Convent, which is at the western termination of the mountain, we proceeded along the top of its main ridge to the opposite extremity, the *Mohhrakah*, undoubtedly the locality of Elijah's miraculous sacrifice in presence of King Ahab with the priests of Baal and of the groves; thence we returned to encamp for a time at the cleanly Druse village of *'Esfia;* after which a few hours' ride westwards led us by the village of *Dâliet el Carmel,*[*] also inhabited by Druses, to the romantic *'Ain ez Zera'ah* and over the sites of ruined places, *Doomeen, Shelâleh,* and *Lubieh,* where the hewn stones lying scattered over the ground were indications of much better buildings than those of modern villages.

Then down the long and wearisome descent to *Teeri* on the sea-coast south of Caiffa.

For topographical purposes chiefly, let me give an outline of a few other journeys made about the same neighbourhood.

I. FROM SAFED TO CARMEL.

Sept. 1846.

Going in the direction of the sea, that is, from Naphtali downwards into Zebulon, we crossed westwards the *Jebel Rama,* a long hilly range ending in the south at Rama, and richly wooded, but to our surprise there were numerous fires left by the people to consume trees and large shrubs at discretion, for the making of charcoal. Fortunately for us there was no wind blowing, but several times as

---

[*] It is worthy of note, that in this single place the ancient name of Carmel is preserved among the people. This being called *Dâliet el Carmel* to distinguish it from the Dâlieh of the Rohha district, yet the denomination Carmel is not otherwise given to this mountain by the Arab population. Dâlieh signifies "a vine," this, therefore, is the "vine of Carmel," and Carmel itself signifies "God's vineyard."

the fiery ashes had been drifted upon the road, our horses had no choice but to step into them. On that eminence I picked up specimens of Geodes which abound there, being lumps resembling fruits outside, but when broken found to be a crust of bright spar, and hollow in the centre; some of these were remarkably large. The hills were fragrant with wild herbs, and the views from them delightful.

After *Semwan* we strayed from the right road and got to *Shemuâta*, where we procured a guide to conduct us in the direction of Carmel; he undertook to conduct us as far as *Abu 'Atabeh*, from which Carmel would be visible, and the distance equal either to Acre or to Caiffa. From the heights we descended to *Ekwikât*, and there found ourselves too tired to get further that night.

In the morning we passed the *Bahhjah*, which had been the luxurious summer residence of Abdallah Pasha, but was in a ruinous condition, and came to *Abu 'Atabeh*, which is not a village but a collection of a few houses, perhaps formerly some outlying dwellings belonging to the Bahhjah. Here was a fountain, and a small aqueduct for conveying water to gardens.

Crossed the *Naamân* river, anciently named the *Belus*, on the banks of which, according to Pliny, the primitive idea of glass-making was discovered by accident. Along the beach we came to the Mokatta' or Kishon, found it deep for fording, but got over to Caiffa, and mounted to the Convent of Carmel.

2. NAZARETH TOWARDS ACRE.

Oct. 1849.

Passing *Sefoorieh*, (the Sepphoris so often mentioned in Josephus) with a distant view of Carmel on the left, like a huge rampart of dark blue, we came to the ruined Khan with a fountain called the *'Ain el Bedaweeyeh*, then through delightful wooded glades, on issuing from which we saw *Shefa 'Amer*, a handsome-looking place, with which I made better acquaintance in after years.

On the plain of Acre I picked up a cannon ball, probably a twelve pounder.

(This journey was repeated in March 1852, and in March 1859.)

3. FROM TIBERAS TO ACRE.

March 1850.

From *Hhatteen* to *'Eilaboon*, a quiet and pretty village, after which we had a long stretch of " merrie greenwood" with furze in golden blossom, birds singing, and the clucking of partridges. At one place where the old trees echoed the shouts of country children at their sports, there rose above the summits a bold round tower, which on nearer approach we found to be an outwork of the fortification of a venerable convent called *Dair Hhanna*, which in comparatively recent times had been converted into a castle, but convent, castle, and tower are now become a picturesque ruin.

Esdraelon Plain and its Vicinity. 241

Near this we saw squatted on the ground a family of three generations, almost entirely naked; they had a fire lighted, and the women were washing clothes in the water heated by it, a great rarity in Palestine, for they usually wash with cold water at the spring. Some Metâwaleh peasants ran away from our party when we wished to make some inquiries of them.

From an eminence we saw before us a flat plain inundated like a lake, left by the wintry floods. This occurs there yearly around the flourishing village of *'Arâbet el Battoof*, at which we soon arrived, after which we galloped for miles over green pastures of grass interspersed by trees.

In three quarters of an hour further we came to *Sukhneen*, a large village with good cultivation extending far around. Still traversing green undulations with wooded hills to the right and left, in another hour we were at a small place called *Neâb*, where the scenery suddenly changed for stoney hills and valleys. In a little short of another hour we saw *Damooneh* at half an hour's distance to the left. In twenty minutes more we stopped to drink at the well *Berweh*, then pressed forwards in haste to arrive at Acre before the gates (being a fortification) should be closed. We got there in fifty minutes' hard riding from *'Ain Berweh*.

II. THE REVERSE WAY FROM WEST TO EAST.

1. ACRE TO TIBERIAS.

March 1850.

Crossed the river Naamân, and paced slowly over the extensive marshes, making for *Shefa 'Amer*.

Among these marshes was a herd of about two hundred horses at free pasture upon the grass, weeds, and rushes, so succulent at that season of the year; these were on their way from Northern Syria, and were intended for sale.

Also among the marshes was a temporary village of tabernacles or huts made of plaited palm-leaves, and papyrus canes or reeds, such as one sees on the line of the Jordan or about the lake Hhooleh, with the same class of proprietors in both cases, the Ghawârineh Arabs. Strange that this race of human beings should prefer to inhabit feverish marshes.

We came upon a paved causeway (called the *Resheef*) leading from a large mill towards the sea, but only the portion nearest to the mill now remains entire. Probably this was turned to some account during the French military operations against Acre in 1799.

At Shefa 'Amer we had *'Ebeleen* in sight. Both places are conspicuous over the district around. At some distance from the town is a large well for its supply, and along the broad road between the well and the town, the Druse women are constantly passing with their horns over the forehead and their jars on the shoulders.

Shefa 'Amer is crowned by the remains of the Palace Castle erected by Shaikh Daher, (celebrated in Volney's " Syria,") and the shell of a large old Christian church; near these are some very ancient wells cut into solid rock, but now containing no water.

The majority of the inhabitants are Druses. There are a few Moslems and a few Christians; but at that time there were thirty Jewish families living as agriculturists, cultivating grain and olives on their own landed property, most of it family inheritance; some of these people were of Algerine descent. They had their own synagogue and legally qualified butcher, and their numbers had formerly been more considerable.*

I felt an especial interest in these people, as well as in the knowledge of a similar community existing at a small village not far distant named *Bokea'h.*

Upon the road that day, and in half an hour from the town, I met a couple of rosy-faced, strong peasant men, with sparkling Jewish eyes, who set to speaking Hebrew with some Rabbis in my company. It was in a scene of woodland and cornfields under the blue canopy of heaven; their costume was that of the ordinary Metâwaleh peasan-

---

*They afterwards dwindled to two families, the rest removing to Caiffa as that port rose in prosperity.

try, *i.e.*, a scarlet and embroidered short coat with large dark blue trousers. I shall never forget this circumstance, of finding men of Israel, fresh from agricultural labour, conversing in Hebrew in their own land.

Our road then led through glades of exceeding beauty: an English park backed by mountains in a Syrian climate. The gently undulating land was clothed with rich grass, and sprinkled (not thronged) with timber, chiefly terebinth. Linnets and thrushes were warbling among the trees.

Cuf'r Menda was on our left; *Sefoorieh* at a distance on the right; *Rumâneh* and *'Azair* before us. Then we entered upon the long plain of *'Arâbet el Battoof*, and rested a short time before sunset at *'Ain Bedaweeyeh* for refreshment. Carpets were spread upon long grass which sank under the pressure. The horses and mules were set free to pasture, and we formed ourselves into separate eating groups; one Christian, one Jewish, and one Moslem. Some storks were likewise feeding in a neighbouring bean-field, the fragrance of which was delicious, as wafted to us by the evening breeze.

On remounting for the road to Tiberias, several hours beyond, we put on cloaks to keep off the falling dew, and paced on by a beautiful moonlight, at first dimmed by mist or dew, which afterwards disappeared; the spear carried by one of the party glimmered as we went on; and the Jews whiled away the time by recitation of their even-

Esdraelon Plain and its Vicinity. 245

ing prayers on horseback, and conversing in the Hebrew language about their warrior forefathers of Galilee.

2. CAIFFA TO NAZARETH.
July 1854.

Passing through the rush of 'Ain Saadeh water as it tumbles from the rocky base of Carmel, and by the *Beled esh Shaikh* and *Yajoor*, we crossed the Kishon bed to take a road new to me, namely, by *Damooneh*, leaving *Mujaidel* and *Yafah* visible on our right, upon the crests of hills overlooking the Plain of Esdraelon. We passed through a good deal of greenwood scenery, so refreshing in the month of July, but on the whole not equal in beauty to the road by Shefa 'Amer.

3. CAIFFA TO NAZARETH.
Sept. 1857.

By *Beled esh Shaikh* and *Yajoor*, where threshing of the harvest was in progress in the Galilean fashion by means of the *moraj*, (in Hebrew the *morag*, Isa. xli. 15 and 2 Sam. xxiv. 22,) which is a stout board of wood, with iron teeth or flints on the under surface. The plank turns upward in front, and the man or boy stands upon it in exactly the attitude of a Grecian charioteer: one foot advanced; the head and chest well thrown back; the reins in his left hand, and with a long thonged whip, he drives the horses that are attached to it at a rapid pace in a circle, shouting merrily or singing as they go, —a totally different operation from the drowsy creeping of the oxen or other animals for threshing in our Southern Palestine.

In due time we crossed the bed of the Kishon, which was quite dry in that part above the *Sa'adeh*, except where some green stagnant puddles occurred at intervals.

We passed a herd of camels belonging to the Turkomans, walking unburdened, whereas all other animals that we met were laden with grain for the port of Caiffa. At the commencement of the ascent on the opposite hills we rested under the *Tell el Hharatheeyeh*, beneath a noble tree of the evergreen oak; and near there we passed alongside of a camp of degraded Arabs called *Beramki*, in a few tattered tents, but they had some capital horses picketed around them. The villagers regard these people with ineffable disdain, as "cousins of the gipsies." It seems that they subsist by singing songs among real Arab camps, and by letting out their horses as stallions for breeding, with variations of picking and stealing. We saw some of their women and children, filthy in person, painfully employed in scraping away the ground wherever black clay showed itself, in the hope of reaching water, however bad in quality.

There was threshing at *Jaida* as we passed that village. We halted at the spring of *Samooniah*, and at *Ma'alool;* the priest of the village was superintending the parish threshing: his reverence was covered with dust from the operation.

Esdraelon Plain and its Vicinity. 247

4. CAIFFA TO SHEFA 'AMER.
June 1859.

From *Bcled esh Shaikh* and *Yajoor*, across the Kishon channel, upon the plain of Acre, and rested a short time at the *Weli of Jedro*, (very like a Hebrew name,) and then near us, all close together were the three villages of *Cuf'r Ita*, *Ja'arah* and *Hurbaj*. Thence to Shefa 'Amer, first diverging somewhat to *'Ebeleen*.

III. SOUTH SIDE OF ESDRAELON.

1. PLAIN OF SHARON TO CAIFFA.
Oct. 1849.

At *Baka* we leave the plain of Sharon, at its northern end, if indeed the extensive level from the Egyptian desert up to this point, may come under this one denomination; and we enter upon the hilly woodlands of Ephraim and Manasseh, so clearly described in Joshua xvii. 11, 17, 18.

In mounting to the higher ground, there is obtained a fine view of the sea, and the oak and karoobah trees were larger as we advanced; from certain stations we obtained a totally unexpected prospect of a stretch of large forest scenery below us, extending towards *Sindianeh* in the west.

At one spot we passed among scattered stones of excellent masonry, large and rabbeted at the edges, lying confusedly about, enough for a small town, but evidently belonging to a period of ancient date; a few mud huts were adjoining these.

Thence we descended into a long valley, several miles in extent, called *Wadi 'Arah*, fully occupied with cotton crops, and stubble of the last harvest of grain. The valley was bounded on either side by well timbered hills, and its direction was N.E by E.

After an hour in this long enclosure, the pleasing features of the scene became less defined in character, and, uncertain of our way, we climbed up to a village called *'Arârah*, where, after an hour's trouble, we got a guide at high price for the rest of the day's journey. The evening was then advancing, and the gnats from the trees and shrubs plagued the horses. Among these trees were grand old oaks of a kind that bear gigantic acorns with mossy cups. At length the verdure ceased, and we had only stoney hills. There was, however, a weli with a spring of water, and fruit trees by the roadside, crowded with a shoal of singing birds all rustling and chirping at once among the boughs as the sun was setting, and throwing a glorious red over the clouds which had been gradually collecting during the afternoon.

We left the village of *Umm el Fahh'm*, (" Mother of Charcoal "—a name significant of a woodland district) upon the right, and night closed in; our old guide on his little donkey singing cheerily in front, till darkness reduced us all to silence.

Esdraelon Plain and its Vicinity. 249

We crossed the small rivulet at *Lejjoon* by starlight; and the rest of the journey in the night was not only monotonous, but even dangerous, over marshes and chinks in the Plain of Esdraelon. Our course was in a direction N.-E. to Nazareth, which we reached in sixteen hours from the morning's starting at *Cuf'r Saba*.

There were fortunately no roaming Arabs to molest us in this night passage across the *Merj ibn 'Amer*.

2. PLAIN OF SHARON TO CAIFFA.

June 1859.

As before, we left the northern extremity of the plain of Sharon, but this time at the eastern and minor village of *Baka*, and thus we missed the ruined town before noticed, but got into the same valley of *'Arah;* and in the great heat of summer, confined between the two ridges of hills, we crept on to the extremity of the valley, and mounted a hill to the village of *Mushmusheh*, opposite to *Umm el Fahh'm*. All the villages in that region are situated on hills, and are of no easy access.

This place enjoys abundance of water springing out of the ground, and at any risk so precious a treasure ought not to be lost; therefore, although the houses were abandoned and the people scattered, they come there stealthily, and as opportunity arises, to do the little service to the ground that it required, and watch its oranges, lemons, and pomegranates, (from the name it would seem that formerly this place was famous for apricots.) As we halted and pitched tents there, one by one some of the people came about us, although they had been preparing to leave for the night, in order to sleep at "Charcoal's Mother," (the village opposite.) They stayed under our protection, and got for us certain supplies from over the way.

Close beside us was a gigantic mulberry tree, around which two very large vines climbed to a great height, and a channel of running water almost surrounded the roots.

I never heard such sweet-toned bells as the flocks about there carried, and which gave out their music near and far at every movement of the goats and sheep.

In the morning we left this very pleasant spot and went on to *Lejjoon;* crossed the Sufsâfeh and the other streams with their oleander borders, and enjoyed the magnificent prospects of Hermon, Tabor, and the plain; rested on the hill of *Kaimoon* under the fine oak-tree of former aquaintance, and at length arrived in Caiffa.

IV. FROM CARMEL SOUTH-EASTWARDS.

April 1859.

The usual way by *'Ain Sa'adeh, Beled esh Shaikh* and *Yajoor;* the woody sides of Carmel diversified in colour at this season of spring; there was the dark green of the bellota oak, the yellow of the abundant broom, the dark red-brown of the sprout-

Esdraelon Plain and its Vicinity. 251

ing terebinth and the pale green of young-leafed trees of many other kinds. There was, moreover, the fragrance of an occasional pine, and of the hawthorn, (Za'aroor,) which is of stronger scent than in England; and the ground was sprinkled with purple and yellow crocuses; also with anemones of every shade of purple and white, besides the scarlet, which alone are found in Judæa, but there in profusion.

Turning off from the road to Jeneen, I rose upon high ground, and came to *Umm ez Zeenât*, (mother of beauties.) Our people were of opinion that this name did not apply so much to the daughters of the village as to the landscape scenery, for near it we commanded an extensive prospect, including Hermon with its snows one way, and the "great and wide sea" in the opposite quarter.

We lost our way for a time, leaving *Rehhaneeyeh* on our left, and straying as far as *Dâliet er Rohha;* on recovering the right road we arrived at *Cuferain,* (the "double village") and to *Umm el Fahh'm,* marching among silent woods often tangled by neglected growth, and abounding in a variety of unknown trees, besides the Seringa and the oaks with much broader leaves than are ever seen in the south; also, for a long period we had frequent recurring views of snowy Hermon in the N.E.

The considerable village of *'Aneen* we found almost entirely broken up, by the recent warfare between the partisans of Tokan and 'Abdu'l Hadi.

At length our repeated calls and promises echoing among the apparently forsaken houses, brought out an old man, and he promised to procure a guide to take us within sight of '*Arâbeh*, after which several women peered out of their miserable dwellings.

The guide conducted us through large woods on heights and in depths, among fragrant herbs and blossoming trees growing wild, till some time after sunset, when we stopped for the night at a poor village called *Harakat;* we were all tired, but especially the two women of a Christian party going to Jerusalem, who had attached themselves to us all the day for the benefit of our protection.

The ground on which the tent was set up was wet, as there had been some rain at the place that day, and springs of water were running to waste near us; the village people served as guards around us, on being fed at our expense; the pilgrims spread their beds in one direction outside the tent, and the kawwâses in the opposite.

By the light of a brilliant morning we marched forwards to '*Arâbeh*, which was being besieged by the Turkish government, in force of infantry, cavalry, and artillery.

VIII

BELÂD BESHÂRAH.

THIS is the mountainous district lying east and south of Tyre, probably the "Galilee of the Gentiles;" bounded on the north by the river *Kasimîyeh*, the ancient Leontes; on the west by the plain of Tyre; on the east by the plain of Hhooleh and of the Upper Jordan; on the south by hills around Safed: the district is very little known to Europeans, and was much less so in 1848.

In that year I entered it from the North, after traversing the Sidon country, crossing the pleasant river with its rose-coloured border of oleander and wild holly-oak at a ford wider than the average breadth of the Jordan.

There we found abundance of noble trees, and some cottages near them, the vines belonging to which climbed up those trees to a surprising height; and the thickness of the vines exceeded any that I had any where or at any time seen.

In front was the village of *Boorj*, and we mounted into a high table-land commanding prospects of indescribable grandeur, which comprised parts of both Lebanon and Anti-Lebanon, the extreme heights of Sannin and Hermon being visible at once.

The day was one of hot shirocco, and there were fires of lime-kilns visible in several directions, this season (late in autumn) being that appropriated to such employment, after all the harvests are gathered in.

There were innumerable villages appearing in every direction. We passed *Abâsiyeh* on our right; *Dar Meemas* and *Izereiriyeh* distant on the left; *Tura* on the right; *Dar Kanoon* we almost entered; *Bidias* near us on the left; *Dair Thecla* on our right; *Bursheen* on the right; *Durtghayer* on the left; *Arzoon* further on the left; then we rested under some olive trees, with *Dar esh Shems* on the right; *Mezra'a* on the left; *Dar Zibneh* with a castle on our right.

In the distance appeared the mighty old castle of *Shukeef* (*Belfort* of the Crusaders) upon an eminence, with Jebel esh Shaikh, or Hermon, rising majestically behind it.

As we descended into a deep glen between verdant hills, the partridges were clucking in multitudes, and so unaccustomed to intrusion, that sometimes they came running up towards us; magpies were flying about, and we were told that the glen abounds in wild beasts, which there seemed no reason to doubt. For hours we wound round

Belâd Beshârah.

and round within this cool and refreshing labyrinth of arbutus, bellota or evergreen oak, aspen, clematis, broom, and what looked like the sloe, besides other and unknown vegetation. The bellota was often respectable-sized timber in girth, though of no considerable height; sometimes our path was overshadowed by their branches stretching across, and we had to stoop beneath them. On the sides of the hills were many fires of the charcoal burners.

As evening came on, we could our see lofty green prison walls tipped with the setting sun.

At length the glen seemed to be terminated by a fine round hill, crowned with a village standing across the passage. The appearance improved as we drew nearer; inhabitants were not few; large flocks and herds were winding by several ways towards it. The people named it *Khirbet Sellim*, (Sellim in ruin) but how could all this cheerful scene belong to a ruin?

The sun set and we had another hour of the lovely glen to thread by starlight. At last we emerged by a gently inclined plain, which gradually became rougher, and we mounted the steep hill on which *Tibneen* is built. There we determined to halt for the night, as our cattle were unable to hold on to *Bint el Jebail*.

We pitched on the threshing floor between the village and the castle.

This castle is the citadel of all the Belâd Beshârah, from the Leontes to Safed, and Ahhmad Bek, its owner, is called by his people "the Shaikh of Shaikhs;" by the Turkish government he is recognised as Kaimakam of the province.

The people were of ill behaviour, and talked about quarantine, but the population of the district are at all times a churlish race, being of the Sheah or 'Ali sect of Moslems; they curse and loathe our Mohammedans, and oppress the sparse families of Christians within their reach. They are called the Mutâwaleh.

At first they refused to let us have anything, till the governor, on ascertaining who we were, sent us down some lemonade; still we got but few articles of food, and our horses were left without water.

My kawwâs Salim was then taken ill from the effect of having slept the preceding night with his head uncovered, and with reluctance our own people put up the small tent that travelled with us on purpose for them; they always prefer sleeping in open air, only covering the head well with the cloak.

This was Saturday night, and we had not an agreeable prospect for a Sabbath rest on the morrow.

The wind was strong all night on that lofty situation, but there was no dew.

In the morning, the people would not supply us with milk, even for the horses, and so it was impossible to stay there; we marched on towards

Belâd Beshârah.

Bint el Jebail, about three hours' distant, a considerable place, which often contests with Tibneen for supremacy in the local government, and where the governor is a distant relative of him at Tibneen.

From the tents, before starting, we could see the following villages in a curved line from S.-E. to N:—

    Haddata or Haita ez-Zoot.
    Bait U'oon.
    Berasheet.
    Hhooleh.
    Shakrah.

And they told us of *El Yehudiyeh* on the N.-W. behind the castle. The Mediterranean in sight. [I became better acquainted with Tibneen, and on better relations with the people in after years.]

Passed on through a pretty country, like all the Belâd Beshârah, with numerous villages in sight; excellent beaten roads, and plenty of them; with everywhere the magnificent objects in view of Mount Hermon, and part of the Lebanon, but not always the Mediterranean.

Rested at half-way of our short journey under a large evergreen oak on the summit of a rising ground, with a refreshing breeze blowing; thence descended to a plain where there were about a dozen wells, and people drawing water for large herds of neat cattle. Here our horses got drink.

Arrived at *Bint el Jebail*, a nice-looking place, with a commanding house for the governor, (Hhusain Sulimân,) but the people were at first even more inhospitable than those at Tibneen, for they drove away our man Khaleel from the village fountain, and covered up their mouths and noses, in fear of cholera.

On application to the Bek, we got permission to draw water for ourselves, and he allowed us eggs and bread, with barley for the horses, and it was with difficulty they accepted any money in return.

The Bek also invited me to visit him in his house, but stipulating not to shake hands.

On coming near the Serai, (governor's house,) the ladies of the Hhareem were looking out of the lattices upon the cavalcade. A crowd of servants were at the door to receive us, in attendance on one of his sons, who had a large hunting-hawk upon his wrist; silver bells upon her legs.

We were shown into a large baronial-looking hall, and chairs were placed for us *upon* the divân.

The great man sat in the right-hand corner, upon a panther skin, one of the prey of the country, his brother at his right hand, and his sons ranged on his left. He wore a robe of the true Moslem apple-green, with a Cashmere shawl round his waist, and another on his turban. His countenance and deportment were truly aristocratic; he and all his family were handsome, with intelligent expression of countenance.

The son who had been outside came in, and put his hawk upon her perch, then took his place.

They gave us sherbet, coffee, and abundant compliments: we talked of hawking in England, and English ladies riding to the sport. London, and the Queen on the throne were discussed; also Jerusalem, where the Bek had never been. On the whole the reception was satisfactory. Pity that the people were afraid of cholera; they did not exhibit the virtue of resignation to Divine predestination any more than our Sooni-Moslems of the south had done.

Our tents were in a sunny situation, but still we had in them a rest for Sunday afternoon.

At sunset the Bek sent me a present of grapes, those that were purple were of large size.

Starlight night, but no dew; jackals were howling in troops, sometimes very close to us. An armed nominal quarantine was placed over us during the night—ridiculous enough after a pretty free intercourse of the people all day.

The morning very cool. A poor Maronite priest from 'Ain Nebel came to me in his black robes and dark blue turban, and, leaning on his staff, gave a lamentable account of persecutions suffered by the four or five Christian villages about there, and imploring English help on their behalf. Alas! nothing could be done for him, only the case of the servant of the governor of Tibneen shooting a poor Christian, while on compulsory work at the lime-kilns, got inquiry made into it at Bayroot. On asking his name, and writing it down, the miserable man said to the secretary, "Tell the consul that I have already written his name on my heart."

Hitherto our journey had been entirely novel—there is no record published of any traveller passing through that country, from the Leontes, its northern boundary, before that date. Going forwards, we passed through pretty green lanes along the sides of hills. From the crest of a hill, whence the view was very extensive, we had *Yaroon* on the right, and beyond it the ruined convent of St George. I afterwards learned that the church there exhibits proof of great size and magnificence.

By the roadside was a huge undecorated sarcophagus, in excellent preservation, standing on a raised platform of masonry; single and alone in a wide expanse, no village or remnant of human works near it. The masonry in front had been wilfully damaged, enough to make the sarcophagus lean, but not to fall, and the ponderous cover was removed from its place—total length, eight feet by five, and four in height, the hollow cut out from the body left the thickness of a foot all round it. No inscription gives any record of the doubtless important personage for whom it was prepared, and no embellishments even provide a clue to the period to which it belongs. It stands well-preserved, great in its simplicity and position.

Villages of *Fârah* and *Salchah* on our left.

Thence we descended into a glen of blazing

white stone, without any verdure, in which were a diversity of paths, and a petty runlet of water issuing from the ground, but soon showing only stagnant green pools and mud, with frogs in abundance, then evaporated altogether. Near this, Salim was taken with vomiting and purging, and was hardly able to remain on his horse; the dragoman also fainting and giddy, and the rest frightened with the terrors of expected cholera. Our guide wanted to desert us and return home.

The muleteers and luggage had taken another road, but after a time we met again. Moving on, the ground became a gradual rise, and a stream coming down it toward us, became clearer as we ascended, and fruit-trees were rather numerous.

Under some fig-trees the kawwâs laid himself down, and we stayed there three hours with him; water was poured over his head to obviate fever, and I administered some pills.

During the interval I found some sculptured stones with Hebrew inscriptions, which I have elsewhere described, and took pains to decipher the words, but without much result. They were lying in a ploughed field by the roadside. We were now entering on classic ground of the Talmudists, and upon a precipice above us, upon wide table-ground, was the village of *Jish*, the Giscala of Josephus.

When evening brought coolness, we proceeded towards Safed.

A peasant passing us was carrying home his plough upon his shoulder, except the iron share, which his little daughter, of two or three years old, carried on her head.

Some of our horses were so stung by flies that the blood flowed to the stones under their feet as they went along.

There were traces of ancient pavement along the road, and cavern holes in chalk-rock sides. Then traversing a few miles of dark volcanic stone we neared a crater in the ground, whose gloomy aspect was fully in keeping with the destruction which such a phenomenon bespeaks as having occurred—silent as the death it produced, and void of all pleasurable features, of wild flowers, or even the thorns of nature.

The whole vicinity bore traces of the earthquakes that have often occurred there, especially that of 1837.

After this a glorious prospect burst upon us of Safed, "set upon a hill," and the gloomy hill of Jarmuk beside it. Tabor also in view far in advance, throwing a vast shadow of late afternoon-time over other hills, and glimpses of the lake Tiberias.

Encamped on our former site among the great old olive-trees north of the town. Some Jewesses gleaning olives from the ground were frightened away. Visitors were out at once to welcome us in English, Arabic, and Jüdisch, (Jewish-German.) We were surrounded by fair and rosy complexions of Jews, the effect of the pure bracing air of the mountain.

My sick people took to their beds, and only after a week's care (medical such as we could get) were able to continue the journey, one remaining behind to recover strength. The complaint, however, had not been cholera, it was rather what is denominated "Syrian fever."

IX.

UPPER GALILEE.—FOREST SCENERY.

TIBNEEN has been already mentioned as one of the two capital villages of the Belâd Beshârah, and lying S.-E. from Tyre. We have now before us the Galilean country that lies southwards between that place and Nazareth.

July 1853.—After honourable entertainment and refreshing sleep in the Castle of Tibneen, I awoke early to look out on the dark and broad mass of Mount Hermon by starlight.

Coffee was served, and I was mounted on my "gallant gray," still by twilight, parting with some friends who had been rambling with me for three weeks over Phœnicia and the Lebanon. I set my face in the direction of Jerusalem.

We were guided by the Shaikh of *Rumaish*, a Christian village that lay upon the road before us, he being furnished with a written mandate from Hhamed el Bek, the ruler of Tibneen, to take four men of his place as our escort through the forest.

In the outskirts of the forest belonging to the

castle we found peasants already proceeding to the threshing-floors; women in lines marching to the wells with jars cleverly balanced upon their heads; and camels kneeling on the ground munching their breakfast of cut straw, with most serious and unchanging expression of countenance, only the large soft eyes were pleasant to look at.

In half-an-hour we were at *Aita*.

This country is famous for the quality of its tobacco, a plant that is most esteemed when grown among the ruined parts of villages, because the nitre contained in the old cement of houses not only serves to quicken the vegetation, but imparts to the article that sparkling effect which is admired when lighted in the pipe.

Vines are also extensively cultivated, and the people take pleasure in training them aloft upon the high trees, as oak, terebinth, poplar, &c., and allowing them to droop down in the graceful festoons of nature, which also gives an agreeable variety of green colour among the timber trees.

We were entering the gay woodland and reaching the top of a hill, when the sun rose at our left hand, and the glory of that moment surpassed all common power of description. Crowds of linnets and finches burst suddenly into song; the crested larks "that tira-lira chant," * rose into the merry blue sky, with

---

* Shakespeare; or as Ronsard has it :—
"qui *tire l'ire*
" Des esprits mieux que je n'écris."

the sunlight gleaming on their plump and speckled breasts; the wood-pigeons, too, were not silent; but all, in harmonious concert, did their best to praise the blessed Creator, who delights in the happiness of His creatures.

Forwards we marched with light spirits, through dense woods, varied by the occasional clearings, which are called "the rides" in old English forests, and sometimes we drew near to snug villages, or got glimpses of such, by the names of *Teereh*, *Hhaneen*, and *'Ain Nebel;* the latter at two hours from Tibneen; the people there are Christian, and they cultivate silk and tobacco. In some places we observed ancient sarcophagi, hewn into solid rock without being entirely detached, they had therefore been left unfinished, though partly ornamented.

On a ground rising opposite to us I saw the screw of a large press, standing out of the field; this I was told is used for extracting resin from the red berries of terebinth trees for domestic lamp-lighting—a circumstance which of itself bespeaks the prevalence of woodland round about, and is a variation from the practice of that unhappy thin population on the plain of Esdraelon, who are obliged to use castor-oil for the same purpose, because the *palma Christi* plants which produce the oil are of less value to Bedaween marauders than olive-trees would be, and damage done to them is of less importance than it would be among the latter.

Arrived at *Rumaish*, the Shaikh rode up to his village while we awaited him under the branches of an old oak overshadowing the road. Rumaish is a neat little place, but, like almost every village throughout Palestine, oppressed by the heavy debts incurred with the forestallers of their produce (generally Europeans) in the seaport towns.

Our friend returned with another horseman, and three men on foot, all armed with guns, as our future way lay through a Druse neighbourhood.

These men for our escort were Maronite Christians, and they showered upon me abundant salutations, expressing their satisfaction at the circumstance of a Christian (myself) being treated with such distinguished consideration in Tibneen Castle, and concluding with the hope that I would visit them yearly, in order to give countenance to poor, depressed Christianity. The two priests of the village had desired to come out and greet me, but their people had persuaded them that the distance was too great for their walking in the sun—near mid-day in July.

Resting for a while before resuming the journey, the newcomers sat round in a circle to smoke their fragrant local tobacco, and find some relief to the mind in relating tales of suffering under persecution. They said they had more reason to be satisfied with the rule of my host, Hhamed el Bek, than with that of Tamar Bek at Bint Jebail, which they described as most cruel and capricious. That I could easily believe after the incident that came to my knowledge in that vicinity five years before,—that of the wanton murder of a poor Christian, at the lime-kiln works, by a servant of that governor. I have already mentioned that it was narrated to me by the village priest of 'Ain Nebel. An inquiry was instituted into the case by the authorities at Bayroot; but there must be many such instances occurring that are never known by those who would or could bring them to light and justice.

At length the signal was given for mounting. The mules weie collected together, after straying about for such pasture as could be got, their bells gently ringing all the time, and the pipes were stowed away: those of the muleteers being placed down the backs of their jackets, with the bowls uppermost, reaching to the men's necks.

We then plunged into the forest of *Tarshcchhah*, where the Shaikh of the principal village, that which gives name to the district, is a fanatic Moslem, who was then preaching religious revivals, and was said to engraft upon his doctrine the pantheism of the Persian Soofis. This was not considered improbable, seeing that the Moslems of the Belâd Beshârah are all of the Sheah sect, (here called *Metâwala*,) out of which the Soofi heresy is developed. The new doctrines had spread rapidly in various directions, and were professed by several of the Effendi class in Jerusalem—the old story repeated of Sadducean principles obtaining among the rich and the luxurious. This Shaikh was described as excessively intolerant of Christianity, and at that period, viz., the commencement of the Russian war, was in the habit of travelling about with a train of disciples, all carrying iron-shod staves in their hands, and distinguished by having a portion of the muslin of the turban hanging loosely behind, doing their utmost to excite tumult and hatred of the Christians by shouting aloud the Mohammedan formula of belief, "There is no God but Allah, and Mohammed is the Apostle of God," striking the ground with their iron-shod staves by way of emphasis.

Among the evergreens, and the gall-oaks, and karoobah-trees, our path often became very narrow —sometimes subsiding into sunless hollows, then mounting afresh into a chequered brilliancy—but always passing between woods of dark and glossy foliage. At one place was a pretty spring of water, where one of the party halted to drink while the rest proceeded. On finding him fail to come up with us, a horseman and two footmen were despatched in search. Their shouts gave animation to the scene, but gradually became fainter as the distance between us increased.

The whole of the day's journey hitherto was remarkable for absence of human population.

Came to *Herfaish*, a Druse village, in the very heart of the forest, but passed on, still toiling in the hot sunshine. Occasionally the paths were so rocky that we had to dismount and lead the horses.

It was evident from the deportment and conversation of our guides, that whenever Christians (who in that neighbourhood are all Maronites) enter that division of the forest where the Druses of Herfaish prevail they find it necessary to travel in companies and armed. Fortunately we encountered none of the fanatics of Tarshechhah. The escort told me that they themselves only became acquainted with these cross roads in the direction of Nazareth by means of their journeys thither at the ecclesiastical festivals of Easter, Christmas, &c.

At this hot season there were not many flowers to be noticed, beyond some varieties of salvia, yellow broom, bright-coloured thistles, the pink flax, blackberry blossoms, and one kind of heath, together with some plants unknown to me.

The trees were not of large dimensions, but mostly evergreen and of slow growth; many were very wide-spreading, and all dense enough to afford good shelter from either sun or rain.

After six hours and a half of uninterrupted forest we arrived at a small trickling spring called *'Ain Noom*, when large trees began to give place to shrubs and underwood, and human inhabitants

Upper Galilee.—Forest Scenery.

again cheered the sight, they bringing cattle to the water for drinking.

At *Bait Jan* we were overtaken by the missing member of our party. At this place there is considerable vine cultivation. Very soon afterwards we were suddenly upon the brow of a deep descent—sheer steep down to the plain of *Battoof*, and the prospect from that spot was amazing, not only beyond expectation, for we had not expected any remarkable scene to come in our way, but beyond all previous experience.

The whole of Lower Galilee, Samaria, and Gilead, was laid like a map at our feet; and from so great an elevation the Mediterranean and the Sea of Galilee were brought close together Among the most conspicuous geographical points were Tabor, a very small object beneath; then the line of Carmel; and Ebal in Samaria; there was Hhatteen, the last battle-field of the Crusaders; King Baldwin's castle of Cocab; the entrance of the Jordan into the lake, and both the supposed sites of Capernaum; also Acre with her blue bay, and a small amount of shipping off Caiffa. Pity that I had no aneroid barometer for ascertaining the elevation of that site.

The map-like appearance of the wide panorama suggested to memory the song of Deborah the prophetess, with her recapitulation of the succours furnished or omitted by the several tribes of Israel at the battle of the Kishon and Harosheth of the Gentiles. From such a site she would turn to the left hand for expostulation with Reuben, and to the right for rebuking Dan and Asher upon the seacoast, after that the Lord had defeated the national foe without them, and sold Sisera into the hands of a woman.

Our descent was by a narrow path of zig-zags, veering alternately towards Acre or Tiberias, although those towns were soon concealed by intervening hills; the plain below was a large dark patch of olive plantation.

In an hour and ten minutes of wearisome toil in leading the horses down, with no possible interval of rest, we came to the village of *Rama;* having long before lost sight of the Mediterranean.

We took refuge from the sun in the house of a Christian named Ibrahim Hhanna, and after an hour's sleep rose up to a feast of eggs, olives, bread, and cream cheese, after sharing in which our guides from Rumaish took their leave, with kindly wishes on both sides.

Next we hired a guide for our crossing the plain to 'Arâbeh el Battoof on the way to Nazareth, and travelled over alternate corn stubble and balloot underwood. In one short valley that we crossed there were six *jeldeh* or short aqueducts to watermills.

The weather was still extremely hot.

Passed near *Dair Hhanna,* a large ruin of a fortification upon a hill rising out of the plain; probably, as the name would seem to intimate, an old

Upper Galilee.—Forest Scenery. 273

castle of the Knights of St John of Jerusalem. A few poor people here have built huts for themselves within the great walls, in the manner of the Italian peasants in Goldsmith's "Traveller," who do the same within the confines of a Cæsar's palace—

> "And wondering man can want the larger pile,
> Exult and own their cottage with a smile."

Two small towers, now also in ruin, flank the castle at short distances. These were erected by Shaikh Daher about eighty years since, who employed the whole for military defence in his revolt against the Turks.

Near this 'Arâbeh lie some time-eaten fragments of large old columns. There we dismissed the guide, as he wished to be at home again before dark, and we traversed the plain of *Sefurîyeh*, the celebrated Sepphoris of Josephus' wars.

It is to be observed that in that afternoon we had crossed three narrow but long parallel plains, all running east and west, and divided from each other by lines of rocky hills. The northern one contains *Rama* and *'Arâbeh*; the middle one has *Sefurîyeh*; and the southern one has *Tura'ân* and *Cuf'r Cana*, the place of the miracle at the marriage in St John's Gospel.

Hoping to reach our destination by a shorter track, after passing *Rumâneh* and *Jerjer* we mounted a hill to *Mesh-had*, that was in sight, but as darkness came on, lost our way for a considerable time;

S

rain threatened and fell a short time. Once we came near a large cattle-fold, which we afterwards learned belonged to the Latin Convent of Nazareth, but no people appeared to answer us; then we got a gloomy view of Mount Tabor; at length, however, we were cheered with discovering the window lights of Nazareth, after being fourteen hours in the saddle, omitting the two hours' rest at Rama, and the half-hour at Rumaish.

The whole country we had traversed is particularly interesting; but at the close of the day the company were all too tired to sing aloud, as might have been performed under other circumstances, that Arab song well known over the country, with its wild high note (not cadence) at the end of each line:

> "If thy horse be indeed
> A creature of speed
> Thou wilt lodge for the night in Nazareth."

In December of the next year (1854) I traversed the Rama plain lengthwise, that is to say, from Tiberias to the plain of Acre.

After *Mejdal* and the *Wadi el Hamâm*, or "Valley of the Doves," we soon struck out due westwards, and passed under a hill with ruins on its top called *Sabâneh;* then some more considerable ruins in a similar position called *Memileh*. At a good way to our left a small village was pointed out called *'Ailabool*, containing, among other inhabitants, a few Christians, who have their chapel and a priest.

The whole road was extremely picturesque—the scenery consisting of broken rocks of ochreous tinge and shoots of balloot oak; and for a long distance at every turn, in looking backwards, there showed itself the still lovely lake of the Gospel narratives—that object which no one can ever forget who has had once the privilege to be near it.

We kept *Mansoorah* steadily before the eye, but on arriving at the hill upon which this stands, the road deviated a little, and rose over an eminence side by side with the village. Here we got a view of those several separated objects—Tabor; the Sea of Galilee; and Dair Hhanna.

We were accosted by some Druse peasantry when the village of *Moghâr* was somewhat on our left.

While passing the large olive plantations of *Rama*, we gazed up at the long and steep ladder of the precipice by which we had descended last year.

Rama is at some height above the level of the plain, although low in proportion to the mountain at its back.

Just before sunset we halted under the trees for refreshment about a quarter of an hour, then engaged a guide to conduct us to *Yerka*, on the plain of Acre.

The man purposely led us up to the village of Rama, over a very stoney road, hoping to induce us to stay there for the night on the way to Yerka.

When I refused to remain, and insisted on going forwards, he took us into places even worse for travelling, to the peril of limbs to ourselves and the horses and mules: and great was our just wrath on finding ourselves every few minutes in augmented trouble in utter darkness; for there was no moon, and the stars were hid by clouds. The horses' feet were sometimes caught between close-wedged rocks, so that we had to lift them out with our hands, and our boots were with difficulty extricated from the same catch-traps; nevertheless the traitor trudged on nimbly a-head of us, heedless of our embarrassments. Had he not led us up to Rama at the beginning we should have kept upon a pleasant, well-beaten road on the level of the general plain.

At length by our own efforts we got down to this highway, and trudged on at a good pace, the guide still trotting on in advance, out of reach of our hands, fearful of consequences, until we reached *Mejdal Croom*, (or *Migdol*, or Tower of the Vineyards in Hebrew,) where he swore that Yerka was still three hours before us, and that he was exhausted with fatigue. As we were so in reality, we halted, and with great trouble obtained a room in the village for the night.

In the morning it was discovered that Yerka was only half-an-hour in advance, but the mischievous fellow was already gone back to where we had unfortunately picked him up.

In the house of our lodging I was amused by seeing rude paintings upon the white-washed walls, rather good for native Palestine artists of the nineteenth century. The principal object was a three-masted ship, actually containing what were intended for human figures; (perhaps it was a Christian, not a Mohammedan house.) On the masts were very large flags of no special nationality, but one of them flying in exactly the opposite direction from the others. The three men, (constructed of lines for limbs and a dot for the head,) looking through telescopes, were taking observations in different quarters; but perhaps this may be allowed—two men formed the crew. There were no sails, and the mainmast had one yard-arm, the rest had none. Up in the air, near the ship's masts, were two Arabs on horseback carrying spears; the whole tableau was coloured, as such works in the East always are, of a uniform dull red.

N.B.—We were within sight of the sea and the fortress of Acre.

The three previous chapters, and this one at its commencement, relate in no inconsiderable proportion to woods, glens, and glades included in proper forest scenery; but inasmuch as travellers in Palestine, describing only what they have themselves seen along high-roads from town to town, under the guidance of professional dragomans and muleteers, generally deny the existence of forest scenery in Palestine, I may subjoin some remarks on this particular subject.

Passing over the extensive olive plantations of Gaza, and the Sahara of twenty square miles between Bayroot and Saida, as not exactly belonging to the class of timber trees; and the "pine forest" near Bayroot, which is of artificial formation for accomplishing a preconceived design; also the neb'k and other thorny trees unfit for mechanical purposes, extending for miles in wild profusion beyond Jericho, and adding beauty to the scenery; there remain the veritable forests of Gilead and Bashan beyond Jordan, seldom visited by European travellers, and the two large forests in Western Palestine, accessible to the tourists who have leisure and will for knowing the country.

First, the Belâd Beshârah to the north, northeast, and east of Tibneen, and also west and southwest of Safed, through all of which I have travelled with unceasing admiration and indulgence of the early taste implanted in childhood among old forests of England. The verdure and the shade from the Syrian sun were delightful, with the glades and vistas, as well as the amusing alternations often occurring of stooping to the horse's neck in passing below the venerable branches that stretched across the roadway. Those sylvan scenes abound in game, and are known to contain formidable wild animals.

Secondly, the forest extending in length at least

thirty miles from below Cæsarea, northwards to the plain of Battoof beyond Sepphoris. This was designated the "ingens sylva" by the ancient Romans. I have crossed this in several lines between Nazareth and Acre or Caiffa; and twice from the Plain of Sharon to Carmel through the *Wadi 'Arah* by *Umm el Fahh'm*, a village, the very name of which ("mother of charcoal") belongs to a woodland region; besides the line from Carmel to *'Arâbeh*.

The portion of this forest immediately contiguous inland from Carmel is named "the Rôhha," clearly from the fragrance exhaled by the pine and terebinth trees, with the wild herbs upon the hills; this, together with the dark wooded sides of the long mountain, constitutes "the forest of his Carmel" mentioned in the boasting of the King of Assyria, (Isa. xxxvii. 24; also x. 18, in Hebrew,) and it is the *Drymos* of the Septuagint and of Josephus, (Wars, i. 13, 2,) in the which a battle was fought by those Jews who were aiding the Parthians on behalf of Antigonus. No wonder that the loss of men was considerable among the woods and thickets there. I note the accuracy of assigning the name $\Delta \rho \acute{v} \mu o \varsigma$ to this region, consisting as it does almost exclusively of oak.

Besides these wide tracts of woodland, there are also the summit and sides of Tabor, with woods along its north-eastern base.

And the district south and south-west of Hebron, in which, besides oak, &c., pine timber is frequent,

—I should rather say *was*, for of late years it has been much devastated, and that too in an unmethodical manner, to meet the increased requirements of Jerusalem, Bethlehem, &c., for fuel ; nay, as I have been told, shiploads of it are constantly conveyed away to Egypt, especially for works on the Suez Canal. In like manner, in creeks of the sea between Acre and Bayroot, may frequently be seen small vessels loading with wood for Egypt.

Throughout all the period of my experience in Palestine, I have had reason to deplore destruction of the growing timber by charcoal-burners in various provinces. I have seen the sides of whole hills in a blaze, purposely kindled and then left by these men to perform the work with least trouble to themselves: the Government takes no heed in the matter, and no care is employed for propagation of new trees to succeed the blackened ruin thus produced.

So it would appear that in ancient periods, when the land was well peopled, the very wants of that population would, as in every other country, keep down the growth of forests. In the military periods of Roman and other invasions, large timber was required for offensive and defensive operations; and in our generation, when the population there is exceedingly diminished, the ignorance, the bad government, and the wastefulness of uncivilisation, produce the same result of destroying or hindering the increase of timber growth.

There are not many parts of Palestine more bare of timber trees than the interval between Jerusalem and Bethlehem; yet there are old houses in the latter town whose owners pride themselves on the strong, stout rafters and planks they contain, of a quality known far around by the name of Bethlehem oak, and there are persons still living who can remember oak-trees near Solomon's pools.

That this neighbourhood was formerly well wooded is still proved by the tufts of evergreen oak which spring up everywhere over the hills. These tufts of brushwood are found to come from immense roots, each one enough for several camel-loads of fire-wood. They are dug up by the peasantry, and sold in Jerusalem for fuel, under the name of Carâmeh.

It is popularly said that "once upon a time" a man of Jerusalem went to reside at Hebron, and the usual chequered events of life occurred, ending in the calamity of losing his eyesight. In extreme old age he resolved upon returning to his native city, and when he reached the Convent of Mar Elias, half-way between Bethlehem and Jerusalem, the weather being hot, he took off his turban to rest it on the saddle before him. "Oh, our father," said his sons, who were walking by his side, "why art thou uncovering the bareness of thy head?" "It is," he replied, "that I may enjoy the coolness that is to be enjoyed beneath the trees that I remember to have been by the roadside all the way hence to Jerusalem." They assured him that not only did no such avenue exist, but that not a tree was to be seen in any direction, right or left, and that much of the change was owing to the hostilities that had been carried on among the villages under the laxity of the Turkish government. "Is it so?" said he: "then turn back, my sons, and let me die where I have lived so long; Jerusalem is no longer what it was."

This anecdote, current among the peasantry, describes strongly, by its very simplicity, the process that for centuries has been in operation to reduce that country to the condition in which we now find it.

I ought not to leave the subject of forest scenery in Palestine without inviting attention to the eloquent passages in Dr Thomson's "Land and the Book" upon that subject. This veteran missionary of the Lebanon knows the whole country well, and being an American of the Far West, has been accustomed to large forests, huge trees, and charms of woodland scenery; yet he speaks with rapture of the groves about Banias—the solemn glens and verdure of the Belâd Beshârah, and the magnificence of the Sindiâneh. This author has a keen relish for all the varied beauties of nature, and possesses the faculty of describing them so as to enable us to share in its healthful gratifications.

X.

A TEMPLE OF BAAL AND SEPULCHRE OF PHŒNICIA.

ABOUT midway between Tyre and Sidon lies what has been called by Porter and Tristram a kind of Syrian Stonehenge ; but neither they nor Vandevelde, who likewise mentions it, really visited the spot.

The remains are not even mentioned in Carl Ritter's elaborate compilation, the " Erd-Kunde," nor in Robinson or Thompson; but as I have visited them five times, namely in October 1848, October 1849, September 1855, October 1857, and September 1859, I may as well tell what I know of these monuments, which I believe to be of some importance.

The site on which they stand is a large open cultivated ground, nearly opposite *Sarafend*, (Sarepta,) between the high-road and the sea, a quarter of an hour south of the vestiges of *Adloon*, whose broken columns and large pieces of tesselated pavement lie actually upon the highway, so that our horses and mules walk over the household pavements, or the road pavement of hexagonal slabs.

Adloon may be at half distance between Soor and Saida. It has been conjectured that the name is an Arabic modification of *Adnoun*, and that again derived from *Ad nonum*, meaning the ninth Roman mile from Tyre; but as far as my memory serves me, that does not correspond with the real distance.

There are upright stones standing from four to six feet each above the present level of the ground, but which may not be the original level. There may have been a considerable rise accumulated in process of time. The largest stone still shows six feet by a breadth of two. They anciently formed a parallelogram, (not a circle, which is commonly believed to be an emblem belonging to Baal-worship,) as may be seen in the following plan, which represents their present appearance:—

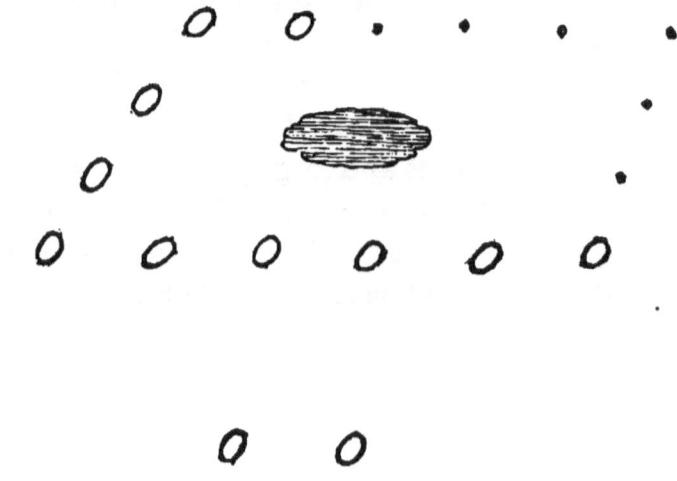

The twelve stones marked *O* are still erect; the rest, whose places are marked by dots, are either pros-

A Temple of Baal, etc. 285

trate on the ground, or have entirely disappeared. Between them all are spaces of two or three yards each. The stones appear to have been carefully hewn originally, though now the edges are worn off, or pieces have fallen away from the substances of most of them. They bear, however, no chisel-indications of having been connected by lintels across the tops: they have not been placed as trilithons.

Outside the parallelogram, at the distance of six yards, stand two other stones of the same description, which probably served as a portal of approach.

Within the enclosure is a depression of ground, in an oval shape, almost filled up with weeds, which demands but little effort of imagination to suggest the position of an altar now removed, leaving only the hollow orifice of a channel for carrying away blood or ashes. This may be worth an examination hereafter.

There are tokens of buildings having stood near, but these may have been of later date. I picked up a fragment of tesselated pavement there, but that may have come there by means of any conceivable accident from Adloon.

Such is my simple account of what I cannot but believe to have been a temple of Baal-worship for the old Phœnicians, certainly of earlier period than any Greek or Roman architecture in the country; and vestiges such as these, of antique Syrian monuments, may, on careful examination, furnish us with data, useful in enabling us to understand the Celtic remains still found in Europe.

The nearest village to these remains, though at some distance upon the hills, is *Sairi*, hence the place is named *Sook Sairi*, from the circumstance of a "market" of cattle and general goods being held there periodically for the district around. But why should this spot above all others in the long-deserted plain be used for such a market? Is it not a traditional continuance of some remote custom in connexion with the importance conferred by the ancient temple and its now-forgotten worship? Who can tell us through how many ages this rural fair has been held at Sairi or Adloon?

The peasant account of the stones is that they were formerly men, whom God, or a prophet in His name, turned into stones for their wickedness, while they were employed in reaping a harvest; further my informant could not tell. The narrative closely resembled the explanation given me by country people in England respecting some almost similar stones at Long-Compton, on the border between Oxfordshire and Warwickshire; and I think I remember to have read of similar instances in other parts of England.

Vandevelde was told that this miracle was wrought by Nebi Zer, (whose weli is in the neighbourhood,) and that this prophet Zer was nephew to Joshua, the son of Nun,—*i.e.*, if he understood his interpreter aright.

A Temple of Baal, etc.

I cannot well leave that vicinity without mentioning the long lines of sepulchres excavated in the cliff-line which runs parallel to the sea, eastwards of the highway, and upon the crest of which line Sarafend and other villages are posted. These sepulchres have been noticed by travellers generally, even while merely passing along without leaving the beaten track, others have taken the trouble to visit them, but without finding any inscriptions. I have seen one inscription, the following in Greek, and apparently unfinished :—

ΠΑΤΕΡ
ΑΡΙΣΤΟ

Although in some respects these resemble the sepulchres near Jerusalem, they are not so elaborately formed into passages and inner chambers as the latter. Many of the excavations high above the ground have been at some era adapted to residences for hermits.

Near Saida I have been shown sepulchres that were entered by steps and passages, and coated with very hard stucco, on which were pictures in fresco of festoons of olive and vine leaves alternated, these leaves being diversified sometimes with tints of autumnal brown, also trees of palm or olive, with birds upon their branches; the birds being all of one kind, with long tails, and coloured bright yellow and red, with brown backs. Inasmuch as these portray living creatures they must be ascribed to some classical, *i.e.*, ante-Islamitic epoch. The designing and colouring of them are excellent, and the work remains in good preservation; they are most likely of Roman art, for their style much resembles the wall pictures of Pompeii.

I have met with no mention of these decorated sepulchres, but in Ritter's quotation from Mariti, (Saida's Umgebungen in vol. iv. 1, page 410,) and that only lately.

The sepulchre which I entered consisted of one principal chamber, at each side of which were three smaller recesses, besides two such opposite the entrance. These latter have others proceeding further within them. There are no low shelves as in the Judæan sepulchres, but the dead were laid in shallow trenches sunk in the rocky floor. The stucco has only been employed to the right and left of the principal chamber.

I pass over, as not belonging to this subject, the more recent discovery by others near the town in 1855 of the two sarcophagi, one of them bearing a Phœnician inscription.

XI.

JERUSALEM TO PETRA, AND RETURN BY THE DEAD SEA.

DURING the last twenty years there have been many English and other visitors to Petra; but they have usually taken it in the way from Egypt towards Jerusalem, which is probably convenient with respect to the season of the year, inasmuch as they thereby get a warm winter before the "sights" of Jerusalem (as some irreverently speak) begin. It would not be so well to take Egypt after Easter.

But, on hearing that several travellers had been unable to reach Petra even after 'Akabah, on account of hostilities arising between the Alaween and the Tiyâhah Arabs, or on account of the exorbitant demands of money made by the former of these, I thought the time had arrived for me to show the practicability of getting at the wonders of Petra from Jerusalem, under escort of the Jehâleen Arabs near Hebron.

I went accordingly, and treated with the Fellahheen of Wadi Moosa in the place itself; and numerous travellers have since availed themselves of this

T

advantage, though none have published an account of their expedition.

On looking back at my notes of the journey, I am astonished at the rapid flight of time; for although my recollection is on the whole very vivid, these notes are dated in April 1851. Full occupation during the intervening period has seemed to shorten the interval. The scene, too, is now changed; for instead of the arid desert and the blasted porphyry cliffs of Edom, then before my eyes, these lines are penned among the bright green meadows of England, with the broad Thames in view, bearing large three-masted ships on its tide, freighted with imports from the most distant parts of the world.

With an officer of dragoons, being a traveller in Jerusalem, and under escort of Hamzeh, the Hebron agent for the Jehâleen, we proceeded across country to meet the Arabs in their wilderness.

Leaving the Hebron road at *'Ain Dirweh*, we ascended the lofty hill to the little village and weli of *Nebi Yunas*, (Prophet Jonah,) which is so conspicuous an object far away in every direction,—the minaret which rises from the building giving it very much the appearance of a rural church in Europe. Thence through well-cultivated fields of wheat and barley,—green at that season,—towards the village of *Beni Naim;* but at quarter of the intermediate distance, passed considerable remains of good masonry, named Khirbet *Bait Ainoon*, (ruins of Beth Enon.) At *Beni Naim* is the reputed sepulchre of the Prophet Lot, according to the Moslems; that of his daughters being on an opposite hill at no great distance. This village commands a grand prospect of the Dead Sea, although there is no view of the kind from all the country around. Is not this the place whence Abraham, after the departure of the angels, saw the smoke of Sodom and Gomorrah rising as the smoke of a furnace? (Gen. xix. 27, 28.)

Here was a travelling durweesh, fantastically dressed, amusing the peasants by dancing and cracking a long whip; while a lad accompanying him thumped a large drum,—both the thonged whip and the large drum being rare objects in that country.

In a quarter of an hour we terminated our short day's journey (about six hours and a half) in a meadow of long green grass. The site is called *Beerain*, from the two wells there. Selâmeh, the brother of the Arab chief, with several of his people, were awaiting our arrival; and they were to lead us forward in the morning.

April 2.—My right knee was much swollen from the strain of a sinew, caused by an unexpected step down a bank taken by my horse when near *Hhalhhool*, on the road from Jerusalem; consequently, feeling feverish, and with a headache all night, I was not soothed by the camels groaning, quarrelling, or champing their food close to my tent.

In the morning we made our bargain with Selâmeh, for the hire of camels, the escort, &c. The captain and I, with my attendants, were to ride our horses in the desert,—taking camels to carry an extra supply of water for them.

We started, but in a very short time became disgusted at the slow travelling of our caravan, as we were compelled to moderate the pace of our riding to suit the leisurely tread of the camels. Selâmeh bestrode a very young colt of the K'baishi race; but I rated my pony, of the Jilfi stock, still higher than his.

The wide expanse before us was sprinkled with wild flowers, including the yellow furze, (I have beside me, while writing this, a bunch of the same, of English growth;) and the ret'm, or juniper, seven or eight feet in height, covered with white blossom, the fragrance of which resembled, or, if possible, was an improvement upon, the smell of a bean-field in flower.

Near *Ziph*, the rocks have many ancient wells cut into their solid substance. About noon we halted at a rough natural cistern, for the purpose of filling our barrels and kirbehs (goat and camel skins) with water. This task occupied an hour, during which I contrived to find just enough shade for my head under a big stone, but took refuge in the cistern itself while the camels were being reloaded.

Leaving this, we found the waste plains abounding in locusts innumerable, and not full grown. As a natural consequence, there were storks hovering about and feasting upon them. On account of the benefit thus conferred on mankind by these birds, the Arabs call them *Abu Sa'ad, i.e.,* " Father of good fortune."

In the middle of the afternoon we arrived at the encampment of the Jehâleen, under the north-east side of Tell *'Arâd*, the site of the Canaanitish city in Num. xxi. 1, xxxiii. 40; Judges i. 16. It was a cheerful green site, though the verdure consisted merely of a thin and poor grass.

We had to be introduced to the real shaikh on his own territorial domain, namely, Hadji Daif Allah abu Dahook,—a sharp fellow in driving a bargain,—a taller and stouter man than any of his people, who were all extremely dirty in person and dress, and several of them but small, withered-looking old men. One of the women, however, was tall, and walked with exceeding dignity of manner.

Our European tents were pitched at some distance from the black hair tents of the Arabs; and we observed, soon after our arrival, that three strangers came up on horseback, carrying spears tufted with black ostrich feathers, on a visit to our shaikh. They were well received; and songs, with clapping of hands, continued during a great part of the night, with a monotonous accompaniment of the women grinding corn in their hand-mills!

April 3.—We rose early, enjoying the indescribable beauty and purity of starlight in an oriental desert, thermometer, Fahrenheit, 53¼°, at sunrise; but before sunrise I mounted to the summit of the hill, where I found no vestiges of a city, only the foundation of a castle, or some such edifice, of about a hundred feet by sixty. In fact, this covered nearly the whole surface of the summit. The city must, therefore, have been situated on the plain, the metropolis of a petty Canaanitish king; but every trace of it is gone.

Low hills bounded the view on every side, over which some peaks of the Moab mountains showed themselves in the east.

When fairly started on the march at 10 past 6 A.M., we went along very cheerily, accompanied by Hadji Daif Allah and the three strangers, till, on a sudden, the latter wheeled about, and required from us the ghuf'r, or toll, for our future passage through their country. The shaikh recommended us to make them a present of a couple of dollars, as they were neighbours of Petra, and without their good-will we should not be able to succeed in the expedition.

We complied, and they rode off southwards. Abu Dahook returning to his camp.

Wearisome indeed is travelling with camels; but what would it have been had we been mounted upon them, as is generally the case with travellers from Sinai and 'Akabah! We horsemen frequently imitated the practice of old Fadladeen in *Lalla Rookh*, when he rode ahead of his caravan, and alighted now and then to enjoy the spectacle of the procession coming up and passing, then mounted again to repeat the pleasure.

The strongest and worst tempered one of our camels having the barrels of water to carry, suddenly lay down and rolled them from him. Had his burden been the skins of water instead, they would have burst, and we should have lost their precious contents. Our Arabs not being accustomed to the convoy of travellers, were as yet unskilful in loading the camels, or in poising the burdens in equal divisions; and most extraordinary noises did they make in urging the beasts forward,—sounds utterly indescribable in European writing, or even by any combinations of the Arabic alphabet!

We had about half a dozen men, mostly trudging on foot, and but slightly armed, commanded by Selâmeh; and one of them, named Salem, was the merry-andrew of the party, full of verbal and practical jokes. The ride was exhilarating,—over a level plain, green with thin grass or weeds, and low shrubs, whose roots extended to surprising distances, mostly above the surface of the ground; the morning breeze delicious, with larks trilling high above us in the sky, and smaller birds that sang among the bushes.

Sometimes we caught distant views of innumerable storks devouring the infant locusts upon the hill-sides.

Passed '*Ain Mel'hh*, (Salt-fountain,) which Robinson identifies with the Moladah of Joshua xix. 2, by means of the transition name of Malatha in Greek. The only building now remaining is a square weli, surmounted by a dome. Here we were not far from Beersheba, upon our right, and fell in with the common route from Gaza and Hebron to Ma'ân. Finding a flock of goats, we got new milk from the shepherd; when diluted with water, this is a refreshing beverage.

On coming up to a camp of Saadeen Arabs, our cook, a vain-glorious Maronite from the Lebanon, and ignorant of Arab customs, attempted to fire upon a watch-dog at the tents for barking at him; and it was judged necessary to deprive him of his pistols for the rest of the journey. Had he succeeded in his folly, we should have got into considerable trouble; for an Arab watch-dog is accounted so valuable, that to kill one of them might have entailed upon us a long delay, and a formal trial in a council of elders of different tribes, collected for the purpose; followed by the penalty awarded by the unwritten laws which obtain in the desert, namely, a payment of as much fine wheat as would entirely cover the dog when held up by his tail, and the nose touching the ground, and this is no small quantity; such delay would have probably thwarted our whole journey.

At a narrow pass, called *Daiket 'Arâr*, was the shell of an old building, now roofless. Near this, and by the wayside, as we advanced, were considerable remains of foundations of houses. There must have been a town of note at that place, it is the 'Aroer of 1 Sam. xxx. 28. Our course now suddenly trended towards the east, instead of southwards.

In less than another hour we came to *Kubbet el Baul*, merely the foundation of a small weli. Selâmeh told us that this had belonged to a tribe called Bali, (or Baul in the plural.) I have no doubt that this is the site of *Balah* of Joshua xix. 3; and that from it the Arabs, settling near it afterwards, derived their appellation.

We soon afterwards, 3 P.M., passed *Curnub*, a ruined place on the right, and descended the slope of *Muzaikah*.

In another hour and a half, namely, at half-past four, we halted for the night, after a journey of ten hours. It was on a smooth, pebbly plain, dotted with shrubs, having lines of chalky hills to the south-west, for which our people had no other name than *Jebel el Ghurb*, or the "western mountain." The whole scene was that of a mere desert; no creatures were to be seen or heard but ourselves. No Turkish authorities ever intrude into this purely Arab wilderness; still less was the landscape spoiled by the smoke of European factories. No speck of cloud had we seen the whole day through.

Not far from this must have transpired the incidents recorded of Hagar and Ishmael,—incidents that might have occurred yesterday, or last week; for a few thousand years count but little in so primitive a region.

Our ragged fellows ran about singing, in search of thorns or long roots, or even the straggling plants of bitter colocynth, as fuel for our cooking-fire.

Stars arose, but such stars! not like the spangles of the English poet's conception, those "patines of bright gold," though that idea is beautiful; but one could see that they were round orbs that flashed streams of diamond light from out their bigness.

So luxurious a bed as that spread upon the desert sand, amid such pure air for breathing, is scarcely to be obtained but in exactly similar circumstances; and we were undisturbed by cries of any wild beasts, although jackals and hyenas are common at night in the more cultivated parts of Palestine.

April 4.— Thermometer, Fahrenheit, $53\tfrac{3}{4}°$ at sunrise. We had our breakfast, and were off again by sunrise. It is said that

> "Early to bed, and early to rise,
> Makes a man healthy, wealthy, and wise."

Jerusalem to Petra, etc. 299

It remained to be seen what the effect would be upon us.

The groom being left behind a short time for packing up the kitchen utensils, allowed us to get out of sight without his observing the direction we had taken; and, when mounted, he took a wrong course. It was therefore necessary to give chase towards the hills to recover him.

In an hour we reached two tul'hh (acacia or mimosa) trees, from which, I believe, the gum-arabic is obtained, and the stump of a third. These were the first that we had seen. Then descended, during about half an hour, to the broken walls of a town called *Sufâh*, below which commenced the very remarkable nuk'beh, or precipitous slope into the great Wadi 'Arabah. Before commencing this, however, we paused to survey the savage scenery around us, and the glorious expanse of the plain, which extends from the Dead Sea to the Red Sea, and is bounded on one side by the hills of Judea, and on the other by the mountains of Edom,—on an average of 3500 feet above the level,—including Mount Hor, the most conspicuous peak among them. At that time, however, the range was capped with rolling mists of the morning.

This *Sufâh* is most likely the *Zephath* of Judges i. 17,—the frontier town of King Arad the Canaanite, which the tribes of Judah and Simeon destroyed, and called the site Hormah, (*i.e.*, "devoted to destruction.") If so, it is strange that the

Canaanitish name should outlive the one intentionally given by the early Israelites. Probably, the surrounding tribes never adopted the Hebrew name, and preserved the original one.

We were standing among crevasses of shivered mountains, whose strata are tossed about in fantastic contortions; and what we had yet to traverse below this, was something like a thousand feet of very slippery rock, lying in flakes, and sloping two ways at once. The greater length forms a rough line, at an angle of what seemed to the eye to be one of forty-five degrees, —not so steep as the Terâbeh that we came to afterwards, but longer and more perilous. Yet this is the only approach to Judæa from the desert for many leagues around. Was it here that King Amaziah destroyed his Edomite prisoners after his victory in the "valley of salt?" (2 Chron. xxv. 12.)

Half way down, one of our barrels of water slipped off a camel, and rolled into a chasm with noise and echoes like thunder. Wonderful to relate, it was not broken, and we were thankful for its preservation.

At the bottom of the precipice, just beyond the shingle or débris of the mountain, the captain and I rested, and drank some camels' milk. This the Bedaween consider very strengthening. There were several tul'hh-trees in a torrent-bed beside us, and some neb'k. With some twine that we gave him, and a stout thorn of tul'hh, one of our Arabs mended his sandal, which was in need of repair. We, having preceded the beasts of burthen over the slippery rock, sat watching them and the men creeping slowly down, in curved lines, like moving dots, towards us.

Upon the ground we found some dried palm-branches and slips of vine, which must have belonged to some former travellers, passing from the western towns to Ma'ân, for neither palm nor vine grows in this wilderness, of which it may be truly said, "It is no place of seed, or of figs, or of vines, or of pomegranates," (Num. xx. 5;) and it is now become like a past dream, that Virgil and Lucan mentioned the palm-trees of Idumæa.*

So at length we were upon the great 'Arabah, or "wilderness of Zin," of the Israelitish wanderings; and our path was to be diagonally across this, pointed direct at Mount Hor in the south-east.

On crossing a shallow wadi named *Fik'r*, they told us of a spring of water to be found in it, at a good distance to the north-east.

After some hours, we came to *Wadi Jaib*, sometimes styled the Jeshimon, as well as its corresponding plain on the north of the Dead Sea, and in Arabic both are called "the Ghôr," in the shallow

---

* Yet there was a "city of palm-trees" towards the south, which the Kenites abandoned for this district south of Arad,—probably the present *Nukh'l;* the name has that signification.

bed of which were receptacles for water, concealed by canes and brushwood laid in the utmost disorder, so as to produce the appearance of mere random drift of winter storms. Without the Arabs, of course, we should never have suspected the existence of such valuable stores. Probably also the Bedaween from a distance would not be aware of such resources there. The covering would, besides, serve to prevent a speedy evaporation of the water by the sun's heat. These spots were shaded likewise by tul'hh, sunt, and neb'k-trees. There we watered the cattle and filled our vessels.* In another half hour we rested for the night, having made a march of nearly twelve hours, over more tiring ground than that of yesterday.

'Ain Weibch was to our right, which Robinson conjectured to be Kadesh Barnea.

We perceived footprints of gazelles and of hyenas.

April 5. Sunrise, Fahrenheit, 62¼°. Our Jerusalem bread being now exhausted, we took to that of the desert-baking, which is very good while fresh and hot from the stones on which the improvisation of baking is performed, but not otherwise for a European digestion: and our servants, with the Bedaween, had to chase the chickens

---

* There are many such *cachets* of water in the desert, but known only to the tribes of each district. During the Israelitish wanderings, Hobab, a native of the desert, may have guided them to many such.

every morning. The survivors of those brought from Jerusalem being humanely let out of their cages for feeding every evening, the scene of running after them, or flinging cloaks in the air when they took short flights, not to mention the shouts of the men and the screams of the birds, was very ludicrous, but annoying, when time is precious. The merry little Salem enjoyed all this, as well as the amusements of our people, during the monotony of daily travelling : as, for instance, the captain rolling oranges along the ground, as prizes for running, or his mounting a camel himself, or riding backwards, &c.—anything for variety.

The desert may be described as a dried pudding of sand and pebbles, in different proportions in different places,—sometimes the sand predominating, and sometimes the pebbles,—with occasionally an abundance of very small fragments of flint, serving to give a firmer consistency to the sand. Round boulders are also met with on approaching the hill-sides. In one place large drifts of soft yellow sand were wrinkled by the wind, as a smooth sea-beach is by the ripples of a receding tide. These wrinkles, together with the glare of a burning sun upon them, affected the eyes, so as to make the head giddy in passing over them.

Wild flowers and shrubs are not wanting ; and the former are often very fragrant. I observed among those that are so, a prevalence in their names of the letter غ (gh) ; as Ghurrah, Ghubbeh, Ghurkud, Ghuraim, &c. They brought me a handful of *mejainineh*, which was said to be good for pains in the stomach; and the starry flower, called *dibbaihh*, not unlike a wild pink, is eaten by the people, both petals, calyx, and stalk.

The tul'hh, or mimosa-tree, has a strange appearance, very like an open fan, or the letter V filled up.

The green foliage of it is particularly vivid at the season when we saw it, and the thorns long and sharp.*

Distances are hard to judge of in such exten-

* It is not to be supposed, however, that this is a just representation of all that "great and terrible wilderness" through which the Israelites were led for forty years. It is indeed "a land not sown," (Jer. ii. 2,) and a land of pits and drought fearful to contemplate, as a journey for a wandering population of nearly two millions of souls, especially in the hottest seasons of the year; but the peculiarly *terrible* wilderness must have been among the defiles, hemmed in by scorching cliffs in the Sinaitic peninsula.

In that direction also were the "fiery flying serpents," concerning which I have never been able to learn anything more satisfactory than that, in the hot and unpeopled gorges west of the Dead Sea, there is a thin and yellow serpent called the Neshabiyeh, which flings itself across from one point to another in the air with astonishing velocity and force. It is therefore named after Neshâbeh, a dart or arrow in Arabic. The natives also apply to it the epithet of "flying." The wound which it inflicts is said to be highly inflammatory and deadly, and from this effect it may be called "fiery." It may be also that, from being of a yellow colour, it may glitter like a flame when flying with rapidity in the sunshine.

It is only in Isaiah xxx. 6, that the epithet "flying" is used for these serpents. Observe, however, in Hebrew Lexicons the several applications of this word עוף.

sive plains and in so clear an atmosphere. We had been nearly two days in sight of Mount Hor

TUL'HH TREES.

straight before us; yet the mountain only grew in size as we approached it, not in distinctness.

As we came nearer to the eastern mountains, we found innumerable and huge blocks of porphyry rock scattered over the ground. The Arabs called the range of Seir by the name of *Jebel Sherreh.*

At about eight hours from our last night's station, we turned off the Wadi 'Arabah by the narrow *Wadi Tayibeh* into the heart of the mountains, at the foot of Hor.

Ascended a series of precipices, and, at some elevation, met two young English gentlemen, with a pair of double-barrelled pistols shared between them, and their fingers ready on the triggers. They had a tale to relate of grievous exactions made by the Fellahheen of Petra,—which, however, seemed to me, by their account, to have been

U

brought on unconsciously by themselves, in having taken an escort of Tiyâhah Arabs from Nukh'l instead of the Alaween; and they informed me that a clergyman from Cambridge was still detained there, as he refused to comply with the excessive demands of the people.

On what a stupendous scale is geology to be studied in Mount Seir, where you have masses of red sandstone 1500 feet in depth; yellow sandstone extending miles away in ranges of hills, and the sandy desert beneath; all of this incapable of cultivation, and inspiring a sensation of deep sadness, in connexion with the denunciations of God's prophecies!

At a quarter before four we caught the first glimpse of the Mezâr of Aaron's tomb, and at five pitched our tents on the rugged side of Hor, among crags and scented plants, enlivened by numerous cuckoos, and the sweet warbling of one little bird. What reminiscences of dear old England the song of the cuckoos awakened! Now, however, from henceforth, being in England, their song will infallibly recall the memory to large bare mountains, extreme heat of climate, and the fragrance of Elijah's ret'm plant.

During the last hour we had seen some blue pigeons, one partridge, and, separately, two large eagles, to which our attention had been drawn by their shadows moving on the ground before us; then, on looking upwards, the royal birds were seen sailing along, silently and slowly, against the blue vault of ether.

This had been the hottest day of our whole journey; and the atmosphere became thick as the evening stole over the hills.

April 6th.—Sunrise, Fahrenheit 77°. In the morning we advanced upwards towards Aaron's tomb. Walking in front of the luggage, we met the clergyman of whom we had heard the day before. He had been allowed to leave Petra on suffering the people to take money out of his pockets,—reserving to himself the intention of complaining against them officially to the consul in Jerusalem.

He had been to the summit of Hor, and pronounced the view from it to be more grand and striking than that from Sinai. On bidding him farewell, we took Selâmeh and one kawwâs, for clambering on our hands and knees to the summit, leaving the luggage to proceed and wait for us farther on; but had to rest occasionally in the shade of large trees of 'Arâr, which Robinson considered to be the true juniper, and not the ret'm. The latter (the *rothem* of the Hebrew Bible, under which the Prophet Elijah reposed) was very abundant, and covered with white blossom, shedding the richest perfume. Is it possible that all this fragrance, and the warbling of the birds, is but " wasted in the desert air?"

The mountain is all of dark-red colour; and the

higher we ascended, the more difficult we found the progress to be. At length all farther advance seemed impossible, till, on looking round, we observed an excavation for a well, with masonry around it; and beyond this were steps cut into the rock, which rock was sloped at an angle of between fifty and sixty degrees. This encouraged us to persevere.

Still higher, I picked up some tesseræ of mosaic, and morsels of marble and alabaster,—a piece of the latter now lies on the table before me.

At length we attained the highest peak, where there was scarcely more space than sufficient to contain the small weli-building, which was at the time untenanted, though we had expected to find a Moslem devotee in permanent residence there.

I utterly despair of being able to describe the prospect around us; and can only say that extensive mountain-peaks lay in lines below, and might be compared to those made upon embossed maps, but that the whole scene was vast, savage, and abandoned to sombre desolation—both the hills and the desert—in every direction.

Jerusalem to Petra, etc.

The atmosphere was too thick and hazy to allow of very distant views. Neither of the two waters —the Red Sea or the Dead Sea—was visible.

Let those who take pleasure in doing so, doubt that on that peak lies interred Aaron, the first high priest of Israel, "the saint of the Lord," and that there was effected the first personal transfer of the pontifical office from him to Eleazer his son. Rather let me believe that there my unworthy footsteps have been placed on the same pieces of rock with the two venerable brothers who led up the redeemed people from Egypt, "the house of bondage," and that it was there they parted, leaving Moses to carry on the task alone.

> "Three Hebrew cradles, the Nile-palms under,
> Rock'd three sweet babes upon Egypt's plain :
> Three desert graves must those dear ones sunder,
> Three sorrowful links of a broken chain.
> Kadesh and Hor, and Nebo yonder,
> Three waymarks now for the pilgrim train." *

I seated myself, and wrote a brief letter to a dear relative in England.

Entering the weli, we found near the door a common-looking tomb, with an Arabic inscription, —which, however, I found too illegible to allow of its being copied; and over the tomb was spread a pall of silk, striped in red, green, and white, but much faded. Against a pillar, which supports the roof, were hung rows of coloured rags and threads of yarn, with snail-shells and sea-shells strung

---

* Dr H. Bonar.

among them by way of further ornament. A wooden bowl, at one end of the tomb, was probably intended to receive alms for the support of the devotee who claims the place, and who practises the curing of diseases by charms among the wild Arabs.

The floor of the chamber has been handsomely paved with tesselated bits of coloured marble, much of which still remains. Over the tomb are suspended some ostrich eggs on a line, as is common in oriental churches; and near it is a mihrâb, or niche in the wall, to indicate the southerly direction for Moslem prayers.

In a corner of the floor, a flight of steps leads down to a crypt; and, providing ourselves with a light, we descended thither, in expectation of finding there the more ancient tomb, believed to be genuine, as it is the usual practice in Moslem welies to have an imitation tomb on the common floor at the entrance, while the true one is exactly beneath it. But we only found an iron grating, swinging loose to the touch, and within it a plain wall, from which part of the plaster having fallen away, allowed to be seen the corner of a kind of stone sarcophagus. The portion visible was not, however, sufficient to enable us to judge of its probable era. The ceiling of the crypt is blackened by the smoke of lamps.

I then mounted, by the outside of the building, to the top of the dome, but could see nothing thence of Petra, so deeply sunk is that valley betwixt high hills.

Descending the mountain by the opposite side of that of our arrival,—namely, on the side next to Petra,—we discovered that more pains in road-making had been bestowed there, and that the ascent in that direction would be comparatively easy. Cuckoos and partridges were heard plentifully; and, on looking back, I saw a very large raven hovering over the weli.

In an hour's descent we rejoined our servants and horses, but were not yet at the foot of the mountain.

Entering a valley of red rocks, much streaked with blue in wavy lines, the first work of antiquity that met our view was a square turret on each side of the road. Then we passed some tombs, or chambers, cut into the massive red cliffs with architectural cornices, pediments, and pilasters, some of them very handsome. Next was what Laborde marks in his map as "the solitary column." It is standing solitary; but then near its base lie other columns of the same edifice, with the circular slices (or *drums*, as architects term them) that composed them, scarcely disturbed as they slid down in falling.

In five minutes more we halted for the night close to what Laborde designates the Acropolis, where a pile of fine building lies prostrate, and the columns on the ground, in their segments, still touching each other.

At the foot of this heap stands what is named the Palace of Pharaoh; and our station within it appeared, from the black relics of fires there, to be a frequent resting-place for travellers.

Here, then, we were fairly lodged among the wonders which so deservedly excite the curiosity of the world, and proceeded to improve time, before the Fellahheen of the district should arrive to annoy us, by crowding and importunity.

It is not my design to recount in detail the marvels of the place,—this has been done by Laborde, Lord Lindsay, Wilson, and Robinson,—but just to say, that having with me the small edition of Laborde and some manuscript notes extracted from other books, by their help I saw most of what was to be seen. I wandered through streets of the middle town; surveyed and entered palaces hewn into crimson rocks; sat reading on the solid benches of the theatre, and walked along its stage; then gazed with unwearied admiration on the beautiful Khazneh, its delicate tints and graceful proportions, and went to rest upon a green bank opposite to it, with a running stream at my feet, bordered by gorgeous oleanders, where I chatted with some wild Arabs arriving from the south. Such a harmony of ruddy tints, from the darkest buds of the oleander, through gradations on the rocks, to the most delicate pink, was truly a feast of nature for the eyes.

These are incidents never to be forgotten, and

the memory of them is unspeakably charming. I made a few rough sketches; but it may be sufficient here to give only a specimen of the capitals of columns that are peculiar to Petra.

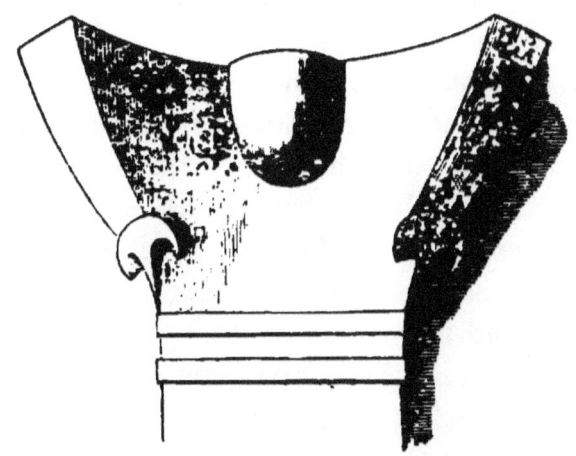

During the afternoon the thermometer stood inside the tent at 95° Fahrenheit.

The captain, my companion, went alone to explore the chasm called the *Sik*, as my slight sprain, after being almost forgotten during the journey, had become painful again from the effects of climbing upon Mount Hor.

But I had come to Petra for business; and the indigenous peasantry of Wadi Moosa were gathering around our tents from different directions. They had not been prepared for the reception of guests arriving from the north, *i.e.*, Jerusalem, as travellers usually come from 'Akabah or Sinai, through Nukh'l.

Our Arabs, both Jehâleen and some strangers, set to making themselves comfortable. There arrived a large body of the Fellahheen, headed by Shaikh Sulimân es Saïd, a ragged and ugly crew, he as dirty as the rest, but strutting about in a robe of bright scarlet.

Then commenced the negotiations and disputes between them and ours; noise and menace speedily ensued, alternated with diplomatic manœuvres, for our champion, Selâmeh, was an able practitioner in such matters, at least he had a reputation for it. The stormy scenes were not concluded till late in the night, and they ended by an arrangement that travellers, arriving by the new road from Jerusalem, should pay the same pecuniary acknowledgment to the territorial owners as had been hitherto claimed from those arriving under Alaween escort from Nukh'l or 'Akabah; and this agreement I ratified orally, as writing or sealing would have been altogether out of place there. One might think that so simple a matter could have been finished in five minutes; but just as in European business of that nature, it is always necessary for the contracting parties to be allowed scope for the display of their professional talents.

April 7th.—Sunrise, Fahrenheit $65\frac{3}{4}°$. An inundation of strange Arabs from the desert had arrived during the night, and it was computed that there were not less than two hundred guns round our tents, while our party had not more than five, with a few pistols. We were hemmed in by the newcomers, and the crags over us were occupied by men with guns laid in position between crevices. Some men were scattered about, shooting at birds; but it seemed to me their real object was rather the making of signals.

These people were 'Ali Rasheed's branch of the Alaween, from a district not so distant as 'Akabah. Our Jehâleen party looked very insignificant among them; they had evidently not expected this turn of events.

As soon as we Europeans showed ourselves after breakfast, the Fellahheen rushed forward to serve as guides in exhibiting the curiosities. Feeling rather lame, I decided on remaining at the tents with my two kawwâses as sentinels; the more disposed to do so, as the strangers had, during the night, purloined some articles from the Jehâleen.

It was a warm, misty morning, and in the absence of my companion I found considerable amusement in the screams of multitudes of wild birds, high aloft "among the holes of the rocks, and the tops of the rugged rocks,"—probably all of them birds of prey,—which echoed and reverberated with sounds closely resembling the laughter and shouts of children in their vociferous games.

On their return, the Fellahheen were rapacious in demands for remuneration of their services, but were at length contented. This was the signal for the others to take their advantage. They wanted toll to be paid for crossing part of the desert on which they thought the Jehâleen had no right or precedent for bringing strangers. So, on our preparing to leave the ground, they rushed up the bank, secured commanding points for their guns, and thus exacted their fee. The screams and hubbub were at length terminated by some small backsheesh, (to our surprise, how little was required,) and we all marched away in a northern direction, the opposite to that of our arrival.

This gave us an opportunity of passing again in front of the principal edifices, if they may be so denominated, including what I had not before seen, the sepulchre with the Latin inscription in large letters, QVINTVS. PRÆTEXTVS. FLORENTINVS.

It is to be noticed that Petra itself is called by the Arabs, Wadi Pharaôn,* not Wadi Moosa. The two valleys are adjoining, but in the latter there are no antiquities or wonders. At a distance, however, the journey to Petra is usually called a journey to Wadi Moosa, because the Fellahheen of the region about there, and to whom toll is paid, are cultivators of the Wadi Moosa.

Before leaving the place, it may be observed that the neighbourhood must have been kept in a high

* They take a pride in attributing everything of antiquity here to Pharaoh, the cursed king of Egypt,—as those about the Euphrates attribute all their old wonders to the cursed king Nimrod. These names are learned from the Korân.

state of cultivation during the Roman empire for the maintenance of so numerous and luxurious a population of the city, instead of the absence of necessaries of civilised life that we now see there; and that good state of things must have continued in later Christian periods, when the district formed "the third Palestine," and deputed bishops to the synods of Jerusalem and elsewhere.

With respect to the colouring of the hills and rocks, it is truly surprising to behold such huge masses of deep red colour, variegated with wavy lines of violet and purple and blue, especially in the direction towards Mount Hor. We did not, however, remark so much of yellow and orange as Laborde or Irby and Mangles describe.

I find since that Dr Wilson states these rocks to be highly saliferous, and says the Arabs scrape them with knives to obtain saltpetre for making their rude gunpowder. He is of opinion that in some geological era the whole place has been formed in a salt-water lake. Few people have had so much leisure for making researches there as he had.

The temperature was high in the valley, because closely confined between lines of hills; notwithstanding that the elevation is supposed to exceed 2000 feet above the Mediterranean. What it may be in a more advanced season than April I cannot tell; but I perceived neither scorpions nor serpents there, (as some represent the place to abound in,) no creeping things worse than earwigs.

When on the march, we learned that the robbery of the night by 'Ali Rasheed's people, amounted to one camel, one gun, and old Selâmeh's sandals. Also, that those three men whom we saw on the 2d April at Abu Dahook's camp were of the same faction, probably also my visitors of the Khazneh yesterday. Selâmeh thought that for a couple of gazis (about three shillings and sixpence) he might succeed in a redemption of his goods. These I gave him, and he trudged back over the hills with one of his people, while we kept on our way. He was to meet us at our night's station.

The last glance given to Petra showed us the palace of Pharaoh, and the peak of Hor with Aaron's tomb.

Our way led us over a tolerable plain, made agreeable by the fragrance of the ret'm, as wafted along by the breeze; this plant sometimes almost covering the small branch valleys.

Soon after noon we were in the *Wadi Nemela*, through which we travelled for nearly two hours, —a scene of broken rocks on each side, and the intermediate space with a profusion of oleander, ret'm and 'arâr, all in flower, some of the latter having trunks of ten feet in circumference.

Thence we issued upon a heath covered with low fragrant herbs; our Arabs singing, and the camels striding on famously, followed by a poor little lamb that we had bought at Petra. This, of course, we did not intend to convey all the way to Jerusalem;

but his presence constantly reminded me of the text, (Isa. xvi. 1,) "Send ye the lamb (to) the ruler of the land from Sela [*i.e.* Petra] to the wilderness, unto the mount of the daughter of Zion." This is no longer the time when the king of Moab paid tribute "to the king of Israel, 100,000 lambs and 100,000 rams, with the wool," (2 Kings iii. 4.)

Soon after two P.M. we were passing over ledges of porphyry mountain-cliffs, dark and gloomy, but enlivened by large yellow salvia in bloom, and plenty of flowers visible in the hollow below; the whole scene most romantic and fantastic in formation. Such huge piles of porphyry I had not seen since those of the coast of Peterhead and Buchan, lashed by the great billows coming from the Baltic Sea. Occasionally we came to standing pools of water, which, lying on this hard kind of stone, could not filter away or be absorbed, as in our Palestine limestone would be the case. From these settlements our water vessels were supplied. Thermometer in shade of a rocky cliff, $75\frac{3}{4}°$ Fahrenheit.

We were soon again upon sandstone cliffs, but wildly broken, and descending into lower ground with its juniper and oleander. Then ascended again, and attained our greatest elevation by half-past three, at least equal to Robinson's calculation of 1500 feet above the 'Arabah. For two hours more we had to traverse cliffs, gullies, crags, and precipices of red porphyry or green syenite alternately, in enormous masses, split by convulsions of nature, and next arrived in a valley strewed with huge fragments, angular, not rounded boulders, yet fallen from the adjacent mountains. But we were still high above the wide level of the 'Arabah.

Halted at half-past five; thermometer, Fahrenheit $71\frac{1}{4}°$, and, during our dinner, old Selâmeh rejoined us, having failed in his dealings with the Alaween, who refused to restore their plunder, as they said their object was to punish the Jehâleen, for bringing travellers through their country, instead of making them go by way of Egypt.* He reported that thirty more Arabs had arrived at Petra, half-an-hour after our starting.

April 8th.—Sunrise, Fahrenheit 59°. Moving again at six o'clock. In half an hour we were clear of the mountains of Seir or Edom; but for another hour the ground was still strewn with blocks of porphyry and green syenite, too hard for any of our implements to break off bits from them, and fragments small enough to be carried away were very difficult to find; however, we got some. These large stumbling-blocks, together with dry watercourses, rendered our travelling unusually troublesome to the horses and camels, and wearisome to ourselves.

At length we got upon the free 'Arabah, among green shrubs and trees of tul'hh and neb'k.

* Numerous travellers, however, have since gone from Jerusalem in virtue of the agreement made on this occasion by me, and returned without molestation from these people.

Jerusalem to Petra, etc.

At nine o'clock we came to a high sandbank, beneath which was a verdant line of tamarisk, and ghâr, and tall canes, with frogs croaking among them. All of these were indications of water; and, accordingly, we found a spring named '*Ain Taäsân*, being one of those which together form the stream of *Buwairdeh*. Here we filled our water vessels to the utmost, as it was not expected we should find any more good water for two days to come.

The surrounding prospect was one of utter desolation, and I took out my Bible and read the words of 2 Kings iii. 8, 9, and 20: "And he said, Which way shall we go up? And he answered, The way through the wilderness of Edom. So the king of Israel went, and the king of Judah, and the king of Edom; and they fetched a compass of seven days' journey: and there was no water for the host, and for the cattle that followed them. .... And it came to pass in the morning, when the meat-offering was offered, that, behold, there came water by the way of Edom, and the country was filled with water."

On the spot, as well as at the present time, I remembered with pain the deplorable weakness and wickedness of the remarks on this event contained in Paine's "Age of Reason," and which I do not choose to repeat. The most charitable opinion that one can entertain of such writers is that they know nothing of the nature of the country under

x

consideration. Thank God that the world at large, and that land in particular, is now better known than formerly, and, as a consequence, our evidences of the truth of the blessed Bible are daily the more confirmed.

We then proceeded northwards along the bed of that stream; but in a few minutes its water was lost in the sand. In another hour we entered the dry bed of the *Wadi el Jaib*, and continued along its course in the direction of the Dead Sea.

The hills were misty on both sides, and the ground hot beneath, as we tramped along, all our voices hushed during the "strength of the heat," (according to Arab expression,) and the footfall of the camels entirely without noise.

Who can sufficiently admire the adaptation of this creature to the desert, in which the Maker and Ruler of all has placed him? No heat exceeds the power of his endurance; steadily, patiently, silently he stalks his long strides over the yellow ground—one animal following another in regular military step. And during our travels at least he never flagged—the large eyes never lost their brightness; and who ever saw a camel, even though his master may seek rest or shade as he finds opportunity, shrink from the blazing brightness of the sun?

Halted for the night shortly before five P.M., the journey having been one of eleven hours. But the Arabs insisted on our being placed behind the corner of a re-entering valley, in order that our fire and smoke might not be seen during the night by hostile people from a distance.

Thermometer at sunset, $81\frac{1}{2}°$ Fahrenheit.

We found footprints of gazelles, storks, and hyenas.

Mount Hor at that distance, and in that direction, very much resembles the Salisbury Crags of Edinburgh.

April 9th.—Sunrise, Fahrenheit $63\frac{1}{2}°$. Tents struck, and all on the march by half-past five. Losing sight of Mount Hor.

At a quarter to eight a breeze sprung up from the north, so refreshing in that hot and dry wilderness as to merit the praise of the Bedawi poem, beginning—

"Shemâli, ya hawa ed-deeret shemâli."
"The north! O thou wind of the northern direction,
  It has increased my blessing, and all that belongs to me,
  And after weakness of state, has changed my condition."

I find, however, that this literal translation gives but a very poor idea of the feeling concentrated in the words of the original, and only feebly expresses the reminiscence of that time as still preserved at the moment of this writing.

Soon after eight o'clock we were out of the Wadi el Jaib, that is to say, the high cliffs of marl on each side abruptly terminated, previous to which, they had been at first more than a hundred feet above our heads, and then gradually diminishing in height as we advanced. We descended gradually into the semicircular expanse of marshes called El Ghuwair or the Little Ghôr, with the large Dead Sea and the *Khash'm Usdum,* or salt mountain of Sodom, spread out before us.

The course of the wadi we had left trended from south-east to north-east, on issuing from which we took the line on the western side of the Ghuwair, and easily descended over small eminences. This place is most probably the "ascent of Akrabbim," (Num. xxxiv. 4, and Josh. xv. 3,) the southern boundary of the land given to Israel, and named after its abundance of scorpions. In our hasty passage over it we saw none of these.

Among the marshes we found several palms growing wild. They were stumpy in stature, and ragged in form for want of cultivation, or perhaps of congenial soil. The miasma was strongly perceptible to the smell, and our horses were plagued with flies and gnats. How great was this change from the pure dry air of the mountains!

Quarter to ten at *'Ain 'Aroos,* (the bridegroom's fountain,) but the water was brackish.

Thermometer in the shade, $83\frac{1}{2}°$ Fahrenheit.

For an hour past our people had been on the alert, on account of a feud between them and the Ghawârineh Arabs. On coming up to the print of a human footstep, this was carefully examined as to its size, direction of the tread, &c. The circumstances were not, however, exactly parallel to the occurrence in Robinson Crusoe, which naturally came to mind.

At twenty minutes to eleven, having completed the western curve of the Ghuwair, we fell in with the *Wadi Hhuggereh*, which came up from the south-west, and on looking back, perceived a distinct mirage visible over the dry sands which occupy part of the Ghuwair, probably the effect of a salty deposit.

About noon we arrived at a clear, running stream of water, but which proved, on tasting, to be highly impregnated with salt. The surface of the plain was in a great measure covered with a white efflorescence. Along the middle of this plain there was a sunken channel of a mile and a half in length, occupied by an overflowing of the Dead Sea, which, however, did not interfere with our track.

At the end of this, and on approaching the corner of the salt mountain, we had an *incident* to enliven the tediousness of the hot journey. A party of Arabs came in sight. Our men discovered them first, and running forwards, primed their guns, or lighted the match of the lock, drew their swords and screamed, making bare the right arm, as if prepared for awful deeds. The others took up position behind low rocks, unslung their fire-arms, and screamed *not*. Presently a real or fictitious recognition took place, the guns on both sides were fired up in the air, and swords were brandished for very joy. Both parties rushed into each other's embraces, smiling and kissing with the greatest fervour.

The comers proved to be some of their own

Jehâleen, escorting some Hebron townsmen to Kerak. There were two women among the latter, some old men, and some conjurers with monkeys, who thereupon set up a dance to the music of tambourines. Upon something like equanimity being restored, the strangers informed us of certain doings that had taken place, on our account, since we had passed by there, and which nearly concerned us.

The two parties soon separated, taking opposite directions.

As we were close upon the western side, there was the southern end of the Dead Sea at our right hand, coming up imperceptibly upon the land, flush with it, so that no limit could be distinguished between water and the wet beach.

At a few minutes past one we all alighted before the large cavern which runs into the heart of the salt mountain; and a picturesque group our party formed, spread about in some shade of the hill, with a great variety of costumes and colours—the camels kneeling and the horses picketed upon the bay of the sea of Sodom and Gomorrah.

Entering the cavern, we found relics of the recent French expedition thither, under M. de Saulcy, such as egg-shells and torn paper coverings of candles, with French shopkeepers' names upon them. We did not penetrate far inwards, but could see traces of occasional overflowings of the lake into the interior.

The mountain itself is a wonder: five miles of salt above ground, and a hundred feet, probably in some places two hundred feet high. The colour is not bright, but of a dull gray. The best parts of it are very hard to break, and with difficulty we brought away some pieces for curiosity.

As for Lot's wife,—the pillar of salt, mentioned and portrayed by the American expedition in 1848, and of which it is said they took a fragment for a museum at home,—after a good deal of search, we only discovered a crooked thin spire of rock-salt in one place of the mountain; but it would not have been very remarkable if many such had been found to exist in similar circumstances.

It was a place for inducing solemn reflections and intense sensations, such as one could hardly venture to record at the time of being there, or endeavour to repeat now after so long an interval. Much may, however, be imagined by devout readers of the holy Scriptures—not only as contained in the records of the Book of Genesis, but also as inculcated with intense emphasis in the Epistle of Jude in a later period. Still, there is a vividness of impression to be derived only from being actually on the spot, and surveying the huge extent of water that differs from any other in the world,—placid and bright on its surface, yet awful in its rocky boundaries. But where are the cities and their punished inhabitants, except in the Bible, and the traditions preserved by Tacitus, the

Korân, and by the present inhabitants of the country?

Some morsels of bitumen were found upon the beach; but the principal season of the year for finding it is in winter, especially at the commencement of winter, when the lake becomes unusually agitated, and breaks off masses of it from the bottom, often of very large size—the peasants of Hebron, with exaggeration, say, "As large as ships;" but I have seen many camel-loads of it brought up to Jerusalem at a time, for export to Europe. It is, however, a monopoly of the crown.

We should note that in Gen. xiv. 10, the district was full of bitumen pits previous to the overthrow of the cities of the plain.

At twenty minutes to three we came to a rude heap of stones called *Zoghal* or *Zoghar*. This cannot well be Zoar, among other reasons, because it lies upon the beach, and is not upon an eminence. It is well to mention that M. de Saulcy's extravagant ideas of the Pentapolis of Sodom, &c., had not then been published.

In another quarter of an hour we had reached the extremity of the "Salt Mountain," with all its distorted, sometimes even perpendicular stratification. By this time we were convinced that the whole of the mountain is not salt, but that a good deal of the upper length of it is a mixture of salt and marl or sand. Between it and the water's

Jerusalem to Petra, etc.   329

edge we frequently saw blocks and spires of rock-salt protruding through the flat beach.

There can be no doubt that the Arabic name, *Usdum*, is identical with Sodom, by a well-known custom of the language to invert the consonant and vowel of the first syllable. But even this is brought back to the original state in the adjective form. Thus I heard our guides speak of the Jebel Sid'mi, meaning the Khash'm or Jebel Usdum, or promontory of Sodom.

The *Wadi Netheeleh* comes up from the south-west to the shore at this northern end of the mountain, parallel to the Wadi Hhuggereh at the southern end.

We kept along the sea-side, and on rising to a higher level, near five o'clock, halted for the night at the mouth of a valley where some water was to be procured, and near us was a broken tower. This site is named *Mobugghek* or *Umm-Bugghek*. As we were scarcely out of the reach of the Ghawârineh Arabs, our people had to go out in armed detachments for collecting firewood.

During the process of pitching the tents, one of our men, named 'Odeh, perceived a stranger at a great distance, and half stripping himself, ran nimbly up a steep sand hill, ready for whatever operation might be necessary. Our European, I might rather say, our civilised eyes, could not have discovered the ill-omened object at that distance, but those of desert Arabs are far more powerful than ours. I do not know that I shall ever forget the ardent brilliancy of Shaikh Selâmeh's eyes at all times, as witnessed constantly during our excursion.

While we rambled on the beach in search of bitumen or sulphur, we suddenly heard a furious screaming in the direction of our tents, and hastily returning, found a number of strangers coming down a winding path. Our men were gathered together, and armed. The captain also examined the state of his double-barrelled pistols. However, on their arrival, the newcomers were recognised as people *not hostile* to the Jehâleen, and their general location is near 'Ain 'Aroos. So, after some squabbling and arrangement, they agreed to share our supper with us in peace. Had the case been otherwise, our position was not an enviable one; for we were shut in between their hills and the sea, they were more numerous than our Arabs, and they had entire command of our spring of water. Our camels, too, were all unloaded, and the packages scattered on the ground.

The scenery was desolate and gloomy in the extreme, undoubtedly blasted by the wrath of Almighty God, although a place which had at one time been " well watered everywhere . . . even as the garden of the Lord, like the land of Egypt," (Gen. xiii. 10;) and it required strong faith to expect the possibility of this " wilderness " (*'Arabah*) being again made " like Eden, and her desert like the garden of the Lord,' (Isa. li. 3.) Indeed, that promise does not seem to apply to this peculiar locality, by comparing it with Ezek. xlvii. 10, 11, although these unwholesome waters are to be healed, and are to have fish of various kinds in them, with fishermen's nets employed there.

It deserves observation, that now the sea is so utterly lifeless that the American explorers there were unable, by the most powerful microscopes, to find any animalculæ in its water. Yet Lynch was of opinion that the atmosphere or vapour there was not in any way prejudicial to human health; and since then, Mr Holman Hunt spent a considerable time near the brink without injury derived from it.

The air was very warm all night, with no freshening dew, and the sound of slow, rippling water on the strand, during the still starlight hours, was one to which our ears had not been of late accustomed.

The Arab figures and conversation round the watch-fire were romantic enough. Thermometer at eight P.M., $90\frac{1}{2}°$ Fahrenheit.

April 10*th.* — Sunrise, Fahrenheit $70\frac{1}{4}°$. In taking this last note of the thermometer at sunrise, I may observe that the marking of it at that moment gives but a feeble idea of the heat that we experienced during the days' marches throughout this excursion, — the temperature rapidly increased after sunrise, and at later hours within the confined hollows, such as Petra and the basin of the Dead Sea, rose to that of (I suppose) an Indian climate—but above all the effects of heat was that produced by the weight of atmospheric pressure at probably the lowest position in the whole surface of the globe: about 1300 feet below the Mediterranean.

Before six o'clock we were on the march, over broken and precipitous rocky paths, on which the progress was slow and toilsome. Then down again upon the beach. I am sure that if the Dead Sea were already covering the ground that it now does, before the time of Chedorlaomer, the "four kings against five" could not possibly have mustered or manœuvred their armies on any side or place between the mountains on each side of the water.* At a quarter past seven the thermometer stood at 86° Fahrenheit.

There is always a close, heavy heat in this depressed region, inducing profuse perspiration.

At ten minutes past nine we were at the spot where the great eastern peninsula projects nearest to us, having in view the two extremities, north-east and south-west, now named on the maps, the former as Point Costigan, after the unfortunate explorer of 1835, and the latter, Point Molyneux, after my friend, the lieutenant of H.M.S. *Spartan*, who was there in 1847. But at that season of the year we could perceive no traces of the shallow or

---

* This I repeat after having travelled at different times on most parts, north, west, and south of the lake, and read all that has been printed about the eastern side. (1867.)

Jerusalem to Petra, etc. 333

ford by which the Arabs occasionally pass over to it on the way to Kerak.

At half-past nine we were in front of *Sebbeh*, with a view of the ruins of Masada on its summit, to which, however, we did not climb, but contented ourselves with recalling to memory the heroic events of the Jewish defenders, as related by Josephus. Here the sea, retiring towards our side, forms a semicircular bay, terminating at *'Ain Jidi*, (Engeddi,) where we arrived at two o'clock. There we were at a considerable elevation above the shore, which we now abandoned, not only because all further advance in that direction is impracticable, but because our route towards Jerusalem lay in a different direction.

We were upon a platform abounding in springs of water and luxuriant neglected vegetation. The pleasure derived from the sound of gushing streams can only be appreciated by those who have been in our circumstances. The contrast is not to be understood merely from words laid before a reader, between this and the dry wilderness of Edom or the salt beach of Sodom. One of our camels not only drank his fill, but rolled himself in the water.

There were some neb'k trees, some trees of the *'osher*, (apple of Sodom,) and some of the shrub *solanum melongena*, all of which may be found near Jericho, though not peculiar to that region. Canes and large weeds almost filled the watercourses, but not a blossom of any wild-flower could I find upon the ground.

The streams abound in petrifactions of vegetation, which would show that the water cannot be very wholesome for drinking. A monster crab was brought us out of a channel; my horse in drinking had been startled at the sight of it.

There were traces of buildings about the place, such as foundations of walls almost razed to the ground, and one broken tower.

But the prospect eastwards, including the peninsula, and the mountains and huge crevasses of Moab, or southwards, including Sebbeh and the Salt mountain, are magnificent beyond expression. We could not be sure that Mount Hor was distinguishable. At a quarter past three, and under shade of trees, the thermometer was at 86° Fahrenheit.

After considerable repose and some feeding there, we prepared for the remaining ascent, called by our people "The Ladder of *Terâbeh.*" This was a very toilsome climbing of near two hours up a nearly perpendicular cliff, by means of curves and zig-zags turning away four or five yards. Most of the way we were dismounted, but still the horses and camels were greatly distressed by the effort of the ascent. At first the camel-drivers sang to cheer their animals. This, however, dwindled into occasional prolonged notes, which again were deteriorated into groans instead of music.

It was a curious sight for us who were untroubled

with the care of camels, and consequently getting on faster than they, to look down upon the wavy lines of moving creatures, and hear the echoes of their voices from below.

Reached the summit at half-past four, and after an hour's progress upon level ground, we halted for the night. Poor old Selâmeh fell down flat, not so much from the effect of mere fatigue, as from having had his ankle bitten by a spiteful camel in the morning, and then the long climbing in addition.

This was to be our last night together, and we enjoyed to the utmost the social gathering round the bivouac fire with our Arab companions, to whom, after ten days' association, to the exclusion of all the rest of the world, we could not but feel something of temporary personal attachment. There was Selâmeh, with his mended shoe and his bitten ankle, who had been our officer and diplomatist, ready for fun or a row at any minute; 'Odeh the champion, called out upon emergencies; Khamees, the slave boy, a general domestic, if this latter word may be allowed for a Bedawi Arab; and Salem the merry-man, short in stature, and drawing into the vale of years. We chatted over the fire about the events of the expedition, while some of the men were kneading and baking fresh bread upon stones made hot in the fire.

Yet this is a sad aimless life that such people lead—of course our excursion under their protection was an event to supply matter for many a conversation afterwards.

As for religion : they seem to have little or no sense of its responsibility or benefit, or even its formalities. I asked Selâmeh about prayers or reading, and all he had to say was that annually in Ramadan they hire a reader from some mosque of a town to come and read the Korân to them; but not one, not even Abu Dahook could read for himself. I never heard these Jehâleen mention either the word *Moslem* or *Ghiaour*, much less the technical words *Mushrakeen* or *Seerat el Mustakeem*. Thermometer at sunset, $79\frac{1}{4}°$ Fahrenheit.

April 11*th.*—Our camels were loaded for the last time, as usual grunting, groaning, and tossing the head backwards while the burdens were placed upon them, and, as must be known to all desert travellers, the smell exhaled from these animals after a long journey is particularly disagreeable.

We were marching forward at half-past five, and in an hour and a half we caught a distant view of our old familiar Frank mountain, which was lost again afterwards. About ten o'clock, we saw in a valley at our left an encampment of Saïr Arabs, and soon afterwards in a valley at our right, a circle of the Ta'amri tents. In another hour we arrived at a square enclosure of very large ancient stones, which was denominated '*Arkoob Sahâba*. The breezes on this high land were most refreshing after our southern excursion.

Passed *Thekua'* or Tekua', (Tekoa,) and at some distance forwards, to the north-east, some ruins called *Abu'n-jaib*, or perhaps Abu N'jaim.

Then we approached the well-remembered fragrance of the wild herbs on the uncultivated hills about Urtas and Bethlehem, redolent of homeward associations, and between two and three o'clock were at Jerusalem, grateful for special and numerous mercies of Divine Providence.

Jewish friends were much interested in my report of Aaron's tomb on Mount Hor, and regarded it as a great achievement to have visited and returned from "Joktheel," as they called Petra, in compliance with 2 Kings xiv. 7, where King Amaziah restored its more ancient name from *Selah*, (see Joshua xv. 38.)

In conclusion of this expedition to Petra, I have a few observations to make, arising from local peculiarities connected with it.

A. *On the payment of toll, or ghufr, as it is termed, for traversing unfrequented districts.*

Of course, this custom could never obtain in a country enjoying the benefits of a vigorous central government; but it is, and perhaps always has been, common in the far East. In Persia or Tartary, wherever a chief is able to lay hold of a tower, and collect around him a band of followers, he invariably exacts this tribute from strangers; just as in our middle ages of Europe was done by the same class of persons in countries where feudal institutions prevailed. The petty barons were the shaikhs of their place and period.

But some considerations may serve to show that there is, after all, something useful in the practice.

1. In such countries, the payment of this toll exempts the traveller from the violence of all other claimants.

2. Those who get the toll, (I speak now of Palestine,) are always ready to perform small services in return, which would be assuredly missed if omitted, independently of the price paid for hire of camels.

3. If there were a better government existing, the traveller would expect that government to provide good roads and bridges, and to establish military posts for guarding them. This expense would be defrayed from tolls, or some such mode of taxation, and so the fee or duty would be only removed from one receiver to another. This is done at present, and probably has been for many centuries, at the *Jis'r benât Ya'koob*, between Safed and Damascus.

One cannot be surprised at the peasantry of Wadi Moosa exacting a toll from travellers on entering the valley of Petra, to see the wonders of antiquity which are attracting the attention of the most remote nations; remembering, too, the position of the place, viz., in a hollow, surrounded by crags and hills, where no Turkish rulers have ever been.

In like manner, we shall only be in a condition to remonstrate on paying ghuf'r in the shape of presents to the Adwân beyond Jordan, when we are able to find our way to Ammân and Jerash without them, or to keep off the Beni Sukh'r and 'Anezeh, either by our own right hand or by means of the Turks.*

Finally, it must be borne in mind that the Turkish government itself pays ghuf'r to the Eastern Bedaween for allowing the Hadj pilgrims to pass from Damascus to Mecca.

B. *On the Fellahheen, or peasants of Wadi Moosa.*

The most experienced travellers that have visited Petra, have remarked that these men are of a different race from the Bedaween Arabs around them. They are ugly, bad in expression of countenance, and have a reputation for cruelty and treachery.

Laborde says, that the Alaween looked upon them "with contempt *and fear.*" Lord Lindsay says, that Shaikh Hhussain, from 'Akabah, " was *in fear* all the time of being there." Irby and Mangles were told by the Jehâleen that these

* Since writing the above, we learn from Lieutenant Warren's very interesting letters that the Turkish Government have sent a large force into the trans-Jordanic region, with a view of chastising the Arabs: it remains to be seen whether this measure will leave any permanent effects.—(*Nov.* 1867.)

Fellahheen murdered thirty Moslem pilgrims from Barbary, the year before their visit.

Dr Wilson stayed among them longer, I believe, than any other European, and he did not like them, yet found them gradually improve under civil treatment, which always, like some other things,

"Emollit mores nec sinit esse feros."

He divides them into two classes as cultivators of land. First, Those residing in a village called *Eljy;* and, second, Those residing in tents under one Abu Zeitoon.

He describes them as a very exclusive people, never intermarrying with Arabs, nor burying in common grounds with them; and having a different set of personal names among them from those used by Arabs, which names greatly resemble those found in the Old Testament Scriptures.

He concludes that they are descendants of the ancient Edomites.

A most remarkable circumstance that he observed, was their calling themselves children of Israel, (Beni Israïn.) This he regards as a feeble traditional reminiscence of their prosleytism to the faith of Israel by the sword of the Maccabæan conquerors.

For my own part, I distinctly aver that during the altercation upon my arrival there, between them and my Jehâleen, I did hear the words "children of Israel" used. I had not chosen to take a part in the conference, or to remain long at a time among the disputants, but only passed occasionally in and out of the tent, and my mind was chiefly engrossed with the subject-matter in hand, so that on hearing the words, "children of Israel," I thought they were alluding to some history or tradition of the Hebrew people. But afterwards, on connecting the fact with Dr Wilson's assertion, I cannot but consider it very remarkable.

But the whole subject of these Fellahheen seems to merit closer attention from those who have leisure and opportunity for it.

I know that numerous travellers, including ladies, have been there in safety; and it is probable that some of the disputes which have arisen were occasioned either through ignorance, or from insolence of the dragomans. It would be interesting to compare the accounts of those who have suffered annoyances in Petra, so as to ascertain how far the Fellahheen were to blame, or whether difficulties are not rather due to the Arab tribes who are in the habit of tyrannising over the Fellahheen from the outside.

C. *On the 'Arabah and the Dead Sea.*

While on the spot, I had wished to believe in the theory of Leake in 1822, and afterwards turned almost into poetry by Lord Lindsay, notwithstanding the demonstrations of Bertou in 1838, and of the American expedition of 1848, namely, that the Jordan formerly flowed the whole length from the Anti-Lebanon to the Red Sea, and that the

Asphaltite Lake, or Dead Sea, is only formed by a stoppage of its stream.

Two facts, however, which militate against this theory, were visible to our eyes on this journey.

1. That the valleys south of the Dead Sea all point towards it, and incline the slope of their beds in that direction. This was most particularly the case with the Wadi el Jaib, where the banks between which the torrents had cut a channel became higher, which is equivalent to saying that the water fell lower as it passed northwards.

2. That wherever there were trees or shrubs to arrest the currents of water, we found that all the rushes, thorns, or reeds carried on by the streams, were arrested on the south side of those trees, and there they remained in the dry season.

The course of the torrents was therefore from the south, towards the Dead Sea.

The best dissertation on the relative levels of lands and seas, bearing on this subject, and that which I believe to be exhaustive on the subject, till we get more of scientific realities, is contained in vol. xviii., part 2, of the Royal Geographical Society's Journal of 1848.

Still, allowing the facts that I myself observed, as well as all the scientific calculations in the Journal above referred to, (indeed, making use of them,) there seem to remain certain considerations undisposed of, in favour of the theory that the Jordan formerly ran into the Red Sea.

1. The 'Arabah, south of the Dead Sea, and the Ghôr on its north, are one continued hollow between the same parallel lines of hills; and Robinson has shown that by the Arabian geographers they are both called the 'Arabah; the native Arabs also still call by the name of Ghuwair, or little Ghôr, a space at the southern extremity of the water.

In the Hebrew Bible also, the northern part is called 'Arabah, as in Joshua iii. 16, where it is said the Israelites crossed "the sea of 'Arabah, namely, the sea of salt." In 2 Sam. iv. 7, the murderers of Ish-bosheth went all night from Mahanaim to Hebron along the 'Arabah, this was clearly not south of the Dead Sea. Josh. xii. i., "From the river Arnon to mount Hermon, and all the 'Arabah on the east," going northwards; this is explained in the 3d verse as "the 'Arabah, (beginning at Hermon,) unto the sea of Chinnereth, (sea of Tiberias) on the east, and unto the sea of the 'Arabah, the sea of salt, on the east." The same words occur also in Deut. iii. 17, and iv. 49. That the present Arab 'Arabah on the south of the Dead Sea bore the same name, may be seen in Deut. ii. 8, where Moses speaks of "the way of the "'Arabah' from Elath, and from Ezion-gaber."

Therefore, according to Hebrew and Arabic authorities, the 'Arabah and Ghôr form one line from the Lebanon to the Red Sea.

2. The Book of Job takes cognisance of the

river Jordan, and describes river scenery in the land of Edom, *i.e.*, south of the Dead Sea.

3. No lake existed in that locality before the catastrophe of Sodom, although a river may have traversed it. This I deduce from the march of the army of Chedorlaomer, shortly previous to that catastrophe, (Gen. xiv.) After the taking of Seir and Paran, he crossed the valley to Hazezon-Tamar, which is Engedi, (2 Chron. xx. 2,) and the confederates were met by the kings of the plain in the vale of Siddim. And I have heretofore shown that this is utterly impossible to be done with the present lake in the way. The words, therefore, of Gen. xiv. 3 obviously signify, as given in the Latin Vulgate and in Luther's German, "the vale of Siddim, which is *now* the Salt Sea."

The inference from all these points is, that between the time of Chedorlaomer and Moses, some tellural convulsions took place which impeded the course of the river towards the Dead Sea, and thereby formed the present lake. There is no mention of a river in the lower 'Arabah during the wanderings of the Israelites under the leading of Moses.

It is another matter to discuss whether the overthrow of the guilty cities of Sodom and Gomorrah is connected with that convulsion of nature, with or without miracle, which formed the depression of the great valley; yet it is remarkable that the deepest part of the lake is at the spot which tradition has always pointed out for the site of those cities, and nigh to the salt mountain, which still bears the name of Sodom.

To this spot the slopes both ways tend, and there they meet. Calculating the whole line of depression, as. Petermann does, at 190 miles, the slope from the north, *i.e.*, from the "Bridge of the daughters of Jacob," near Safed, is comparatively gradual for 140 miles; and that from the south, *i.e.*, from the elevation in the southern 'Arabah, where the level meets again from the north, is more precipitous for 50 miles. Action and reaction being equal in natural effects, the rapid declivity in the shorter distance is equal to the more gradual declivity in the longer measure.

But that centre of *seismal action* is taken for the site of Sodom—hence the site of the destruction of Sodom and the starting point of earthquake are the same. The record of the destruction is, therefore, the record of some dreadful convulsion capable of stopping the Jordan, so as to form a lake there; and the only *adequate* cause in nature assigned by geologists for such a depression, is earthquake accompanied by volcanic action.

While on the subject of possible depression of the Jordan bed, I may mention an indication which I have often pointed out to others, namely, the remarkable ledge traceable along the face of the Moab mountains at a considerable height, as seen from the neighbourhood of Jerusalem. It is distinctly marked, and forms a curious record of some natural change having occurred on a large scale.

Dr Wilson, in his "Lands of the Bible," contends that an earthquake capable of depressing a straight line of the length of the Ghôr and 'Arabah, must have convulsed all the lands of Canaan, Moab, Ammon, Edom, and the Desert, with their inhabitants; but that no such convulsion took place, for Zoar on the east, and Hebron on the west, are known to have remained.

Does it, however, necessarily follow that seismal devastation spreads in *every* direction? On the contrary, earthquakes act in oscillations from east to west, returning from west to east; or from north to south, returning from south to north: but not in the manner of a flood of water spreading in every direction at once. If so, a mighty earthquake, extending along the whole Ghôr and 'Arabah, would be exactly such a cause as might spare a city on each side of its progress.

The whole subject still admits of much careful investigation on sundry points; but, meanwhile, until geologists have given us more data from which to form conclusions, I must take my stand upon the distinct record of Genesis; that what was the Salt Sea when Moses wrote, had been the Vale or Plain (Emek) of Siddim, containing cities with kings, who fought and were subdued by Chedarlaomer upon that plain in the time of Abraham; and that those cities were the same as those that were penally destroyed soon after.

XII.

ACROSS THE LEBANON.

I HAVE traversed the Lebanon eastwards and southwards of Bayroot several times; once in 1849; again in 1853; and also in 1855: but it seems advisable to narrate the incidents separately, and although on two occasions I passed over nearly the same ground, it will be curious to compare or contrast those journeys, inasmuch as the circumstances were dissimilar.

PART I.—1849.

The course of the first journey was as follows :— From Sidon on the sea-coast we gradually climbed the Lebanon range eastward; then descending by tortuous roads, and turning somewhat to the south, we crossed to where Hhasbeya lies at the foot of Anti-Lebanon; after which we followed the general direction of the streams southwards, and uniting above the waters of Merom form the Jordan. Holding on at the western side of the plain we arrived at Safed in Galilee.

Oct. 25th.—We left Saida for Joon, which had been for many years the residence of Lady Hester Stanhope, and the vice-consul furnished us with a kawwâs who had been a servant of her ladyship.

Turned off from the high road of the sea-coast, at the river Awali, which is believed by the native Christians to have been the limit of our Lord's ministry on earth, when it is said that He went into "the coasts of Tyre and Sidon."

We outflanked the rich scene of fruit plantations belonging to the town, but picked blackberries, hips, and haws, from their hedges alongside the runnels of water which supply those gardens.

On its approach to the sea the river Awali has two separate channels, along either of which it flows in different years, according to the volume of water at the beginning of winter, but never in both at the same time.

Through lovely scenery we gradually mounted higher and higher, till arriving at the village of *Joon*, where rooms were to be prepared for us in a native house.

The nature of the district thereabout is that of numerous round hills, separated from each other by deep valleys. On one of these hills stands the village, on another the large "Convent of the Saviour," (Dair el Mokhallis,) which is the central station of the Greek Catholic sect; *i.e.*, of those who, while retaining their Oriental rites and calendar, acknowledge the supremacy of the Pope

Across the Lebanon.

of Rome; and on the third hill is Lady Hester Stanhope's house, the three forming the points of nearly an equilateral triangle. The village commands a fine prospect of the Mediterranean.

Without dismounting, we proceeded at once to the desolate house of Lady Hester, but, owing to the precipitous nature of the ground, it takes some considerable time to reach it, yet voices are easily distinguishable from one place to the other.

The house presents a melancholy spectacle, though, from the purity of the atmosphere, the walls appear clean and almost new; no roof remains, all timbers having been purposely removed immediately after her death, according to legal right of the proprietor from whom the place was rented. There has been an extensive suite of rooms, not adapted to stateliness, but meant for the reception of guests; these are all of small dimensions, and were mostly built by Lady Hester. We were told that she kept an establishment of a hundred servants, forty of whom were women. For the last five years she never travelled beyond the garden, and during that time the renowned two mares, Leilah and Lulu, (the former of which was the one with the hollow back, reserved for entering Jerusalem together with the new Messiah,) became so broken in health for want of exercise, that when Lady Hester died, they were sold with difficulty for 300 piastres (less than three pounds) each.

The stables still remaining were very extensive.

The gardens and terraces must have been beautiful, for we were told they were carefully kept and arranged. We saw large myrtle shrubs in abundance, besides fruit trees now utterly neglected—

"And still where many a garden flower grows wild,"

for there were red roses blooming without the least care or notice.

No one now resides on any part of that hill.

The eccentric lady is buried in the garden, and in the same grave (we were assured) with Captain, son of General Loustaneau, a crazy French enthusiast who lived for above twenty-five years a pensioner on her bounty. The grave is covered with this simple stone monument, of a pattern very common in the country.

TOMB OF LADY HESTER STANHOPE.

At the distance of a few yards is the monument over a former Moslem proprietor of the house.

Lady Hester died in June 1839, lonely and

miserable, and so ended her wild dreams and fancied importance. During her long residence there she had meddled in local dissensions, patronising the Jonblâts of Mokhtârah against the Ameer Besheer and the Egyptian invaders; she kept spies in the principal towns, as Acre and Saida, and had even supplied ammunition to the citadel of Acre for the Turks, but did not live to see the Egyptians ousted from the country.

There was good deal of exaggeration afloat at the time respecting her and some of her habits of life, though scarcely more extraordinary than the reality of other matters, as we are now able to judge of them; but at that period Syria and the Lebanon were very little understood in Europe, *i.e.*, from 1823 to 1839. She was not so utterly removed from human society as is often supposed. She was not perched like an eagle on an inaccessible mountain, for there are villages near, besides the great Convent of Mokhallis, and she had constant communication with Saida for money and provisions.

The view around is indeed stern and cheerless in character, devoid of romantic accessories, without the rippling streams, the pines or the poplars of either Mokhtârah or Beteddeen; her hill like its neighbours was a lump of stone, with some scanty cultivation in the valley below, very little of this, and her small garden attached to the dwelling.

Before leaving this subject, I may as well state with respect to the common belief of Lady Hester being crowned Queen of Palmyra by the desert Arabs, that from information which I consider reliable this is all a mistake, or as it was expressed to me, a "French enthusiasm," the truth being that in consequence of her lavish largesses among the wild people, they expressed their joy by acclamations in which they compared her to the "Queen of Sheba" who had come among them; and then by her flatterers, or those who were unskilled in the language, the term "Melekeh" (Queen) was interpreted as above: and as for a coronation the Arab tribes have no such a custom; the greatest chiefs, nay, even the kings of the settled Arabs, such as Mohammed and his successors, have never received such an inauguration.

Returning to the village, we found our lodging provided in the house of a Greek Catholic family; unlike to our south country houses, it was built with ponderous rafters of timber in the roofs, and these rafters and planks between them are painted in coloured patterns. It was a cheerful scene as the family sat inquiring about Jerusalem, or chatting otherwise on the mustabeh (a wide stone seat) outside, with the effulgence of the setting sun reflected on the convent before us, and then the twilight pink and violet tints upon the mountain-range behind.

Then again in the early morning, how delicious were the air and the scenery of the mountains!

> "Yet sluggards deem it but a foolish chase
> And marvel men should quit their easy chair,
> The weary mile and long, long league to trace;
> Oh, there is sweetness in the mountain air,
> And life that bloated ease may never hope to share!"

While mounting for the departure, our host pressing his hospitality upon us, adjured us in these words:—"May your religion be your adversary if ever you pass my door without entering it."

Arriving at Dair el Mokhallis we were there also received with cordiality. In the church a service was going on, gabbled over by a priest arrayed in white silk and gold, waving incense before the altar, his congregation consisting of one person, a sort of sacristan or beadle. There were some good pictures on the walls, but others together with them of degraded rank as works of art.

On being invited to visit the President, we found him a jovial, handsome man of middle age, reclining on cushions at a large window with wide views of the sea and the mountains before him, besides *Dar Joon*, Lady Hester's house.

This establishment is not only the largest convent and church of the Greek Catholic sect, but also a college for clerical education; their most celebrated clergy have been trained there. The inmates at this time, of all employments, were 110 in number, exclusive of servants. Those whom we saw appeared very well fed, and we were not a little surprised to find so many women servants employed within the walls.

A nunnery of the same rite, and rules of St Basil, with forty persons under vows, is a good building at half-a-mile distance, between which and the male institution a very excellent road has been made, notwithstanding the hilly nature of the ground; other roads are being improved, and all the contiguous grounds are in a state of the highest cultivation.

As we proceeded on our journey, the scenery became more and more romantic, till on a sudden turn of the road a wondrous picture of nature was opened before us, consisting of mountains, including our own, all sloping down into a plain in which was a river, and a village with its orchards and poplars; cascades rolled down the furrowed sides of these hills, their bounding and dashing were evident to the sight, but no sound audible owing to their distance; it was a fairy scene, or like a beautiful dream.

In the descent we passed a Maronite priest riding, attended by a guide on foot; the former was greeted by our party with his title of Abuna, a novelty to us Jerusalemites.

We forded the river *Barook*, a tributary to the Awali, in front of the above-mentioned village,

Across the Lebanon. 355

which is *Bisrah*, amid tall poplars quivering in the breeze, for their foliage had stalks long like the aspen.

Our luggage having gone on during the visit to the convent, we could get no tidings of it and our people, but a guide was procured for part of the day's journey before us; and we betook ourselves to a hill over which was, what we were assured, the only road to Hhasbeya. A road so steep and thickly entangled by bushes and trees, that we inquired of every passer-by in his turn whether we could possibly be upon the *Sultâneh*, or high road. At first through an olive plantation, then among evergreen oak, and higher still the fragrant mountain pines. The zigzags of the road were necessarily so short and abrupt, that at each turn we had to peer up perpendicularly, guessing which way the next twist would go. Then still higher, towards the frowning sombre cliffs that seemed to touch the brilliant blue sky, the arbutus glowed with their scarlet berries, and the pine-trees became more tall, straight, and numerous. No wonder that the Assyrian king, when he boasted of being able to cut down the cedars of Lebanon, included also "the choice fir-trees thereof," (2 Kings xix. 23.)

Near what seemed to be the climax, we unexpectedly reached a village, named '*Azoor*, where a school of boys hummed their lessons in the open air on the shady side of a house; and near them a plank of wood was suspended, such as serves for a church-bell in parts of the country where the Moslems predominate, and bells are not tolerated. Here in the Lebanon every village and convent may have its bells; and they generally have them, for the Mohammedans scarcely exist throughout "the mountain," as the whole range is popularly termed from Tarabulus to Saida.

The higher we ascended, the more we obtained of a brisk breeze playing and sighing musically among the noble pines, and the ground was clothed with heather and fragrant herbs. Still onwards, "excelsior," the pines were more straight and lofty; there were patches of wild myrtle on the ground, some in white blossom; and we looked down upon the flat roofs of villages below, an appearance so strange to us after the round domes of the south country.

About noon we overtook the luggage, and the servant-boy of the muleteer swore that his head had turned gray since we left him, four hours ago, by reason of the bodily labour and anguish of mind that he had suffered on so fearful a road. He was incessantly calling upon God by epithets out of the Korân, as "O thou Father of bounty!" "O thou knower of former things!" mingled with curses hurled at the mule, or prayers that her back might be strengthened: being a Jerusalemite, he had not been accustomed to travelling of that description. This youth was nicknamed by his fellows as *Abu*

Tabanjah, "the father of a pistol," from his carrying a single pistol in his girdle: it being unusual for persons in his employment to carry any belligerent weapons.

Next came the descent to *Jezzeen*, over a slippery road, with purple crocuses in blossom at intervals.

Jezzeen is romantically situated among broken rocks, with a stream of water, called the *Zaid*, bordered by a profusion of sycamore, (*i.e.*, what is called so in England, a variety of the plane-tree,) walnut, and aspen trees. We halted beneath a spreading walnut-tree, whose leaves had already begun to change colour.

The inhabitants are Greek Catholic, Maronite, and a few Mutâwaleh. Here we had to get another guide for an hour or two forwards—a task not easily accomplished—and he assured us that the road before us was far worse than that we had already traversed—he would on no account go the whole day's journey with us.

Forwards.—Thin white clouds were resting upon the peaks high above us, the vine terraces and poplars were succeeded by whitish-gray rocks and olive-trees, till we issued upon a comparative level of confused chaos of rugged rocks pitched and hurled about in the most fantastic combinations, rendering the road almost impassable for our cattle. Darker clouds than before were around, but not immediately over us; and the atmosphere was hot like the breath of a furnace, with now and then a momentary gush of piercing cold coming between sharp peaks and round summits.

In little more than two hours from Jezzeen we were at *Cuf'r Hooneh,* a pretty village surrounded by sycamore, walnut, poplar, and vineyards, with numerous running streams of water, bordered by oleanders in rosy blossom, very tall—girt in with romantic precipices, and rooks were cawing overhead. A spring of water issuing from the ground, of which we drank, was cold like ice.

After this the road improved, the rocks were more friable, and were often streaked with pink and yellow colour; indicating, I suppose, the existence of copper mineral, (see Deut. viii. 9,) "out of whose hills thou mayest dig brass," *i.e.,* copper.

All about this region fossil shells were numerous.

In half an hour we attained our greatest elevation, with a long line of Mediterranean visible in the west. The Anti-Lebanon stretched before us on the east, and among the hills to the south our guide declared he could distinguish Safed. Here he left us, returning homewards.

Upon this eminence the air was reviving, and as the fervour of the sun abated, our horses recovered energy. Thence we descended to a green level space as void of inhabitants as the wild scenes that we had traversed; and from that to a stage lower, over a very long fertile plain running southwards, where we fell in with two or three of our fellow human beings, and over this the wind blew very cold. Forwards into another level, a glen of wild verdure, then through chalk fissures and red slopes, till in a moment there burst upon our view a prospect beyond all power of description in words; Mount Hermon, (Jebel esh Shaikh,) and the intervening long plain, also the Litâni river on our right, winding between tremendous cliffs, and passing the castle of Shukeef towards the sea.

That river passing the foot of our mountain, and over which we had afterwards to cross, appeared like a narrow ribbon of pale green, so silent was it to us, for no sound from that depth could reach up so high; to this we had to descend by a precipitous path of zigzags roughly made in the face of the hill.

Half way down I first distinguished the rushing sound of the water; a flock of goats upon its margin resembled mere black spots, but the bells among them became faintly audible.

On reaching the river Litâni, (the classic Leontes, and named the "Kasimiyeh" when debouching to the sea near Tyre,) we found it to be a strong stream, and the dark border, which from a distance had seemed to be low bushes, were in truth gigantic and numerous trees; on our way to the bridge, along the river side for some distance, were parapets erected for the safety of travellers and flocks of cattle.

It was after sunset, but we rested awhile to

stretch our limbs after the cramp brought on by the steep and long descent.

The moon was shining as we crossed the bridge, and its light was broken in the heady dashing of the stream; the land swelled gradually upwards as we proceeded S.-E. till we passed a ridge and turned N.-E. to the village of *Cocaba* on the great plain, which has the river *Hhasbâni* flowing through it, from which village we got directions how to find Hhasbeya. Thoroughly tired as we all were, the rest of the way was most wearisome, though not so much so as it would have been in the heat of day, after so many hours on horseback. The night was bright and clear.

Reached *Hhasbeya* in thirteen hours from Joon in the morning.

The town is perched up in the line of the Anti-Lebanon, at the end of a *cul-de-sac* running inwards from the plain, and stands at an elevation of more than 2000 feet above the sea-level, though this is scarcely apparent by reason of the lofty mountains everywhere around, especially Hermon, under the shadow of which Hhasbeya is nestled. This was the cleanest town and the one in best repair at that time that I had hitherto seen in Palestine or Syria; what it may be since the calamities of 1860, I know not. The majority of the inhabitants were Christian, with a good many Druses, and a few Moslems and Jews.

We had a most friendly reception from the native

Across the Lebanon. 361

Protestants, and from the governor, Ameer Saad ed Deen Shehâb and his family.

In the afternoon of the next day we passed on to *Banias*. How different a matter is travelling in that country from merely drawing a pencil line across the map from one point to another, and measuring the distance of that line. By such a method of making a journey it is but a trifle of thirty miles from Soor to Hhasbeya, and less than a hundred and twenty from the latter to Jerusalem. (I mention these places because they belong to the journey here described,) and it may be said by stay-at-home travellers in a carpeted saloon, at a mahogany table, that these distances can be covered on horseback in a determinate number of hours, allowing so many miles to an hour; but Palestine is not so smooth as the greater part of England, and the ways (one cannot well call them roads) are not drawn in direct lines; climate also counts for something; and unforeseen incidents will occur to mar the plans of even those habituated to the country.

To-day's progress, however, was tolerably plain, though not level, and it occupied six or seven hours.

In an hour and a half we caught first sight of the lake *Hhooleh* (the Semechonitis of Josephus) in the due south, and at this point we entered upon a district strewn with volcanic basalt, in dark-brown pieces, porous and rounded at the edges. A peasant directed us forwards to the *Tell el Kâdi*, which at length we reached—an eminence rising from the plain, out of which issues a river all formed at once, gushing from the hill over a stony bed. This is one of the heads of the Jordan, and the place is that of *Dan*, which Josephus erroneously supposed to supply the last syllable of that river's name.

But beyond all question it is the site of the city Dan known throughout Scripture history for many ages, and under a variety of circumstances: among the rest for the forcible invasion of it by a number of colonists from the tribe of Dan in the south of Palestine, where they found their allotted district too strait for their possession; and being established here, they gave the city the name of their patriarchal chief.

That history of their migration reads with peculiar interest and force on the spot, and strange to say that Tell el Kâdi seems to retain their tribal name, inasmuch as *Tell* signifies "a hill," and Kâdi is but the Arabic for the Hebrew word *Dan*, "a judge," (Gen. xlix. 16.) It is not however common, very much the contrary, for names to be transmitted in this way according to their signification through the lapse of ages—they are usually perpetuated through their orthography.

The Amorite or Sidonian people living here "at ease" were worshippers of Baal and Ashtaroth, or Astarte. Suddenly they were assailed by the Dan-

Across the Lebanon. 363

ites, who "smote them with the edge of the sword, and burned their city with fire;" and the newcomers set up "the graven image, and the molten image, and the teraphim," which they had stolen on their way thither over Mount Ephraim, appointing the young Levite, the owner of the images, to be priest of their idolatry. In later times it was a station of the golden calf of Jeroboam's institution, that is to say, the revived emblem of Baal, going back to the practice of the Leshemites; and there is yet an idea prevailing in our days that the Druses of the neighbourhood retain that emblem or idol among them—a remarkable instance of the perpetuity of idolatry, and one form of idolatry under different names, modified only by circumstances in the same locality. I forbear to pursue further the reflections that can be evolved at large from that idea, as they might bring us into other countries than Syria or Palestine.

Riding our horses up the full stream for a short distance, we forded it, and entered into the shade upon the hill, where we reposed under a large evergreen oak, decorated with rags as votive offerings to an Arab shaikh buried beside it. Near this tree is an extraordinary jungle of brambles and gigantic flowering shrubs, through which it seemed impossible to penetrate, but out of which tangled mass the copious stream issues, as also a minor current, which after some deflection meets the other, and forms one stream on leaving the hill, and this, when joined by the waters of Banias, to which we were now going, combines into one river, Jordan, then enters and passes through the Lake Hhooleh. For the present I omit the consideration of the Hhasbâni and its spring, which not only helps to form the Jordan, but actually commences further beyond the springs of Dan and Banias.

It wanted about an hour to sunset when we turned in eastwards, round the foot of old Hermon, for *Banias*, the Cæsarea Philippi of the New Testament, whose hill and ancient castle appeared not far distant.

We observed numerous small runlets of water flowing from the north and east towards the Tell el Kâdi, one especially of nearly four feet wide. Yet with all these blessings the district is mostly neglected, and abandoned to a sparse population of wretched Ghawârineh Arabs and their buffaloes.

We passed through neb'k trees and stunted oaks, some karoobah trees and sumach about twenty feet high, with their red berries, besides myrtles almost as lofty. Signs of the existence of inhabitants appeared in patches of cultivation and an occasional flock of goats. Trees became closer together than at first, and at length Banias stood in face of us, touching the foot of Hermon, which formed a magnificent background of receding heights, but its summit withdrawn from view at that position. An ancient castle crowns a high peak rising above the village, and which for gran-

Across the Lebanon.

deur of situation and noble aspect is unsurpassed by any ruin that I have seen in Syria. Yet how small was all this in comparison with the mighty mass at its back! I regret the having been unable to examine this remarkable fortress, the modern name of which is the *Kula'at es Subeibeh*.

The halt was in an olive plantation, and while the tents were being raised, I rode forwards to the other celebrated source of the Jordan, namely, that issuing from the cavern, and drank of its water, but first had to swim the horse through a strong current.

How beautiful was the evening scene of rocks, trees, blue mountains, and the extended plain, with the thread of the Hhasbâni winding through it on the western side! There were also herds of cattle coming in, and a shepherd boy playing his rural pipes. What a scene for Poussin! I offered to buy the Pandean pipe (of several reeds joined laterally) from the boy, wishing to have it for my own, obtained at the mythological home of Pan himself—

> "Pan primus calamos cerâ conjungere plures
> Instituit,"

but the lad asked an exorbitant price for it, and strode away.

Then rushed up to make use of the fading twilight for catching at least a glimpse of the Greek inscriptions and Pan's grotto, from which the river issues, not in infantile weakness, but boldly striking an echo against the sides of the natural cavity.

"Great Pan is dead!" as the superstitious peasants of Thessaly said, when they imagined they heard the echo formed into words, sixteen hundred years ago; and while musing on the "rise and fall" of the classic idolatry, a bat flew past me out of the grotto, but I saw no moles for the old idols to be thrown to, (Isa. ii. 20.)

Pan was the mythological deity presiding over caverns, woods, and streams, from whom this place received its denomination of Panion or Paneas in Greek, or Panium in Latin; and the word Paneas becomes Banias in Arabic, as it is at this day. Here costly temples and altars were raised, and Herod built a temple in honour of Augustus Cæsar. These edifices have fallen to the ground, the idols have been demolished by early Christians, Jews, and Mohammedans; but niches with pedestals, on which the dumb figures stood, accompanied by inscriptions, still remain in attestation of written history.

Of these inscriptions I took copies next morning, as others have also done, but with special pains to insure accuracy. Every one of them has the name of the god Pan; two of them have the name of Agrippa; one is set up by a priest of Pan, "for the welfare of the lords the emperors;" and another is dedicated by Agrippa, son of

Marcus, who had been for eight years Archon, and had been admonished in a dream by the god Pan. The breaks in the words caused by defaced letters make it difficult to get more signification out of them.

Some further remarks on the same, as well as copies of the tablets, will be found in appendix B.

In a field near our tents, were two prostrate granite columns of about fifteen feet length of shaft by two in diameter; besides a piece of column of common stone three feet in diameter. In another part of the same field was a square capital of pilaster with some plain moulding, and an abundance of squared stones of two to three feet dimensions; such, however, are to be seen scattered in every direction around.

A small ancient bridge crosses one of the several streams branching away from the main course, and all running between steep banks. By this bridge I approached a noble gateway, leading into a very large square fortress, with strong ancient towers at each corner. The arches of both gate and bridge were Roman; parts of the walls remained in their regular courses, and numerous large rabbeted stones were rolled down in disorder upon the slope and into a military trench. But the whole scene, whether of rugged rocks or of the work of man, was fringed and clothed with brambles, ferns, evergreens, and the rosy oleander.

The principal charm, however, belongs to the grotto with the river which it discharges—the site of which may be described as a semicircular termination of a valley on a natural platform half way up a cliff—the water tumbles down in short cascades for some distance; the grotto inside is untouched by chisel squarings or embellishment, just as Juvenal wished the grot of Ægeria to be.

All this is particularly romantic, but a more exalted interest is attached to the town and vicinity of Banias from its being a certainly known station of our Redeemer's journeys—He who in all His travels "went about doing good"—but, inasmuch as some records of His blessed footsteps are connected with incidents of higher importance than others, this one rises into transcendant value, as being the place where His eternal divinity was distinctly enunciated.

At that very time the temple of Augustus, erected by Herod, was in its freshest beauty; the votive inscriptions with the name of Agrippa were newly chiselled; and the priests of Pan were celebrating sacrifices and incense, together with rustic offerings, upon his altar; the worship, too, of Baal was still in existence, under some modifications, upon the mountain overhead. At such a place, and under such circumstances, was the Church universal promised to be founded on the rock of faith to which Peter had given utterance.

It may be here observed that at that period this

Across the Lebanon. 369

Cæsarea Philippi was not a secluded spot, as commentators generally make it, because Banias is so now ; but the town was one of notoriety, adorned, as we have just seen, with expensive public edifices.

On returning to the tents, the shaikh of the village came, attended by some of his relatives belonging to Hhasbeya, begging for some quinine medicine: I gave him eight of my twelve remaining pills. On the adjacent plain there must needs be fever and ague; in fact, so unwilling was I on account of malaria to remain longer at Banias, that we resumed our travelling by night.

At three o'clock, A.M., we were mounted—there was a little rain at the time, and clouds that threatened more of it obscured the setting moon ; there was lightning also in the same direction. I even altered my plan of going on to "the bridge of the daughters of Jacob," (the thoroughfare between Safed and Damascus,) in order to escape from the plain as quickly as possible. For this purpose we turned westwards, and had to struggle through marshes and rough ground by starlight and lightning. Most unwisely we had neglected to take a meal before starting, not expecting the district to be so plashy and unwholesome as it proved to be. The plain, north of the Lake Hhooleh, is traversed by innumerable channels of water, among which rice is grown, of which I gathered a handful as a trophy to exhibit in Jerusalem. And there were lines of tents of the poor Ghawârineh Arabs upon dry ground, besides small scaffolds standing in the rice marshes, from which elevations the people watch the crops and fire upon wild beasts that come to injure or devour the crops; dogs barked as we passed, and fires were visible in several directions.

Arriving at the bridge of *El Ghujar*, my companion and I both felt sick, and had to dismount and rest for a time.

Our guide's account of the river differed from that given in Robinson; instead of the stream being the Hhasbâni and the bridge named El Ghujar, he averred that the river is El Ghujar, and that it rises out of the ground like the waters of Banias and of Tell el Kâdi. Perhaps this may account for Porter more recently placing the bridge El Ghujar in a different situation, much farther north. The circumstance is not without value in inquiries as to the collective formation of the Jordan.

As daylight broke we could see herds of buffaloes among the marshes, or swimming in the water with only their heads raised above the surface; the village of *Khalsah* was half way up the hill-side.

From this point the road was level, dry, and comfortable, running due southwards along the western margin of the plain, but with streams occasionally crossing it, rushing from the hills towards the lake.

Near '*Ain el Mellâhhah* two Arabs rode up to us and planted their spears in the ground near our horses' heads as a warning to stop, and I suppose to pay ghuf'r. I kept on, leaving the kawwâs to parley with them.

Not far from the fountain we rested under a terebinth tree (not a favourable specimen) upon a rising ground; beneath us, but at a short distance, the strong stream turns a mill, passing through a house, and escapes to the plain.

The Arabs met us again, and said they were looking for a horse that was lost, and we saw no more of them.

In another hour my companion was taken with a strong fit of ague, which urged us the more to press onward for Safed. From the hills, as we rose higher and higher, the Lake Hhooleh was perceived to be, above one-third of it, choked up with weeds and rushes. Old Hermon showed himself in surpassing grandeur; not a confused mass—as he does from the plain looking upwards from close beneath him—but as one grand "monarch of mountains."

> "On a throne of rocks, with a robe of clouds,
> And a diadem of snow."

The sun was hot and the hills chalky over which we passed. In one place by our wayside, and at considerable elevation, I found squared masonry stones and traces of houses, with fragments of columns.

A poor Arab peasant, driving an ass laden with a wooden box, was groaning with pain, and implored us for a draught of water, but I fear that our people had neglected to bring any with them, as they expected to be so soon in Safed.

Rested under the shade of some large stones, and sent on a message before us to the town. In quarter of an hour, however, some peals of thunder roused us to pursue the journey; the strong wind that arose at the same time was not good for ague patients. Across the great plain as we looked back was a broad faint piece of rainbow, and the huge mountain, mantled with clouds about his shoulders, but bright below, appeared peculiarly fantastic, with flickering shadows of clouds chasing over his sunny sides.

On the outskirts of Safed we found, as customary at that season, (Bairam,) the newly white-washed graves of the Moslems, adorned with bunches of myrtle.

At Safed we lodged in the house of a Russo-British Jew, and letters from Jerusalem that had awaited us came safe to hand, after which followed the necessary reception of visitors, very troublesome to weary and exhausted travellers, and at last a supper which had been long in preparing—at least so it seemed to be.

PART II.

This, like the journey last described, of six years before, was portion of a much longer tour, but 1 omit all that cannot come under the designation of a Byeway in Palestine. The two routes were very similar to each other, with the exception of the passage from Banias to Safed.

Starting from Saida, and trending south-eastwards towards Hhasbeya, we climbed the mountains, which here rise almost from the sea-shore, and crossed romantic passes of rugged eminences and deeply cleft ravines.

From Hhasbeya the line was due south to Banias, thence westwards by Tell el Kâdi, and Hhuneen, and Tibneen, the capital of the Belâd Beshârah, thus almost reaching once more the plain of Phœnicia on its eastern verge; next by the antiquities of Kadesh Naphtali southwards to Safed; and homewards to Jerusalem, but this latter route is not to be described, for the reason given above.

I was accompanied by my niece and another lady, a settled resident of Jerusalem. The first object after quitting Saida was to visit Joon, and to show my companions the residence of Lady Hester Stanhope in years gone by. This we reached just before sunset, on the 2d of October 1855

The tomb was found much dilapidated; in 1853 it was no longer in so good a condition as it had been in 1849, but it was now even worse, and the whole spectacle of house, stables, and gardens, was melancholy in the extreme: the deprivation of roofs gives a peculiar aspect of desolation to any abandoned dwelling, especially when the gardens have still their cultivable flowers remaining, but running riot within their marked-out beds; these had now been sixteen years neglected, yet the roses and myrtle only required pruning.

We proceeded to the convent, the road was stoney, and we had to find the way by twilight and starlight.

At the great door we were received by the new president, and several of the clergy chanting psalms for welcome, and the great bell was ringing at the same time. I could not but attribute all this unusual display to the operation of political affairs in Europe.

On taking possession of the rooms allotted to us, I received a visit of the Greek Catholic Bishop of Saida, he being there on business connected with the election of a new patriarch in the place of Maximus; his deportment was that of a man of polite society. Our rooms were lighted by huge ecclesiastical tapers of wax.

Next morning, after returning the visit of the bishop at the patriarchal residence in front of the convent, we breakfasted in the corridor with the president and another of the convent clergy. Our ladies then set themselves to sketching the view from the window, and talking about church singing from notes, whereupon the president sent a deacon to fetch his book, and the latter sang for us an anthem, the vociferation and screechings of which was so alarming, not to mention the nasal twang, that my niece had to run away to indulge in an obstreperous laugh, and her senior companion had also much difficulty in refraining from the same kind of expression of opinion. The Oriental system of church musical notation is very complicated, having no stave-lines or bars, but only certain arbitrary marks over the notes to designate high or low, plain or flourishing.

Afterwards we inspected the church; then the refectory, and there they showed us the desk at which one of the community reads to the rest at meal time, triumphantly assuring me that they read the Bible, yet the two books I found on the desk were, one the Apocryphal writings, the other some homilies of St Basil, under whose rule the convent is constituted.

Next we walked over the roof, and looked at the great bell and the gong; the view, as might be expected, repaid the trouble. After this the kitchen and the store-rooms.

On leaving the convent we proceeded to the nunnery in the neighbourhood. The ladies visited the inmates, while I remained in an outer apartment chatting with a priest, till a curtain was drawn aside, and there, behold! were the lady-president and her flock, curious to see a consul, and blaming the servants for not having admitted me together with my companions.

The latter gave me afterwards as their opinion of the establishment, that it very much resembled a comfortable asylum or almshouse for old women.

By this deviation from the high road, we lost the fairy view in that neighbourhood which had charmed me so much in 1849.

There is a pleasing novelty to us non-Lebanonites in being in a native Christian country. Every hill there has its convent, every convent its bells; clergy are continually passing along the road; and on our descent of the hill we met a nice old gentleman in clerical dress, with a very white beard, holding a crimson umbrella over his head, (this is not uncommon in Palestine,) and preceded by a kawwâs with a silver-headed official staff, also accompanied by a few peasants carrying guns,— this was a Maronite bishop.

Crossed the river Barook at *Bisrah*, and ascended the usual highway leading to Hhasbeya.

At the village of *Ineer* we took further directions, and followed over a very wild scene to nearly the summit of a mountain called *Rummet-er-Room*, (the Ramah, or high-place, of the Greeks,) from which the glorious landscape surpasses all power of description—it is one not to be forgotten.

At *'Azoor*, a clean pleasant village, the women and girls ran in crowds to gaze at my ladies; one of the women shouted "Bon soir" in good French, and a man, accompanied by his wife, saluted us in Italian.

Rested in a beautiful wood of pines, though rather late for luncheon, as the sun was falling below the western mountains. Rising higher on the march we got into rolling misty clouds, and the brilliant effect of sunbeams between the hills and clouds could not but be surprising. Our clothes, however, got damp and chill.

At *Jezzeen* our tents were found ready pitched in a grove of noble walnut-trees, with the brook *Zaid* running among them; near alongside was a Maronite convent, with a bridge.

The muleteers having left us in the morning, lost their way, and had taken the more precipitous road by *Dair Mushmushi*.

Here the people behaved with great hospitality to us.

The night was very cold, and in the morning the water for washing felt like ice. The position of our encampment, as perceived by daylight, was so low between hills that the sun could not reach us till the day should be considerably advanced, yet we were at a very high altitude. Pity that we had no aneroid barometer with us to ascertain the amount of our elevation above the sea. The poplar-trees and walnut-trees, with fruit trees of various kinds, showed we were in a totally different region from that of Jerusalem.

Jezzeen is almost exclusively a Christian village, with a Greek Catholic church, besides two Maronite churches, and the small convent mentioned above.

There were clergy walking about; the people cleanly and well clothed, the children modestly behaved, and even when rendering a service, not asking for bakhsheesh.

At the time of our leaving, a party of women were wailing over a dead body under a tree.

The scene gradually became more romantic; and we soon came to a village, if such it may be denominated, where the only dwellings are dispersed among vineyards. These vineyards were, at that autumn season, becoming of a brown and golden tint.

After traversing the wondrous chaos referred to in the former journey, we passed through the villages of *Cuf'r Hooneh* and *Deheedeh*, adjoining each other; where there was abundance of water, and oleander bushes fringing the streamlets, with poplar and maple trees.

The rest of the journey had no remarkable difference from that of 1849, except that on the brow of the great descent to the plain, between Lebanon and the Anti-Lebanon, we rested beneath an olive-tree entwined with honeysuckle, enraptured with the magnificence of the scene, which would

Across the Lebanon. 379

require a Milton to portray it in words, or a Martin in painting. I observed that the prevailing tints of the whole great prospect were of russet and ochreous colours.

Crossed the bridge, charmed with the beauteous verdure and freshening rapid stream of the Leontes river; and when arrived at Hhasbeya, repaired to the house of the native Protestant pastor, (Mr John Wartabed,) till a house could be prepared for us.

Next morning some deputations of the religious sects of the town called upon me; also the Ameer Saad ed Deen and his five sons in rich dresses; and lastly, an old Druse who had distinguished himself as a friend of the Protestant movement. Among all these, my visit there had a beneficial effect upon the existence and progress of native Protestantism. In the Lebanon the Druses have always favoured the missionaries, their schools and their chapels, while the native Christian communities, under the direction of their clergy, have naturally opposed them by every possible means of the direst persecution. In proper time and place I may hereafter have more to say respecting this visit to Hhasbeya.

In the afternoon, Mr Wartabed and the Khoja Bashi, (representative member in the town-council,) of the Protestants, named Naseef er Reis, rode with us to the source of the Hhasbâni river, which ought to be regarded as the origin of the Jordan, even though Banias lower down has been for ages recognised as such. We saw the bubbles at their earliest birth issue from the ground, and in a few yards this becomes a flowing stream. Higher above this spot the bed of a torrent brings down water in rainy seasons, adding to the springs of the Hhasbâni, but this not being permanent, cannot fairly be counted as having part or lot in the Jordan.

The ladies sat down to take sketches, and in haste I pencilled down in short-hand—

> O Jordan, dear Jordan, the feelings that throng
> And press on the heart must awaken to song,
> When the bubbles from pebbles break forth into view
> As clear as the spangles of morn's early dew.
>
> 'Mid the poplars that rising surpass other trees,
> And twinkle as moved by the scarce mountain breeze,
> And the wild oleander in rose-colour'd bloom,
> With trill of the linnet, and shrubs of perfume.
>
> I have drunk from each source that advances a claim
> To share with our Jordan its time-honour'd name;
> Here now at Hhasbeya—and the old site of Dan;
> Or the gush that escapes from the grotto of Pan.
>
> How oft on far banks of its tortuous course,
> In the scenes of repose or of cataract force,
> Where the bulbul, 'mid willows and tamarisk shades,
> Still warbles——

"Now, ladies, the horses are ready, and we have further to go," broke in upon the muse of Lebanon. The day's work had to be finished, and time was short; so we rode away to the bitumen pits in the neighbourhood of Cocaba. These are not worked in warm weather, for the people are afraid of the possible effects of their gas generated under a hot sun. One of the pits is seventy ells, or cubits, deep, and the bitumen is reached through a crust of chalky soil. The property is a government monopoly, rented by natives, and the business is lazily and irregularly carried on; therefore, sometimes the success is greater than at others. We found two men living in a tent as guardians of the place, who were very civil to us, and permitted us to carry away some specimens. These were all of a very soft consistency; but at the bitumen works at four hours north of Hhasbeya, the mineral is of a still softer description, almost liquid.

Next morning, the Kâdi paid us a visit, accompanied by a merchant of Damascus, a correspondent of an English house in India for indigo.

On Sunday we attended divine service at the native Protestant church, which the people call the English church, and in virtue thereof have set up a bell above it; because, although the mission is carried on by American money and under the direction of American agents, the American consuls are forbidden by their home-government from taking any steps in behalf of their undertakings; and thus, but for the protection given them by Mr Wood, British consul of Damascus, and his consular friends at Bayroot, the American Mission, with all their schools and printing-presses, would, upon all human calculation, have been crushed long ago.

In conformity with Oriental usage, the congregation was divided according to the sexes. In the old Eastern churches the women are placed in a gallery above the men, but here the equality of the sexes was maintained by their occupying the same floor, while separated from each other by a wall built rather higher than the usual stature of a man; the pulpit being equally visible from each division. A large jar of water stood in the corner within the door, to which the men repaired occasionally, as they felt thirsty. There were no chairs or benches, except such as were brought from the house for our party, the congregation were sitting on their heels, in which posture they sang the hymns, and remained so during the prayer, only covering the face with the right hand; a few men, however, stood up.

The singing (Arabic) was good, of course all in unison. The first hymn was to the tune of our "Old Hundredth," the chapters read by the minister were Ezek. xviii. and Rom. iii., and the text of the sermon was Ps. lxxxix. 14, "Justice and judgment are the habitation of thy throne: mercy and truth shall go before thy face." The style of language in the sermon was that of good Arabic, but of simple, unpretending character, without admixture of foreign words or phrases: this was insured by the circumstance of the minister being a

Across the Lebanon. 383

native of the country, though originally belonging to the Armenian Church.

At the afternoon service the chapters read were Num. xxiii. and Heb. xiii. The text for the sermon was Heb. xiii. 8, "Jesus Christ, the same yesterday, to-day, and for ever," and the hymn was sung to a sweet plaintive air of American origin.

Afterwards, that is after sunset, we spent some hours with the pastor's family, who all understood English well. Mr Wartabed played the flute to the hymn-singing, and his sister's voice was clear as a flageolet. The evening was one of comfort and refreshment on both sides; it was one of a Sabbath, "a delight, the holy of the Lord, honourable," (Isa. lviii. 13.)

The poor Protestants have not always been in such satisfactory circumstances. Their principal man had narratives to relate of chains and imprisonment endured in past times from the present Ameer, whose policy was now in their favour.

Next morning we left Hhasbeya, and I have not been there since. Little could it be foreseen that in five years afterwards one indiscriminate butchery would be made of the Ameer and his son, notwithstanding their high descent of family and profession of Islam, together with all the Christians of whatever sect in the town, driven like sheep within the walls of his palace—a deed of treachery unexampled even in that period of bloody Turkish treachery. Since then my lady companions are both in their graves, the one at Jerusalem, the other at Bayroot, let me rather say in "a better country," while I am left alone to narrate this in the distant security of England.

On our way towards Banias we met a party of Druses returning from a small lake beyond Hhooleh, carrying leeches in earthen jars and cotton bags upon asses, they themselves walking. A green hill on our right was said to be frequented by wild boars—all the rest of our scenery was bare and stoney.

A weli was a conspicuous object at some distance to the south, and near to the Lake Hhoolch, which the Moslems name after "Judah the son of Jacob." One of the Hhasbeya Protestants, who was with us, quoted in his native Arabic "The sceptre shall not depart from Judah," &c.

At Tell el Kâdi we reposed beneath the great tree near the gush of its branch of the Jordan, the same tree (evergreen oak) as afforded us shelter in 1849. Both this spring of the river and that of Banias are far more striking objects than the humble source of the Hhasbâni, into which stream they run as affluents, making up the Jordan.

It was a beautiful evening of mellow sunlight, and the scene most peaceful at the foot of Hermon.

On nearing Banias we were met by the son of the shaikh of the village, sent out to invite us. It was harvest time of the Simsim, (Sesamé,) and the produce was very abundant; sheaves of it were piled up into large stacks, and the length of the plant in stalk exceeded all I had ever seen before, —a natural effect of growing on these well-watered plains.

There were also my old friends the myrtles scattered about among the other trees.

At Banias our attendants had pitched the tents, to our disgust, near the village, and with the stench of carrion not far off; much better places might have been taken, but this was selected probably in consequence of the invitation from the shaikh. Our short remainder of twilight was employed in viewing the inscriptions and the grotto of Pan.

Next morning I was making fresh transcriptions of the Greek votive dedications before the sun was up, so as to get them as accurately as possible without sunshine and shadows. Then the same once more after breakfast, with the sun full upon them. These, together with the copies taken in 1849 by afternoon sunlight, and consequently the shadows thrown in the reverse direction, ought to ensure for me a correct delineation, saving and except those letters that are defaced by the action of weather during fifteen centuries, or across which small cracks have been made by the same cause.

The shaikh came to transact some business of consequence to him. Before noon we resumed our journey; going due west through the Sesamé harvest and the myrtle trees to Tell el Kâdi; straight across the plain through marshes, frequent small streams, and large fields of rice, which they said would be fit for reaping in twenty days more, that is, by the end of October.

Crossed the Ghujar bridge, but did not as before turn off to Safed; our object now was to reach Tibneen in the Belâd Beshârah, and therefore we kept on due west, ascending up to the great crusading castle and the village of *Huneen*, from which the look back upon Jebel esh Shaikh (Hermon) was indescribably grand.

A little farther on, a glimpse was caught of the Mediterranean Sea! the mountain breeze most delightful. Rested by the roadside for luncheon; came to the village of *Hhooleh*, thence into lower valleys of green woods, often with scarce room to pass ourselves, our horses, and the luggage between branches of trees for some successive hours. Then under the village of *Jahhârah*, where were charcoal burners working at their kilns.

The scene opened into verdant glades, alternated with woodland; the breathing most pure as exhaled from trees upon firm dry ground, contrasted with the noxious vapours from the marshes in the early morning.

Flocks and shepherds appeared, and there was the sound of the axe busy in the woods; not the ringing sound of the bright large English axe, this being wanted in the stroke of the petty Oriental tools.

As evening drew on, and broad shadows fell from

green hills across our way, Tibneen Castle came nobly into view, and there a goodly reception awaited us. A strange medley of splendour, with fleas and dust, obtained throughout the establishment, and our ladies visited those of the Hhareem, concerning whom they brought back no agreeable report.

We remained over two nights at Tibneen; the latter of which was, throughout its whole duration, one of furious storm, rattling the wooden lattices that served for windows; a storm not uncommon in the East, when an adverse wind meets and drives back a strong shirocco. At daybreak the first sound of the morning was that of a large trained hawk near the window, chained to his perch, and screaming out his delight in the bluster of the tempest. Mount Hermon appeared, not in his summer glow, but in solemn majesty, defying the clouds and the winds that raged in vain against his solid substance.

Our progress was thence towards Safed, which, however, we did not reach in less than eleven hours and a half, instead of six, because of our circuit made to see the antiquities of Kadis and Cuf'r Bera'am.

Turning off before Bint el Jebail, we came to *'Ain Atha*, and next to *Aiturân*. At Kadis (Kedesh Naphtali) I found that much of the principal and beautiful temple had been lately despoiled by our late host of Tibneen ('Ali Bek) for the ornamentation of his Hhareem or women's apartments, and balconies or galleries. Then to *Yaroon,* near which was still the ponderous sarcophagus upon a platform in the open country, and likely to stay there for ages to come. It is too plain and devoid of ornament or inscription for antiquarians from Europe to covet it, and to remove it for no particular use would demand too much exertion from the natives of the country. My groom, however, thought it might be useful as a depository of barley in the stable!

We overtook a party of Safed people returning from the weekly market at Bint el Jebail.

At Cuf'r Bera'am we inspected the ancient buildings now bearing Hebrew inscriptions, and I was more than ever convinced in my own mind, that neither these nor any edifices at Kadis have any relation to the Jewish people, in their origin or intention. The Hebrew writing is of inferior style, and very modern character, far, far unequal to the beauty of the architecture; besides having evident traces of animal figures which have been hastily chiselled off.

The sun set, and a bad road had to be traversed in order to reach our destination at Safed.

PART III.

In my two journeys just described, the route was over the southern part of the long Lebanon range, not only on the main ridge, but crossing some of the innumerable spurs thrown out towards the sea. This time, however, we have to deal with a more northerly and higher region; and it is because of its being in a different direction from those of 1849 and 1855 that I have not observed the consecutive order of date—this was in 1853. We shall start from the coast, where the most projecting and western spur subsides into Ras Bayroot, and the climbing begins almost immediately after leaving deep yellow sands and the pine forest.

The object was to reach Mokhtârah, perched high in the heart of the Shoof or central ridge of Lebanon, like an eyrie, as it was then, for the princely house of Jonblât. Mokhtârah lies S.-E. from Bayroot, and to arrive there we had to cross the intervening spurs, climbing as we went.

The town of Dair el Kamar and the palace of Beteddeen, formerly the headquarters of the house of Shehâb, lay upon the road. The remainder of the journey after Mokhtârah consisted in a rapid descent to Sidon, the great port in antiquity for Damascus, Phœnicia, and the Lebanon.

This tour comprised the finest range of the territory occupied by the Druse nation.

1853. *July.*—From Bayroot, with its bewitching scenery and its gorgeous colouring of mountains and the sea, we went to '*Abeih*, the best known of the American missionary stations in the Lebanon.

Through the woods of pines, with their reviving fragrance, and through *El Hadeth*, an entirely Christian village, where the bell of the Maronite convent was ringing as we passed, we came to *Shuwaifât*, and rose still higher towards the mountain pines and the breezes so desirable in Syria in the month of July, leaving below the olive in abundance, the mulberry and the fig-trees.

Beside the fountain called '*Ain Besâba* was a pottery factory. The nature of the rocks around was soft sandstone; a gigantic pear-tree stood conspicuous among the excellent cultivation of the neighbourhood; higher still, between straight tall pines and wild holly-oaks, our road curved round and round the hills.

We overtook a company of Christians, the women riding and the men walking—this circumstance alone would show they were not Mohammedans. The two parties had to pass each other with much caution, as the path was narrow and the precipice deep below.

At '*Ain 'Anoob*, where a copious supply of water issues from three spouts, the fountain has on each side the representation of a chained lion, sculptured in stone. One's first impression would be that this were a relic of the Genoese or Venetian crusaders; but these figures, whatever their meaning or origin, are not infrequent upon fountains about the Lebanon, even when only rustically daubed in red ochre; and it has not been often noticed that there are similar lions facing each other, only without the chains, one on each side of St Stephen's Gate at Jerusalem. Some of the women at the fountains wore the horns on their head, the fashion for which is gradually passing away. The terraces on the hills were in the highest state of cultivation, and gave abundant promise of fruit for the coming season; the sun was near setting, the rooks cawing overhead, and we saw two little girls each bring a lamb to the fountain to drink and then proceed to wash them.

Sidi Ahhmad, a Druse 'Akal, with, of course, a white turban, undertook to be our guide as far as 'Abeih.

Fresh air to breathe! how different from the oppressive heat of Bayroot! We all drank of every spring by the way, and by consequence lifted up the drooping head, (Ps. cx. 7,) thinking each fountain colder than that before it.

The most rugged portion of the road was between *'Ain 'Anoob* and *'Ainab*, and zigzag were the worn tracks of the way. Sometimes a musical jingle of bells announced the coming of travellers in front, who were however invisible till they pounced upon us from between two pinnacles of rocks. On the steepest ascents it was necessary to halt and await the coming up of our baggage mules.

From mountain heights it is often difficult to distinguish the blue expanse of the Mediterranean Sea from the similar blue expanse of the sky, until the actual moment of sunset, when the bright orb becoming suddenly flattened on its lower curve reveals the exact horizon line ; and so it was this evening.

Wearied with the climbing position of the saddle, hour after hour, I passed *'Ain Kesoor* on foot, the 'Akal leading the horse. This was shortly before 'Abeih, but there I rode up to the mansion of Kasim Bek, the local governor, to ask hospitality; it was dark night, and Saturday. My intention was to spend the Sunday in a Christian manner among the American missionaries. The journey had been one of five hours and a half from Bayroot.

We were heartily received into a fine old house, in which were shaikhs and chiefs of sundry grades seated on the divân with the host, and immediately the means for washing were brought by the domestics with great respect. A good supper was prepared, the Bek eating with us, to my surprise, but I afterwards learned that this is not uncommon with a non-'Akal Druse, as he was.

Sunday.—Quiet morning. Bell of the Capuchin Convent almost adjoining the house. From the windows there is a fine prospect of Bayroot and the coast-outline.

After breakfast I went up to the chapel of the American missionaries, and entered just as the Arabic service was about to commence—Dr de Forest in the pulpit; and his sermon was preached with fluency of language equal to that of a native. The subject was taken from 1 Cor. i. 12, 13, concerning those who named themselves followers of Paul or of Apollos. The women were screened off from the men in the congregation.

After service Dr de Forest welcomed me, and led me up the hill to the mission-house, where I found my old friend, Dr Eli Smith, who was unwell, and about to leave them on the morrow for his home at B'hamdoon. With Mrs de Forest there was a young lady just arrived from the United States to be a teacher in the school.

The residence is a good one; with the girls' school on the ground plan, and the dwelling apartments above. The scenery and prospect equal all that the highest imagination could conceive of the Lebanon. Over the sea, the island of Cyprus can occasionally be distinguished from the terrace, that is to say, three peaks of a mountain show themselves at sunset, particularly if the wind be in the north, in the month of May or the beginning of June. This view, therefore, gives the outskirts of "the isles of Chittim," as seen from the Holy Land, (Num. xxiv. 24, and Jer. ii. 10.)

After dinner we all went together to the English service in the chapel. Mr Colquhoun preached a simple but impressive sermon from John x. 4; which text he illustrated by an incident that he had witnessed in a recent journey northwards.

A shepherd with a flock arrived at a river of some impetuosity. He entered it first, trying the depths with his staff, got over at the best place, and then with his voice called over the sheep to him. From which the following points were deduced:—

1. That the shepherd led the way, and the flock waited for his call.

2. That the sheep followed when he called, although not all of them at the precise ford he had discovered. Some of them trusted to their own judgment, and these generally got out of their depths for a time. His way was certainly the best one.

3. That as the shepherd stood on the opposite bank, he showed no symptoms of uneasiness, for he was confident that every one of the flock would get safely across.

4. That the sheep in passing over used each his own efforts to get across, apparently just as much as if there were no one present to help; although no doubt the presence of the shepherd had a good effect upon their exertions. It is beyond our reach to explain the metaphysical mystery of this.

5. The shepherd in first crossing the stream

himself tested the *force* of the stream. Each individual creature had to do the same; but those who followed the closest upon his track had an easy passage, while those who tried new ways for themselves were some of them swept down the current for a distance, and had to make hard struggles to rejoin their companions and to reach the beloved shepherd.

6. All got safely over, for they were his sheep; he knew them all by name; he had tried the way before them and shown it; he then called them to himself.

Of course each of these points was made use of as personally applicable to the hearers. The sermon did me much good from its quiet and truthful character.

At this service, it is needless to observe, that there was no separation of sexes in the congregation. The girls of the school (who are all taught English) were there placed by themselves, and prettily dressed, wearing the Oriental *izâr*, (or large white veil,) with flowered borders, a novelty to us.

Returning to the mission-house, the late afternoon and the time of sunset and twilight were spent in rational conversation of Christian character. And such was our Sabbath-day of devotion and repose.

How glorious were the colours spread over the vast extent of mountain and sea, modified by length of shadows as the sun declined! Oh how deep are such beauties and the perception of their value laid in the innermost recesses of our soul's nature, only to be completely gratified in the eternity to come. Here, below, we have gorgeous tints differing in succession, even after actual sunset, to be followed by a delicate after-glow, which again gives place to the splendour of night. And as in earth, so in heaven, with the exception of night; for surely there will be alternations of beauteous scenes above; surely there will be developments and variety in light, colour, music, harmony, and the rest of those "pleasures for evermore," which are everywhere emanations from the direct love of "Him who first loved us,"—His gifts, who even here bestows prismatic hues upon icebergs in the arctic circle, and a rosy flush to the peaks of Jebel Sanneen in the Lebanon.

Monday.—Letters were brought at a late hour last night in four hours from Bayroot, giving recent intelligence from our fleet—all political affairs going on successfully.

Everybody speaks well of our host the governor, and his family. He is a studious man, and has acquired from the Americans a good deal of history and general knowledge; his youngest brother attends the natural-history class of the mission-school. He is a relative of the famous Abu Neked, and his wife (Druses have but one wife each) is of the Jonblât family. The ancestral mansion he inhabits was built by one of the ancient race called the T'noohh, who flourished there from the 10th to the 17th century, and artists had been brought for the purpose from Constantinople; the symmetry of the masonry is admirable, and consequently the shadows formed from it are particularly straight and sharp in outline.

The village contains specimens of every form of religion to be found throughout the Lebanon; each sect, however, keeps somewhat apart from the rest, which practice being common in the mountain, may account for the villages appearing to a stranger to consist of separate pieces not quite joined together.

Some women still wear horns, although the Christian clergy set themselves strongly against these ornaments; some even refusing the Communion-Sacrament to those who persist in retaining that heathenish emblem derived from ancient mythology.

Among the Druse men, the 'Akâl are not so marked in their difference of costume from the Juhâl as formerly, except in the extreme cleanliness and careful plaiting of the white turban. My host, notwithstanding the antiquity of his family and his studious character, is not one of the initiated, he is but a Jâhel, yet he probably serves his people best in that capacity, as he is thereby enabled to hold government employments.

From his windows we could see on the south side of Ras Bayroot severa small vessels engaged in sponge-fishing; the crews of these are generally Greeks from the islands: yesterday with the telescope we had a good view of the mail-steamer arriving.

We went to take leave of the American friends, who showed us some excellent specimens of English writing, and of drawing from the girls' school.

Returning to the Druse friends, I visited Seleem, a brother of the Bek. On hearing that we were proceeding to Mokhtârah, Naamân, (brother of Saïd Bek Jonblât,) who has retired from worldly affairs, and become a devout 'Akal, requested one of my party to ask Saïd to send him some orange-flower water. I have no doubt that this message (φωνᾶντα συνέτοισιν) covered some political meaning.

The house of Seleem was simplicity and neatness in the extreme, the only ornamentation being that of rich robes, pistols, swords, and the silver decorations of horses, suspended on pegs round the principal apartment; all thoroughly Oriental of olden time.

The Christian secretary of the Bek attended us to *Cuf'r Natta* on a fine Jilfi mare, where he got for us a pedestrian guide to Dair el Kamar. A very deep valley lay before us, into which we had to descend, lounging leftwards, and then to mount the opposite hill, returning rightwards, to an elevation higher than that of Cuf'r Natta. Down we went by zigzags through groves of pine that were stirred gently on their tops by the mountain breeze,

Across the Lebanon. 399

and there was plenty of wild myrtle on the ground; we frequently met with specimens of iron ore, and pink or yellow metallic streaks in the rocks, to the river Suffâr, being the upper part of the river that is called Damoor upon the sea-coast. This is crossed by the bridge *Jisr'el Kâdi,* (so named from an ameer of the house of T'noohh, surnamed the Kâdi, or Judge, from his legal acquirements, and who erected the bridge in old times,) near which the limestone rock of the water-bed is worn into other channels by the occasional escapements of winter torrents. There are mills adjoining.

We all rested in a coffee-station at the end of the bridge. Several parties of muleteers had halted there at the same time. By the little fireside a large hawk was perched, and the owner of the place had his apparatus for shoemaking in the middle of the room.

Flowering oleander and fruit trees imparted liveliness to the scene outside, our several parties in variegated costumes adding not a little to the same.

Crossing the bridge, (which is level, and has no side parapets,) we commenced the great ascent; the hill-side was largely planted with sherabeen, (sprouts,) of a kind of cedar, not the real cedar of Lebanon. At a spring half way up we found a poor Turkish infantry soldier resting all alone, he was a pitiable object in a district so unfriendly to him.

What a different country would Palestine or all Syria be were it like the Lebanon, industriously cultivated inch by inch! How different would the Lebanon be were this industry and its produce never interrupted by intestine warfare!

Higher still we saw a train of shaikhs on horseback, attended by men on foot, coming in our direction longitudinally on the opposite hill from a remote village.

All the distance, I think, from Jis'r el Kâdi forwards, notwithstanding the steep nature of the country, was over a paved or made road. There is no such a thing in the south; here, however, the desolation of Turkish rule is but little known, and the people are not only industrious, but a fine muscular race.

We overtook small groups of village people who had, it seems, gone out to meet the important riding party lately seen by us. Suddenly, at a turn of the road, the cheerful town of Dair el Kamar opened out to view, with the hills and palaces of Beteddeen behind. This was at three hours from 'Abeih, exclusive of the hour's rest at the bridge.

The town appeared to be well built, better than many a European town, notwithstanding the destruction arising from recent warfare, and the people cleanly; it was, however, no proof of the latter quality that I saw a pig being fed at a house-door as we passed along.

We alighted at the best Arab house I had ever entered, namely, that of the influential Meshâkah family. After some repose the host took me and the friends who had accompanied me from Soor and Saida to look about the town. Through streets and bazaars we came to a large open place occupied by silk weavers at work, among whom was the father of Faris, the Arabic teacher in the Protestant school at Jerusalem, he having been instructed by the Americans at 'Abeih, and whose sister I had seen there the day preceding. The silk stuffs of the town maintain a respectable rivalry with those of Damascus.

Turkish soldiers were dawdling about the streets.

We called at some Christian houses, in one of which (very handsome, with a garden) the recesses in the wall of one side of the divân room, containing bedding as usual in the East, were screened by a wide curtain of white muslin spangled with gold. Upon the other sides of the room were rude fresco paintings. Opposite the door on entering was the Virgin and Child; over the door was a dove with an olive branch; and the remaining side was embellished by the picture of a fine water-melon, with a slice cut off and lying at its side, the knife still upright in the melon, and an angel flying above it, blowing a trumpet!

The town is romantically situated upon successive levels of terraces in the hill, and environed by orchards of fruit. As evening approached, the opposite hill was suffused in a glow of pink, followed by purple light, and the Ramadân gun was fired from Beteddeen when the sun's orb dropped upon the horizon. Suddenly the hills exchanged their warm colours for a cold gray, in harmony with the gloaming or evening twilight.

The population of Dair el Kamar at that time numbered 700 full-grown men of Maronites, 220 of Greek Catholics, 150 of Druses, with a few Moslems and Jews—each of the sects living apart from the rest. The silk manufacture was more extensive than that of Saida, and a constant communication was kept up with Damascus, which is at twenty hours' distance. The Christians are far more hardy than their fellow-Christians the Maronites are in their special district to the north. The whole population is industrious, and the Druses maintain their characteristic steadfastness of purpose, secrecy, and union among themselves.

The house in which I was so hospitably received had been almost entirely destroyed in the war of 1841; and its proprietor (brother of the two brothers now its owners) shot dead in his own court, by persons who owed him money, namely, the Druse party of Abu Neked, two hundred of whom had for a fortnight lived at free quarters there.

The two brothers who were my hosts are Christians of the Greek Catholic sect, named Gabriel and Raphael. A third surviving brother is the talented Protestant controversialist residing in Damascus, and practising medicine as learned from the Americans. The one who was shot by the Druses was Andrew; the eldest of all is Ibrahim, settled in Bayroot, and his son named Khaleel is dragoman of the English consulate there—it was he who furnished us with the introduction to this house in Dair el Kamar.

How curious is the domestic life of these Oriental families. Eating takes place in the principal room, with a throng of women and children passing heedlessly about, or visitors entering as they please. Among these, during the dinner time, came in a Jew speaking Jewish-German. He was a dyer, who had known me at Jerusalem, and conversed with remarkable self-possession : it seemed as if the mountain air, and absence from the Rabbis of Jerusalem, had made a man of him. In attendance on the meal was an ancient woman-servant of the family, very wrinkled, but wearing the tantoor or horn on her head.

On retiring from the table, if we may use that expression as applicable to an Oriental dinner, there came in the Greek Catholic Bishop of Saida, and several heads of houses of the Maronites, on visits of ceremony.

The fatigue of the day was closed, and rewarded by a night of sleep upon a bed of down and crimson silk, under a covering of the same.

In the morning our journey was resumed; but

before quitting this interesting town, I cannot forbear quoting Dr Porter's admirable description of Dair el Kamar, from Murray's "Handbook for Syria and Palestine," part ii. page 413 :—

"Deir el Kamr is a picturesque mountain village, or rather town, of some 8000 inhabitants, whose houses are built along a steep, rocky hill-side. A sublime glen runs beneath it, and on the opposite side, on a projecting ledge, stands the palace of Bteddîn. Both the banks, as well as the slopes above them, are covered with terraces, supporting soil on which a well-earned harvest waves in early summer, amid rows of mulberries and olives and straggling vines. Industry has here triumphed over apparent impossibilities, having converted naked rocky declivities into a paradise. In Palestine we have passed through vast plains of the richest soil all waste and desolate—here we see the mountain's rugged side clothed with soil not its own, and watered by a thousand rills led captive from fountains far away. Every spot on which a handful of soil can rest, every cranny to which a vine can cling, every ledge on which a mulberry can stand, is occupied. The people too, now nearly all Christians, have a thrifty well-to-do look, and the children, thanks to the energy of the American missionaries, are well taught."

This was in 1857, and the description corresponds to what I witnessed in 1853; but, alas! how great a change ensued in 1860. I must refrain, however, from enlarging upon the melancholy tragedy that occurred there during the insurrection of that memorable year.

First we went to Beteddeen, and witnessed the sad spectacle of the Ameer Besheer's luxurious palace in a process of daily destruction by the Turkish soldiery, who occupied it as a barrack. Accounts had been read by me in Europe* of its size and costliness, but the description had not exceeded the reality.

The officer in command gave us permission to be guided over the palatial courts and chambers. We wandered through the Hhareem-rooms, and saw baths of marble and gilding, sculptured inscriptions in the passages, coloured mosaics in profusion on the floors, painted roofs, rich columns, brass gates, carved doors, marble fountains, and basins with gold fish. We entered the state reception room, and the old ameer's little business divân, in a balcony commanding a view of the approaches in every direction, of the meidân for equestrian practice, of the inner courts, of the gardens below, and of a cascade of water rolling over lofty cliffs, at the exact distance whence the sound came gently soothing the ear, and from that spot also was obtained a distant view of the Mediterranean; not omitting the advantage of witnessing

* Especially in a book probably little known, but published as "Memoirs of a Babylonian Princess. By (herself) Marie Therese Asmar," who was in London in 1845, and supported for a time by fashionable patronesses of romantic Orientalism.

every important movement that could be made in the streets of Dair el Kamar, across the deep valley.

Beteddeen had been a truly princely establishment, but now adds one more lesson to the many others of instability in human greatness. Fourteen years before, it was all in its glory—the courts were thronged with Druse and Maronite chiefs arrayed in cloth of gold, with soldiers, with secretaries, with flatterers and suppliants; whereas now, before our eyes, the dirty canaille of Turkish soldiers were tearing up marble squares of pavement to chuck about for sport, doors were plucked down and burned, even the lightning-rods were demolished, and every species of devastation practised for passing away their idle time.

I shall not here describe the political movements that led to this great reverse of fortune, or to the present condition of the family of Shehab.

The mountains around were still in careful cultivation, chiefly with the vine and olive; and the aqueduct still brings water from the springs of Suffâr at several miles' distance, and this it is which, after supplying the palace, forms the cascade above described, and afterwards turns two mills.

At short distances are smaller palaces, erected also by this powerful ameer for his mother and his married sons; but the same fate has overtaken them all—Turkish devastation.

Before leaving the place, I visited the tomb of the ameer's mother and that of his principal wife, who was a Christian; they are near the house, and surrounded by five cypresses.

Took the road towards Mokhtârah, the seat of the rival chief, the Druse Jonblât. For some distance after Beteddeen the roads have been carefully constructed, over an unusually level plateau for the Lebanon; but an enormous ridge of mountain stands conspicuous in the N.-E. This is the highest part of the Shoof, near the sources of the river *Barook*, so named from being the first place where the Arab camels *knelt* on arriving in the Lebanon in A.D. 821. The sad spectacle of villages and good farm-houses desolate and blackened by fire, frequently met the view; for this open tract, called the *Sumkanîyeh*, has frequently been a scene of conflict between the leading factions; it was especially the ground of the considerable battle of the Ameer Besheer and the Jonblatîyeh in 1825. At length, from the commencement of a descent, we saw Mokhtârah upon an opposite hill, commanding the view of our approach—a great advantage in times of warfare. Our road lay downwards by odd turns and twists, and over a precipice to the river Barook, with its romantic banks and fruit-trees peering between overhanging rocks.

On our arrival, the great man, Said Bek

Jonblat,* came out with a train of 'Akâl councillors and a crowd of humbler retainers. He was a handsome man of about twenty-eight, and richly apparelled. Beneath a large abai or cloak of black Cashmere, with Indian patterns embroidered about the collar and skirts, he wore a long gombaz of very dark green silk embossed with tambour work; his sash was of the plainest purple silk, and his sidrîyeh or vest was of entire cloth of gold with gold filigree buttons: on the head a plain tarboosh, and in his hand sometimes a cane ornamented with ivory or a rosary of sandal-wood. His gold watch and chain were in the best European taste.

I need not here expatiate on the sumptuous reception afforded us; it may be enough to say, that having some hours to spare before sunset—the universal time for dinner in the East—we walked about, and the Bek shewed me the yet unrepaired damages, inflicted in his father's time, at the hands of the victorious Ameer Besheer's faction, on that palace and paradise which his father Besheer had created there, thus teaching the Shehâb Ameer how to build its rival of Beteddeen,—and the limpid stream brought from the high sources of the Barook to supply cascades and fountains for the marble courts, which the other also imitated in bringing down the Suffâr to his place. We sat be-

* The events of 1860-61 led to a tragical termination of the career of this young chieftain.

side those streams and cascades, so grateful at that season of the year, conversing about the Arab factions of Kaisi and Yemeni, or the Jonblât and Yesbeck parties of the Druses, or his own early years spent in exile either in the Hauran or with Mohammed 'Ali in Egypt,—but not a word about actual circumstances of the Lebanon, or about his plans for restoring the palace to more than its former splendour, which he afterwards carried out. This was all very agreeable, but a curious fit of policy assumed at the time rendered my host to some degree apparently inhospitable to us Christians.

It is well known that the Druse religion allows its votaries to profess outwardly the forms of any other religion according to place and circumstances. The Bek was now adopting Moslem observances; consequently, it being the month of Ramadân, we could have nothing to eat till after sunset. What could have been his reason for this temporary disguisement I have never been able to discover. Even the adân was cried on the roof of his house, summoning people to prayer in the canonical formula of the Moslems, and Saïd Bek, with his councillors, retired to a shed for devotional exercises, as their prayers may be appropriately termed; and I remarked that at every rising attitude he was lifted reverently by the hands and elbows, by his attendants,—an assistance which no true Mohammedan of any rank, that I had ever met with, would have tolerated.

At length the sunlight ceased to gild the lofty peaks above us, and pipes, sherbet, and ice were served up as a preparation for the coming dinner.

There is in front of the house a square reservoir of water, with a current flowing in and out of it; this is bordered by large cypress-trees, and in a corner near the house wall grows a large acacia-tree, the light-green colour and drooping foliage of which gave somewhat of an Indian appearance to the scene.

Lamps were then lit beneath an arcade, and near the water a huge cresset was filled with resinous pine splinters, and the light of its burning flickered fantastically over the pool, the house, and the trees.

Next came the dinner, late for the appetites of us travellers, and tedious in its duration—with music outside the open windows.

After the meal the Bek withdrew to the corner of his divân for transaction of business with his people, as the Moslems do at that season. His part of the affairs consisted in endorsing a word or two upon the petitions or addresses that were produced by the secretaries—these were written on small rolls of paper like tiny cigarettes, pinched at one end. How very un-European to carry on business in so few words, either written or spoken!

Saïd Bek was a man of few words in such transactions, but what he did say seemed always to hit exactly the point intended; and the wave of his finger was sufficient to summon a number of men to receive his commands. He was evidently a person of a different stamp from the coarse leaders of Lebanon factions, the Abu Neked, the Shibli el 'Ariân, and such like; he is proud of his family antiquity, refined in dress and manners, and has always, like the rest of the Druses, courted the favour of the English nation.

On the entrance of his son, named Nejib, probably four or five years old, all the Akâl councillors and military officers rose to receive him.

In the morning we took our departure, when Saïd Bek accompanied us as far as the Meidân, and a profusion of Druse compliments filled up the leave-taking.

We now passed for some hours along the river side, through the utmost loveliness of Lebanon scenery. Among other trees that lined its banks, or adorned the precipitous cliffs, or followed the rising and falling road, were noble specimens of platanus (plane) and lofty zanzalacht, (the peepul of India;) crystal rills tumbled down the rocks, as if sparkling alive with enjoyment; then the usual poplar, walnut, evergreen oak, and a large plantation of olive: the river sometimes smiled with the fringe of oleander. We halted for a time under a wide-branching platanus at the end of a bridge, between the masonry of which grew bunches of the caper plant, then in blossom of white and lilac, and at the piers of which grew straggling blackberry brambles and wild fig-trees in picturesque irregularity, while the water bubbled and gurgled over a pebbly bed or fragments of rock.

Peasantry passed us with ass-loads of wood for fuel, (camels being unknown in that region.) The same features continually repeated themselves as we advanced; large broken cliffs were overhanging us, and birds singing in the solitude; it need not be added that the sun was cloudless the whole day long.

Forward we went to the Convent of the Dair el Mokhallis, which we reached in four hours and a half from Mokhtârah, where we rested a few hours; then visited once more the house of Lady Hester Stanhope.

Thence descending to the sea beach, we crossed the river Awali, and looked back with regret to the heights of Lebanon. Just as the last gun of Ramadân was fired, (for it was the termination of that fast and the commencement of Beiram,) we galloped our horses into the sea-wave near the walls of Sidon, which they enjoyed as refreshing to their heated fetlocks, and we found a luxury in the breeze and in the rustling sound of the endless roll of wavelets upon the shelly beach.

How different were the temperature and the scenery from those of Mokhtârah in the early morning!

Even now in the nineteenth century one can

understand how it was that in ancient Bible times the peoples inhabiting those romantic districts were distinct from each other within a small space, having separate kings and alien interests, for here in the lapse of few hours I had traversed regions where the inhabitants differed greatly in religion, in manners, customs, dress, and physical aspect. The Maronite and the Druse of Lebanon; the Syrian and the Turk of Bayroot, Saida, and Soor; the Metawâli of the Phœnician district, no more resemble each other than if they were men or women of different nations, as indeed they are by derivation; each of these is but a fragment of antiquity, representing to us his several ancient race; yet all these fragments are united for the present by the slenderest of bonds, those of using one common language, the Arabic, and of an unwilling subjection to the Ottoman scymitar.

Alas! for the beautiful country thus parcelled out by peoples, who, cherishing ancient rivalries and modern blood-feuds, have, and can have no national life, or sentiment of patriotism.

XIII.

NORTH-WEST OF THE DEAD SEA.

IN December 1856, I met, by appointment, at Jericho the Rev. A. A. Isaacs, and my friend James Graham, who were going with photograhic apparatus to take views at the site called Wadi Gumrân, near 'Ain Feshkah, where a few years before M. de Saulcy, under the guidance of an ardent imagination, believed he had found extensive and cyclopean remains of the city Gomorrah, and had published an account of that interesting discovery.

It was on Christmas eve that we rose early by starlight, and had our cups of coffee in the open air, beside the *Kala'at er Reehha*, (Castle of Jericho,) while the tents were being struck and rolled up for returning to Jerusalem, where we were to meet them at night.

Only the artistic apparatus and a small canteen were to accompany us; but the muleteer for these was even more dilatory in his preparations than is usual with his professional brethren—and that is saying much; no doubt he entertained a dread of visiting the Dead Sea at points out of the beaten track for travellers; considerable time was also occupied in getting a stone out of the mule's shoe; then just as that was triumphantly effected, my mare happened to bolt off free into the wilderness; when she was recovered, it was ascertained that my cloak was lost from her back; during the search for this, the guide abandoned us, and it was with much difficulty that we hired one from Jericho.

At length we commenced the march, leaving the kawwâs to look for the cloak, (which, however, he did not succeed in recovering; it would be a prize for the thieves of the village, or even, if it should fall in their way, for one of the Bashi-bozuk,) and got to *'Ain Feshkah*, much in need of a real breakfast. There the water was found to be too brackish for use—as unpalatable, probably, as the water of 'Ain es Sultân was before being healed by the prophet Elisha; so we drank native wine instead of coffee, while seated among tall reeds of the marshy ground, and not pleased with the mephitic odour all around us.

Our photographers having ascertained the site for their researches by means of the guide, and by the indications furnished in the work of De Saulcy; they set themselves to work, during which they were frequently uttering ejaculations at the exaggerations of size and quantity made by my French friend. The cyclopean ruins seemed to us nothing but remnants of water-courses for irrigation of plantations, such as may be seen in the neighbourhood of Elisha's fountain, or heaps of boulders, &c., that had been rolled down from the adjacent cliffs by natural causes during a succession of ages.

Mr Isaacs has since published a book descriptive of this expedition, containing illustrations from his photographs taken on the spot. In this he has given the reasons for our differing from M. de Saulcy, and considering his theories unfounded.

At the end of a strip of beach, which the discoverer calls "the plain," the cliffs have a narrow crevasse, down which water rushes in the season when there is water to form a cascade. This is difficult to reach from "the plain," and very narrow; and it is what our Arabs called the Wadi Gumrân. In front of this opening is a hill with some ruins upon it; thither we mounted easily, and saw vestiges of some ancient fort with a cistern.

When all the observations were taken upon points considered necessary, we prepared to return home by way of Mar Saba, hardly expecting to arrive by daylight at Jerusalem. We were, however, desirous of spending Christmas day there rather than in the bleak wilderness.

On the way we fortunately got some camel's milk from a party passing near us. The weather was hot, but exceedingly clear. The Salt mountain of Sodom, (Khash'm Usdum,) showed itself well at the southern extremity of the lake, thirty miles distant; and from a raised level near its northern end we gained superb views of Mount Hermon (Jebel esh Shaikh) in the Anti-Lebanon, capped with snow. This was entirely unexpected and gratifying; but I could nowhere find a spot from which both Hermon and Sodom could be seen at once. Perhaps such a view may be had somewhere on the hills.

We turned aside through the *Wadi Dubber*, as the guide termed it, within a circuitous winding, out of which, at a spot called 'Ain Merubba', I had passed a night in the open air some years before.

Long, dreary, and tiresome was the journey; the two Bashi-bozuk men complained of it as much as we did. At sunset we came to a well with some water left in troughs near it, but not enough for all our horses, and we had no means of getting more out of the well. This was in a wide, treeless, trackless wilderness.

No one of our party felt quite sure of being on the true road, but we followed slight tracks in the general direction in which the convent lay; we guessed and went on. Occasionally we got sight of the summit of the Frank mountain or lost it again, according to the rise or fall of the ground. Conversation flagged; but at length we struck up a Christmas hymn to enliven us.

In the valley of Mar Saba we saw lights in the convent, but passed on. Saw an Arab encampment, with fire and lights glimmering, where the dogs came out to bark at us; another such in half an hour more; and a larger camp in another half-hour, where men were discussing matters with much vociferation in a cavern by a blazing fire; a scout called out, inquiring if we were friends or foes?

The night grew very cold, and I should have been glad had my cloak not been lost near Jericho. The temperature differed greatly from that of the Dead Sea—a keen wind was in keeping with the end of December. The stars were most brilliant: Venus richly lustrous; Sirius, dazzling; and the huge Orion showing to best advantage. The road was alternately rough in the valley, or over slippery ledges. At length, however, we got cheered by coming to known objects. Passed Beer Eyoob, (En Rogel,) and saw the battlemented walls of the Holy City sharply marked against the sky.

The key had been left by the authorities at the city gate, to allow of our admission; but the rusty lock required a long time for turning it, and the heavy hinges of the large gate moved very slowly, at least so it seemed in our impatience to reach home.

It is said above that I once spent a night at the Ain Merubba'—this was on the occasion of an attempt, which ended in failure, to reach 'Ain Jidi

North-West of the Dead Sea. 419

(En-gaddi) from the 'Ain Feshkah in the common way of travelling.*

Hhamdan, Shaikh of the Ta'amra, with about a dozen of his men, escorted me and one kawwâs in that direction. Instead of proceeding to Jericho or Elisha's fountain, we turned aside into the wildest of wildernesses for passing the night. Traversing the length of an extremely narrow ridge, something like the back of a knife, we descended to a great depth below; but the risk being judged too great for conveying the tent and bed over there by the mule, these were left spread upon the ground for the night under the canopy of heaven; while the men carried our food for us to make the evening meal. Crawling or sliding, and leading the horses gently, we got to the bottom, and then followed up a very narrow glen, winding in and out, and round about between extraordinary precipices rising to enormous heights, till all at once the men halted, shouted, and sang, and stripped themselves to bathe in small pools formed in holes of the rock by settlements of rain-water.

This was our halting-place, but the scene beggars all power of description. We were shut into a contracted glen by a maze of tortuous windings, between mountains of yellow marl on either side; but broken, rugged, naked of all vegetation,—referring one's imagination to the period when the

* Mr Tristram has since done this, but on foot, the rugged road being impassable in any other way.

earth was yet "without form and void," or to the subsiding of the deluge from which Noah was delivered.

Looking upwards to a great height we could just see the tops of the imprisoning hills gilded awhile by the setting sun, and a small space of blue making up the interval between the precipices. Those precipices were not, however, entirely yellow, but variegated with occasional red or somewhat of brown ochre. So fantastic in position or shape were the masses hurled or piled about, and the place so utterly removed "from humanity's reach," that it might be imagined suitable to mould the genius of Martin into the most extravagant conceptions of chaos, or to suggest the colouring of Turner without his indistinctness of outline.

The echoes of the men's voices and bursts of laughter (the latter so uncommon among Arabs) when splashing in the water, were reverberated from hill to hill and back again; but there were no wild birds among the rocks to scream in rejoinder as at Petra.

After a time a voice was heard from above, very high, (it is wonderful how far the human voice is carried in that pure atmosphere and in such a locality,) and on looking up I saw a dark speck against the sky waving his arms about. It was one of the Ta'amra asking if he should bring down my mattress. Consent was given, and, behold, down came tumbling from rock to rock the mattress and blanket tied up into a parcel; when approaching near us, it was taken up by the man who followed it, and carried on his back; and when still nearer to us it was carefully borne between two men. Thus I enjoyed the distinction above all the rest of having a mattress to lie upon; the shaikh had a couple of cloaks, the kawwâs had one, and the others were utterly without such luxurious accessories, and slept profoundly.

Our people called the place '*Ain Merubba*', (the square fountain.) I saw no fountain of any form, but there must have been one, for we had a supply of good water, and the designation "'Ain," or fountain, is one of too serious importance to be employed for any but its literal signification.

Very early in the morning we started afresh, and took the beach of the lake towards 'Ain Feshkah.

A great part of the day was spent in clambering our ponies over broken rocks of a succession of promontories, one following another, where it seemed that no creatures but goats could make way; the Arabs protesting all the while that the attempt was hopeless, and besides, that the distance even over better ground was too great for one day's march.

At length I relinquished the undertaking to reach 'Ain Jidi by that way, and for that year had no leisure from business to try it from other directions.

Hhamdan and I sat on a rock in his free open air dominion, discussing possibilities, and what 'Ain Jidi was like, as well as the " Ladder of Terâbeh," (see p. 334.) At length we rose and turned towards Jerusalem. I am not sure that I ever saw him again, for not long afterwards he was drowned in the Jordan while attempting to swim his horse through the stream at its highest, after assisting in a battle on the side of the Dĕab 'Adwân.

XIV.

SOBA.

ON the crest of a high hill two or three hours west from Jerusalem, stands the village of Soba, and it has long been imagined to be Modin, the birth-place and burial-place of the Maccabæan heroes; though I never heard any reason assigned for that identification, except the circumstance of the sea being visible from it, and therefore of its being visible from the sea, which was supposed to tally with the description given in 1 Macc. xiii., 27–30, of the monuments erected there,—" Simon also built a monument upon the sepulchre of his father and his brethren, and raised it aloft to the sight, with hewn stone behind and before. Moreover, he set up seven pyramids, one against another, for his father, and his mother, and his four brethren. And in these he made cunning devices, about the which he set great pillars, and upon the pillars he made all their armour for a perpetual memory; and by the armour ships carved, that they might be seen of all that sail on the sea. This is the sepulchre which he made at Modin, and it standeth yet unto this day."

I never was persuaded that the words implied that ships carved on pillars at Soba, could be distinguished from the sea, or even that the columns themselves were visible from ships off the coast; but only this, that the deliverers of their country from the intolerable yoke of the Syrians, having opened up communication with the Grecians and Romans, marine intercourse had become more frequent than before, a matter that the Maccabæan family were proud of; and therefore they had ships carved on the pillars, as might be observed by seafaring people who might go there; yet, whatever the words might signify, they could not prove that Modin was so far inland, and among the hills, as Soba.

However, in 1858, I went with my son and a couple of friends to inspect the place itself, considering it at least worth while to make one's own observations on the spot.

We passed through *'Ain Carem*, the *Karem* of the Septuagint, to *Sattâf*, and rested during the heat of the day in a vineyard, near a spring of water and plots of garden vegetables, belonging to the few houses that had been rebuilt after several years of devastation by village warfare.

The approach to the place from any direction is through the very rough torrent bed of the Wadi Bait Hhaneena, and along very narrow ledges upon the sides of steep hills, quite as perilous as any that are used for travelling in any part of the Lebanon; too dangerous to admit of dismounting and leading the horse after the risk has once begun, by far the safest method of advancing is to hold the reins very loose, and if you wish it, to shut your eyes.

Opposite to Sattâf, directly across the valley, the Latins had lately rebuilt a small chapel of former times, said to have been the prison of John the Baptist; they name it the Chapel of the *Hhabees, i.e.*, the imprisoned one.

Leaving Sattâf we gradually ascended to Soba; at first through lemon and orange plantations near the water, and then through vineyards with a few pomegranate-trees interspersed.

It is noteworthy how, throughout most of the tribe of Judah, small springs of water are found dribbling from the rocks, (besides the larger sources of Urtas, Lifta, Faghoor 'Aroob, Dirweh, and Hebron,) which were doubtless more copious in the ancient times, when the land was more clothed with timber, and there were men, industrious men, aware of their blessings, and ready to prevent the streams from slipping away beneath the seams of limestone formation.

At Soba we mounted the steep hill to the *Shooneh*, or small look-out tower at the summit, enjoying the breadth of landscape and the stretch of the Mediterranean before our eyes.

In the village we found remains of old masonry, most likely the basement of a fortification of early Saracenic or the Crusaders' era; besides which there was a piece of wall in excellent condition of the best character of Jewish rabbeted stones.

One man invited us to see some old stones inside of his house; but they formed a portion of the basement above-mentioned, against which the rest of his house was built. The people were unanimous in declaring that there was nothing else of such a nature in the village. So that our researches issued in no corroboration of Soba being Modin.

Leaving the place we descended to the high road of Jaffa to Jerusalem, and saw a number of olive-trees dead of age; none of us, however long resident in Palestine, had seen such before or elsewhere; we concluded them to have been withered by age from their bearing no visible tokens of destruction, while the ground was well ploughed around them, and from finding others near them in progressive stages of decay, down to the utter extinction of foliage.

Arrived at *Kalôneh* upon the highway, certainly the site of a Roman garrison or "colonia," (see Acts xvi. 12,) leaving Kustul behind, which is also a derivation from the Latin word for a castle.

Near the bridge of Kalôneh, where there are good specimens of ancient rabbeted stones, one gets a glimpse of 'Ain Carem through the olive plantation; and the return that day was by a cross way from *Dair Yaseen* through vineyards to Jerusalem.

It is only at a comparatively late period that attention has been directed to the text of Eusebius and Jerome in the "Onomasticon," where it is distinctly said that Modin was near Lydd, and that the monuments were at that time (in the fourth century) still shown there.

Porter considers that therefore *Latroon* is the true site of Modin: in this supposition I wish to concur; for the general run of the Maccabæan history becomes peculiarly intelligible when read with the idea in the mind that Modin lay in just such a situation, namely, upon a hill, rising alone from the great plain, but adjacent to the mountain ridge, and to defiles into which the insurgents might easily retire, or from which they might issue suddenly and surprise regular armies in their camp. I know of no place so suitable for such operations as Latroon.

The word ἐπιγεγλυμμένα, used for the armour and the ships, must mean "carved in relievo," and such objects could never be distinguished by persons actually passing upon the sea, if placed either at Soba, Latroon, Lydd, or even Jaffa; it is difficult enough to imagine that the pyramids and columns were visible from the sea at Latroon.

XV.

THE TWO BAIT SAHHOORS IDENTIFIED WITH BETHSURA AND BATH ZACHARIAS.

THERE are two villages in the neighbourhood of Jerusalem bearing the name of Bait Sahhoor. One lies near to the city, beyond En-Rogel, a little way down the valley of the Kedron; the other is farther off, close under Bethlehem. By way of distinction, the former is called "Bait Sahhoor of the Wâdi," and the latter, "Bait Sahhoor of the Christians." I think that it can be shown that these places, though now fallen from their high estate, once played their part in important events, —that Bait Sahhoor of the Wâdi is identical with Bethsura,—and that Bait Sahhoor of the Christians is identical with Bath Zacharias—both of Maccabæan history.

In the year 150 of the Seleucidan era, being the fifth year of the liberty of Zion, (the term used upon the Maccabæan coins,) a vast army of Syrians invaded Palestine from Antioch, headed by King Antiochus Eupator, in the twelfth year of his age, and under the official command of Lysias, one of

The Two Bait Sahhoors Identified. 429

his relatives. The army consisted of both subjects and hired aliens, even from the islands of the sea. They numbered "a hundred thousand infantry, and twenty thousand cavalry, with thirty-two elephants exercised in battle," (1 Macc. vi. 30.)

The object of the expedition was to crush the Maccabæan insurrection, and wipe out the disgrace of defeats already sustained. The first attempt was to be the relief of the garrison at Jerusalem, which was at this time beleaguered by Judas from the temple part of the city.

"The army was very great and mighty," (ver. 41.) "When the sun shone upon the shields of gold and brass, the mountains glistered therewith, and shined like lamps of fire," (ver. 39.) Each of the thirty-two elephants was attended by "a thousand men armed with coats of mail, and with helmets of brass on their heads; and besides this, for every beast was ordained five hundred horsemen of the best—these were ready at every occasion: wheresoever the beast was, and whithersoever the beast went they went also, neither departed they from him; and upon the beasts were there strong towers of wood, which covered every one of them, and were girt fast unto them with devices; there were upon every one thirty-two strong men that fought upon them, beside the Indian that ruled him," (ver. 35, &c.)

This strange host marched along the Philistine plain southwards to Idumea, which is on the south of Hebron : this being the only way for such an army and its elephants to get at Jerusalem. Thence they swept the land before them northwards, "and pitched against Bethsura, which they assaulted many days, making engines of war, but they of the city came out and fought valiantly," (ver. 31.)

Whereupon Judas desisted from his siege of the citadel—which, I may remark in passing, must have been on Acra, not like David's citadel taken from the Jebusites, on Zion—and hastened to attack the royal host, mighty though it was.

Some have supposed that Bethsura is to be found at Bait Zur, near Hebron, the Beth Zur of Josh. xv. 38; whereas this place is more than a hundred furlongs from Jerusalem, being not much more than an hour (north) from Hebron, and is altogether too far removed to answer the description of Bethsura, and the operations carried on there, close to the Holy City.

The 5th verse of the 11th chapter of 2 Maccabees sets the whole question at rest; the words are distinctly, " So he (Lysias) came to Judea and drew near to Bethsura, which was a strong town, but distant from Jerusalem *about five furlongs*, and he laid sore siege unto it." Again, immediately after taking the city of Jerusalem and dedicating the temple, Judas " fortified Bethsura in order to preserve it," (that is, Mount Zion,) that the people might have a defence against Idumea, (1 Macc. iv. 61.) And the accusation which had been formerly

The Two Bait Sahhoors Identified. 431

made to the King Antiochus Epiphanes in Persia against Judas and his men was "that they had compassed about the sanctuary with high walls as before, and his city Bethsura;" also to the present king at Antioch, "that the sanctuary also and Bethsura have they fortified," (chap. vi. 7, 26.) It is clear that one was an outwork of the other, Bethsura being the defence of Jerusalem against incursions from the south.

I know not how to doubt that Bait Sahhoor of the valley is the very place. It lies upon a lofty hill across the valley not far beyond En-Rogel. This is at present a wretched village, only inhabited for a few weeks in the year; but the position is naturally one of great strength. The distance from the city answers precisely the requirements of the history,—a signal by trumpet, if not the human voice, could be heard from one garrison to the other. I have ridden repeatedly to the spot and examined the ground. The south-eastern angle of the temple wall at Jerusalem (where the great stones are found) is distinctly visible from the houses. I sat there upon my horse and remarked how unassailable by cavalry and elephants this site must have been, and how great its value for a military outwork to the sanctuary of the temple. The pediment and moulding of a column lay at my feet,—around and opposite across the valley were numerous sepulchres hewn in the solid rock; yet the infantry of the Syrians were sufficient to overwhelm the gallant defenders. Judas in this emergency resolved to come to their relief, raising the siege of the citadel and outflanking the enemy. For this purpose he "pitched at Bath Zacharias over against the king's camp," (ver. 32.) This was seventy stadia, or nearly nine Roman, or eight and a half English miles distant from Bethsura, (Josephus' Antiq. xii. 9, 4.) I believe Bath Zacharias to be the village which now bears the name of "Bait Sahhoor of the Christians," close to Bethlehem.* I have ridden over the space between the two villages called Bait Sahhoor; the distance upon a well marked and rather winding road, answers well to the description of the historian. The stratagem of Judas becomes here very intelligible, which was to take the invaders in the rear, and placing them between two hostile Jewish forces, to draw away the main attack from Bethsura and Jerusalem; besides cutting off any assistance from the south. Antiochus did face round in order to attack him, and was met in narrow straits between the two localities. This I take to be the broken ground south-east of Mar Elias, where certainly it would be just as impossible now for two elephants to go abreast as it was when Josephus wrote his lively

* Bait Zacâri and Zecarîah lie far away among the mountains in the south-west. Neither of them would command the road which Judas desired to intercept—neither of them therefore answers to the Bath Zacharias of the history any more than Baitzur near Hebron does to Bethsura—all are equally out of the question by reason of their distance.

The Two Bait Sahhoors Identified. 433

description of the engagement that ensued; of the shouts of the men echoing among the mountains, and the glitter of the rising sun upon the polished accoutrements. It was summer, for they excited the elephants with the blood of the grape and the mulberry. The road is to this day defined by true tokens of antiquity, such as lines of stones covered with hoary lichen, old cisterns, especially a noble one called the *Beer el Kott*, with here and there steps cut in the shelves of solid rock. The last part of the road on the south is among slippery, rocky, narrow defiles and paths, half-way down the hill-sides.

Here six hundred of the Syrian army were cut off, and Eleazar, the heroic brother of Judas, was crushed under an elephant which he had killed. Yet the fortune of the day was not decisive in favour of the Maccabæan army, which retired and entrenched itself within the temple fortress.

The outlying post of Bethsura was obliged to capitulate.

Philological grounds for the above identification are not wanting. Bethsura and Bath Zacharias may have easily represented the Arabic or Hebrew form of Bait Sahhoor. The guttural letter in the middle naturally disappears in the Greek text, just as the Greek word "Assidean" represents the Hebrew Chasidim in the same history.

The following is a simple demonstration of the transition :—

2 E

Hebrew.	Greek.	Arabic.
בית סחדה	βεθσουρα	بيت ساحور
בית זכריה	βεθζαχαρια	

It may be asked, why did neither Josephus nor the author of the Books of Maccabees tell us that Beth Zachariah was near Bethlehem? I answer: first, the narrative did not make this necessary; secondly, Bethlehem was then "among the least of the thousands of Judah," her great day had not yet arrived; and thus it might have been quite as necessary to say that Bethlehem was near Beth Zachariah, as to say that Beth Zachariah was near Bethlehem.

The modern name "Bait Sahhoor of the Christians" arises most likely from the fact that a majority of the inhabitants,—thirty families to twenty in the year 1851,—were of that religion, and from its nearness to the field where it is believed the angels appeared to the shepherds announcing the birth of Christ, with its subterranean chapel, the crypt of a large church in former times.

The other Bait Sahhoor (El Wadîyeh) is so named from its position on the side of the Wadi in Nar, or valley of the Kedron. It is only occasionally inhabited, the people who claim it being too few to clear out the encumbered cisterns for their use, but prefer to identify themselves during most of the year with other villages, such as Siloam near at hand, where water is more abundant.

XVI.

THE BAKOOSH COTTAGE.

AT about seven miles from Jerusalem lie the Pools of Solomon, commonly called the "Burâk," upon the road to Hebron, which passes by the head of the westernmost of them, on the left hand of the traveller to that city; while immediately on the right hand, stands a hill with some cultivation of vineyards and fig-trees, with a few olive-trees; apparently half-way up that hill is a stone cottage, roughly but well built. It is of that cottage and its grounds that I am about to speak, for there I resided with my family for some weeks in 1860, and through the summer of 1862.

There is no village close at hand, the nearest one being *El Khud'r*, (or St George, so named from a small Greek convent in its midst,) which, however, is only visible from the highway for a few minutes at a particular bend of the road before reaching the Pools; the next nearest, but in the opposite or eastern direction, is Urtâs, with its profitable cultivation, nestled in a well-watered valley.

After these, in other directions again, are *Bait Jala*, near Rachel's sepulchre, and Bethlehem, the sacred town whose name is echoed wherever Christ is mentioned throughout the whole world, and will continue to do so till the consummation of all things,—"there is no speech or language where its name is not heard."

Adjoining the Pools is the shell of a dilapidated khan, of old Saracenic period, the outer enclosure alone being now entire. Two or three Bashi-bozuk soldiers used to be stationed there, living in wretched hovels inside the enclosure, made of fallen building stones, put together with mud. On account of this being a government post, the peasantry of the country, ignorant of all the world but themselves, denominate this old square wall, "The Castle," and that name is repeated by dragomans to their European employers.

These were our nearest neighbours.

Close to the khan-gate and to the Pools is a perennial spring of excellent water, which, of course, is of great value, and considering how several roads meet at that point, and what a diversity of character there is continually passing or halting there, it would seem to form the perfection of an opening scene to some romantic tale.

Thus the Hebron highway lay between the Pools, with the khan on one side, and the Bakoosh hill on the other, and no person or quadruped could pass along it unobserved from our window.

The Bakoosh Cottage.

From the cottage, the more extended prospect comprised the stoney, treeless hills in every direction, the Pools forming the head of the valley leading to Urtâs, and the outskirt beginning of green cultivation there; then the streets and houses of Bethlehem; also the Frank mountain; and at the back of all the Moab range of mountains.

Within the wall enclosing the property of the cottage, with its fruit trees already mentioned, there is one of the little round towers such as are

ANCIENT SEPULCHRE ON THE BAKOOSH.

commonly seen about Bethlehem for summer residence of the cultivator and his family during the season of fruit ripening, and which are meant by the Biblical term of a tower built in the midst of a vineyard, (see Matthew xxi. 33, and Isaiah v. 2.) It is remarkable how perfectly circular these are always built, though so small in size. We had also a receptacle for beehives, and an ancient sepulchre.

The hill rises very steeply, but being as usual formed into ledges or terraces, upon one of these, in a corner near the wall, the stable was constructed of a small tent, near a big tree, within the shadow of which, and of a bank, the horses were picketed.

Upon the other ledges were arranged the tents for sleeping in at night, and alongside of the cottage a kitchen was made of a wall and a roof made of branches of trees brought from a distance.

Such was our abode in the pure mountain breezes, with unclouded sunshine, and plenty of good spring water within reach.

Inside the stone walls of the house we stayed during the heat of the day; the children learned their lessons there, and I transacted business in writing, when my presence in Jerusalem was not absolutely required by those carrying on the current daily affairs; indeed the reason for resorting to this place was the necessity for obtaining recruitment of health, after a serious illness brought on by arduous labour. Had not unforeseen anxieties come upon us, no lot on earth could have been more perfectly delicious in the quality of enjoyment, both for body and spirit, than that sojourn upon the wild hill; among ourselves were innocence and union, consequently peace; time

The Bakoosh Cottage.

was profitably spent; and our recreations were, practice in the tonic sol-fa singing lessons, with sketching and rambling on foot or on horseback over the breezy heights of Judah.

And whether by evening twilight, or at the rising of the sun out of the Moab mountains, or earlier still, by summer morning starlight, when Sirius and Canopus (the latter unseen in England) vied with each other in sparkling their varied colours to praise their Maker in the firmament, His handiwork; those rambles were sources of delight that cannot be expressed in human language; they were, however, not novelties after so many years' residence in that Asiatic climate, but had become wrought into our very existence.

Our Sabbaths were happy and conscientiously observed; we kept up the services of the Church of England as far as practicable, and sometimes had a visitor to join us in the same, not omitting the hymn singing.

The two domestic servants were of different Christian communities; for the woman was a Latin, and would sometimes repair to her church-service at Bethlehem, and the Abyssinian lad might be heard morning and evening, or at night in the moonlight—such moonlight as we had there!—reading the Gospels and Psalms in his soft native language, or even singing to a kirâr (or lute) of his own making, hymns with a chorus of "Alleluia, Amen."

Another of our gratifications should not be omitted, namely, the hearing of the large church bell of the Latins in Bethlehem on certain occasions, and always on Sunday mornings; at the moment of the sun peering over the eastern horizon that great bell struck, and was followed by a gush of the sweetest irregular music from smaller bells, probably belonging to the Greeks, and then by the nakoos (plank) of the Armenians, a relic of their primitive customs, serving for a bell,*—all these acting with one consent and with one intention, that of celebrating "the Lord's day," as the early Christians delighted to call the first day of the week.

From our window we had the city of David and of David's Lord before us, and over the window on the inside I had inscribed in large Arabic inscription-characters, "O Son of David, have mercy upon us!" we had therefore the writing and the town at the same glance of view.

We were not without visitors: sometimes a friend or two or three would arrive from Jerusalem—travellers along the road would mount the hill to see us—rabbis of Hebron on the way to Jerusalem, or Jews from the distance of Tiberias

* Very common in Oriental Christendom, and called by the Greeks the Σημάντρον (semantron.)

The ancient Britons used to summon the congregation to church service by means of "sacra ligna," is it not likely that these were the same as the above, seeing that the Celtic nations were derived from the East?

The Bakoosh Cottage. 441

passing to Hebron, would turn aside to pay their respects—Arab chiefs, such as Ismaeen Hhamdân of the Ta'amra — Turkish officers, or even the Pasha himself, found the way to the cottage—also officers of the British navy, when visiting the sacred localities from Jaffa. Among these I would not forget the chaplain of one of our men-of-war, who brought up ten of his best men, namely, the Bible and temperance class under his charge, to see the venerated places, Jerusalem, Bethlehem, and the Mount of Olives. On one occasion we had a surveying party with their instruments from H.M.S. *Firefly*, who passed some nights with us.

On the higher boundary the land was still in its natural condition of stones, fossil shells, and green shrubs with fragrant herbs. There might be seen occasionally starting up before the intruding wanderer, partridges, hares, quails, the wild pigeon, the fox, or even

"The wild gazelle on Judah's hills
Exultingly would bound,"

and escape also, for I carried no gun with me.

Mounting still higher we came upon the *Dahar-es-Salâhh*, a mountain whence the prospect of all Philistia and the coast from almost Gaza to Carmel expands like a map—no, rather like a thing of still life before the eye, with the two seas, namely, the Mediterranean and the Dead Sea, visible at once, with likewise the mountains of

Samaria and Gerizim, besides the Moab country eastward, and Jerusalem and Bethlehem nearer home.

Close at hand upon the mountain on which we thus stand, are vestiges of a monastic house and chapel called "Khirbet el Kasees," (the priest's ruins,) and even more interesting objects still, the remains of older edifices, distinguished by ponderous rabbeted stones.

On the mountain top is a large oval space, which has been walled round, fragments of the enclosure are easily traceable, as also some broken columns, gray and weather-beaten. This has every appearance of having been one of the many sun-temples devoted to Baal by early Syrians.

By temple I here mean a succession of open-air courts, with a central altar for sacrifice; a mound actually exists on the highest spot of elevation, which may well have been the site of the altar.

What a vast prospect does this spot command, not only of landscape in every direction, but of sky from which the false worshipper might survey the sun's entire daily course, from its rising out of the vague remote lands of "the children of the East," and riding in meridian splendour over the land of Israel's God, till, slowly descending and cloudless to the very last, it dips behind the blue waters of "the great sea!" Alas! to think that such a spot as this should ever have been desecrated by worship of the creature within actual sight of that holy mountain where the divine glory appeared, more dazzling than the brightest effulgence of the created sun.

Sloping westwards from the *Dahar-es-Salâhh* were agreeable rides over a wilderness of green shrubs with occasional pine and karoobah trees, and rough rocks on the way to *Nahhâleen* or *Bait Ezkâreh*, from which we catch a view of the valley of Shocoh, the scene of David's triumph over Goliath, and beyond that the hill of Santa Anna at *Bait Jibreen*. The region there is lonely and silent, with some petty half-depopulated villages in sight, but all far away; sometimes a couple or so of peasants may be met upon the road driving an ass loaded with charcoal or broken old roots of the evergreen oak. Evening excursions in that direction were not infrequent for the purpose of seeing the sun set into the sea, from which the breeze came up so refreshingly.

The home resources gave us among the fruit trees, goldfinches, bee-eaters in blue or green and gold, and beccaficas, the latter for food, but so tame that they would stay upon the branches while the gun was levelled at them; in fact, little Alexander, returning one day with several of them that he had shot, complained of want of sport, quoting the lines of his namesake Selkirk in Cowper,—" Their tameness is shocking to me."

Occasionally we got water-hens or coots that had been shot upon the Pools of Solomon; only sometimes it was not possible to fish them out as they fell into the water, and so became entangled among the gigantic weeds that grow up from the bottom to the level of the surface, and among which the men were afraid to venture their swimming. Pelicans we did not see, although one had been previously brought from thence to Jerusalem, and was stuffed for the Museum. Then we had water-cresses from the aqueduct, at a place where its side was partly broken between the upper and the second pool. Often for a treat we had water particularly light for drinking brought from the spring of Etam, (2 Chron. xi. 6.) Figs and grapes were furnished from the ground itself, and at the end of August the Shaikh Jad Allah sent us a present of fresh honeycomb, according to the custom on opening a hive at the end of summer, (in that country the bees are never destroyed for the sake of the honey;) presents thereof are sent round to neighbours, and of course presents of some other produce are given in return. Palestine is still a land abounding in honey.

Occasional incidents occurred on the plain at the foot of the hill,—such as a long line of camels kneeling and growling upon the high road, while their drivers were swimming during the blaze of noontide in the parts of the large pool free from weeds; or military expeditions passing on to Hebron during the night, and called up by bugle after resting a couple of hours at the castle-gate;

The Bakoosh Cottage. 445

or camel-loads of pine-branches swinging in stately procession from the southern hills beyond Hebron towards Jerusalem, to furnish tabernacles for the Jewish festival; or an immense party of Kerak people from beyond the Dead Sea, with their camels, asses, mules, besides flocks, for sale, conveying butter and wheat to Jerusalem, encamped below us and singing at their watch-fires by night.

Large fires were sometimes visible upon the Moab mountains at the distance of thirty or forty miles in a straight line. These may have arisen from carelessness, or accidental circumstances, among either standing corn or the heaps of harvest in the open air; or they may even have been wilful conflagrations made by hostile tribes in their raids upon each other. In any case they showed that wherever such things occurred in ancient times, Ruth the Moabitess, when settled in Bethlehem, might still have been reminded in that way of her native country, which lay before her view.

At the Bakoosh we heard the single gun-fire at sunrise or sunset while the Pasha had his camp at Hebron; and from the highest part of our hill could see the flash of the guns in the castle of Jerusalem when saluting the birthday of Mohammed.

For domestic incidents we had the children pelting each other with acorns by moonlight; bonfires made by them and the servants on the terrace to show us the way when returning at a late hour from Jerusalem; large bunches of grapes from the adjoining vineyard, the *Karawcesh*, suspended against the wall, reserved to become raisins. Then family presents upon a birthday, all derived from the ground itself,—one person bringing a bunch of wild thyme in purple blossom,—another some sprigs from a terebinth tree, with the reviving odour of its gum that was exuding from the bark, —and another a newly-caught chameleon.

The latter was for several days afterwards indulged with a fresh bough of a tree for his residence, changed about, one day of oak, next of terebinth, then of sumach, or of pine, &c.

Such was our "sweet home" and family life on the Byeways of Palestine.

But a time came when care and anxiety told heavily upon mine and my wife's health. For some days I was confined to bed in the tent, unable to move up to the house; yet enjoying the reading of my chapters in Hebrew in the land of Israel, or ruminating over the huge emphasis of St Paul's Greek in 2 Cor. iv. 17, $\kappa\alpha\theta'$ $\dot{\upsilon}\pi\epsilon\rho$-$\beta o\lambda\dot{\eta}\nu$ $\epsilon\dot{\iota}s$ $\dot{\upsilon}\pi\epsilon\rho\beta o\lambda\dot{\eta}\nu$. $\kappa.\tau.\lambda.$ The curtains of the tent were thrown wide open at each side for the admission of air; the children were playing or reading on the shady side of another tent; muleteer and camel parties I could observe mounting or falling with the rises and dips of the Hebron road; and the jingle of bells or the singing of the men was audible or alternately lost according to the same circumstances. I lay watching the progress of sunshine or shadow around the Frank mountain as the hours rolled on; then as evening approached the Egyptian groom took down the Egyptian mare to water at the spring, followed by the foal of pure Saklâwi race, that never till the preceding day had had even so much as a halter put across his head, —a Bashi-bozuk soldier with his pipe looking on, —the Abyssinian lad carrying pitchers of water to the several tents, and the pools of bright blue becoming darker blue when rippled by the evening air. All this was food for enjoyment of the picturesque, but at the same time God Almighty was leading us into deep trials of faith in Himself, and bringing out the value of that promise,—"When thou passest through the waters, I will be with thee; and through the rivers, they shall not overflow thee."

As the autumn advanced, some slight sprinkling of rain fell—dews at night were heavy—mists rose from below—mornings and evenings became cooled —new flowers began to appear, such as the purple crocus, and certain yellow blossoms belonging to the season, the name of which I do not know. We therefore began to take farewell rides about the neighbourhood, as to places we were never to see again. One of these was to a very archaic pile of rude masonry, deeply weather-eaten, at a ruined site called *Bait Saweer*, through green woods and arbutus-trees, glowing with scarlet berries; a place which had only recently been brought to my notice, and of which no European had any knowledge.

The old building, whose use we could not discover, was composed, not of ordinary blocks of stone, but of huge flat slabs, unchiselled at edges or corners, laid one over another, but forming decidedly an intentional edifice. It is well worth further examination. At the time we had with us no materials for sketching, and never had an opportunity of going thither afterwards.

It lies among the wild green scene west from the Hebron road, near where, on the opposite, or east side, is the opening of the Wadi 'Aroob, with its copious springs.

Then we went to *Marscea'*, beyond the *Dair el Benât*—equally unknown to Europeans—and, lastly, to the green slopes and precipices towards *Nahhâleen*, where, lingering till after sunset, we became in a few minutes enveloped in a cloud of mist tossed and rolled along by gusts of wind, and several large eagles rose screaming from perches among rocks below us into the misty air, as if rejoicing in the boisterous weather.

Three months before, we had been on the same spot at the moment of sunset, and saw the whole Philistine plain hidden in a white mist in a single minute, but, of course, far below us; and this, we were told, was the usual state of things, and would remain so for another month, after which the plain would have no mist, but we should have it all on

The Bakoosh Cottage. 449

the mountains at sunset—so it was now found to be the case.

From one spot on our own grounds we were able to point out as objects in the magnificent prospect —the Moab mountains, the crevasse of the Jabbok into the Ghôr, that of Calirrhoe into the Dead Sea, Hhalhhool near Hebron, El Khud'r below us, Rachel's sepulchre, Bethlehem, Nebi Samwil, the Scopus, Jerusalem, and our house there, to which we were soon to remove.

Before, however, quitting this subject of the Bakoosh, I may refer to one very special attraction that held us to the place, namely, an agricultural undertaking in its neighbourhood. A friend, of whom I hope to speak more in another time and place, superintended for me the rebuilding of an ancient Biblical village that lay a heap and a desolation, and cleared out its spring of water, which, by being choked up with rubbish, made its way unseen under ground, it thus became nearly as copious as that alongside of Solomon's Pools. I gathered people into the village, vineyards were planted, crops were sown and reaped there, taxes were paid to the government; and the vicinity, which previously had been notorious for robberies on the Hebron road, became perfectly secure.

On one of my visits, a list was presented to me of ninety-eight inhabitants, where a year and a half before there was not one. Homesteads were rebuilt; the people possessed horned cattle and flocks of sheep and goats, as well as beehives. I saw women grinding at the mill, and at one of the doors a cat and a kitten. All was going on prosperously.

Purer pleasure have I never experienced than when, in riding over occasionally with our children, we saw the threshing of wheat and barley in progress, and heard the women singing, or the little children shouting at their games. Sixty cows used to be driven at noon to drink at the spring.

We returned to Jerusalem on the 21st of October, and on the 28th of November that village was again a mass of ruin—the houses demolished—the people dispersed—their newly-sown corn and the vineyards ploughed over—the fine spring of water choked up once more—and my Australian trees planted there torn up by the roots. All this was allowed to be done within nine miles of Jerusalem, to gratify persons engaged in an intrigue which ended in deeds far worse than this.

Our village was *Faghoor*, and had been one of the ancient towns of the tribe of Judah. Its place in the Bible is Joshua xv., where it is found in the Greek Septuagint together with Tekoah, Etham, and Bethlehem, all noted places—neither of which is contained in the Hebrew text, and therefore not in the English translation.

It seems difficult to account for this; but it may possibly be that neither of these towns were ever in the Hebrew of that chapter, that they were not well known at the time of the original Hebrew being written; but that when the translation of the Septuagint was made, the writers knew by other means, though living in Egypt, that Tekoah, Etham, Bethlehem, and Faghoor had been for a long period famous within the tribe of Judah, and therefore they filled up what seemed to them a deficiency in the register.

APPENDIX.

A.—Page 32.

THE signs here referred to were guessed by Buckingham (about 1816) to be possibly some distinctive tokens of Arab tribes; but he seemed rather inclined to connect them with marks that are found in Indian caverns, or those on the rocks about Mount Sinai.

He was thus nearer to the truth than the latest of travellers, De Saulcy, who, with all his knowledge of Semitic alphabets, says of some of these *graffiti*, or scratchings, at 'Ammân, which he copied: " Tout cela, je regrette fort, est lettre close pour moi. Quelle est cette écriture ? Je l'ignore." (Voyage en Terre Sainte. Tom. i. p. 256. Paris, 1865.)

They are characters adopted by Arabs to distinguish one tribe from another, and commonly used for branding the camels on the shoulders and haunches, by which means the animals may be recovered, if straying and found by Arabs not hostile to the owners.

I have, however, seen them scratched upon walls in many places frequented by Bedaween, as, for instance, in the ruined convents, churches, &c., on the plain of the Jordan, and occasionally, as at 'Ammân, several such cyphers are united into one complex character.

+o Abu N'sair.

o—o Leja.

⌐⊓ Koraishah.

⊢ Abu Njaim.

||| Dhullam.

⌐⊓ Dëab.

⊤⊥ Beni Okba.

9|| Obain Zeben.

ſ. Jehâleen.

+⊩⊤ 'Anezeh.

ſ? or o≡ Abu Faiz.

+ Christians of Es. Salt, or Kerak.

+⊩ Caabneh.

⊤ Hhewaitât.

9 Hamid.

|| Tiyahah.

B.— Page 367.

Considerable discrepancy may be found among the transcripts furnished by travellers in their published works, of the Greek votive inscriptions about the entrance of the cavern of Pan at Banias.

I give the following as the result of careful study of

Appendix. 455

them in 1849, and again, after the lapse of six years, in 1855, each time examining the writing, under varieties of light and shade, at different hours of the day.

There are some other inscriptions, which are entirely blackened with smoke, in the niches, made perhaps by ancient burning of lamps or of incense there. This is particularly the case in one large hollow made in the rock, which has almost its whole surface covered with Greek writing. Within this hollow a niche is cut out, now empty.

One small niche has its inscription so much defaced by violence that only the letters ΠΑΝ are connectedly legible.

Appendix.

This sculptured niche has no inscription, but only the pedestal on which the statue was placed.

This ornamental niche has beneath it, on a tablet, the words as at present legible.

ΠΑΝ , ˙ ˙ ˙ ˙ ˙ ˙ ˙ ˙ ΦΑΙC
-ΑΤΗ ˙ ˙ ˙ ˙ ˙ ˙ ΙΕΘΗ
Κ ˙ ˙ ˙ ˙ ˙ ˙ ˙ ˙ ˙ Ν
Ο ˙ ˙ ˙ ΡΙΠ ˙ ˙ ˙ ΟΥΙ
-ΙΩ ˙ ˙ ˙ ˙ ˙ ΟΥ ΚΑΙ
˙ ˙ ˙ ˙ ˙ ˙ ˙ ˙ ˙ Ν

Appendix. 457

The inscription in the highest situation is as follows:—

ΑΓΡΙΠΠΑ
ΜΑΡΚΟΥΑΡ
ΧΩΝ-ΕΤΟΥC
CΚΤ ΟΝΙΡΩ
ΧΡΗCΜΟ -
ΔΟ -- ΘΕΙ
ΤΗΝ Κ -- --
ΗΧΩΑΝ-ΘΗ
ΚΕΝΑΜ-ΓΡΙ
ΠΠΑΔΟΥ- ΒΙ
-Ω ΚΑΙ ΑΓΡΙΠ---
-ΝΩ ΚΑΙ -- ΡΙ
ΚΩ ΚΑΙ ΑΓΡΙΠ
ΠΑ ΒΟΥΛΕΥΤΑΙ
ΚΑΙ ΑΓΡΙΠΠΕΙΝ
ΚΑΙ ΔΟ - ΝΑΤΕ
ΚΝΟΙC ΑΥΤΩΝ

Beneath this is the following:—

ΥΠΕΡ ϹΩΤΗΡΙΑϹ ΤΩΝ ΚΥΡΙΩΝ
ΑΥΤΟΚΡΑΤΟΡΩΝ
ΟΙΛΑϹΡ-Ο -- ΠΑΝΟϹΙΕΡΕΥϹΘΕΟΥΠΑΝΟϹΤΗΝ
ΚΥΡΙΑ - Ν - ΕϹΙΚΑΙΤΟΝ -- ΝΤΗ- ΑΥΤΟΥ ΚΟΙΛΙΑΜ
ΘΕΙΟΝ Π - … ΕΛΕϹΙΟΥΡ - ΝΤΑ … ΑΥΤΗϹ
· · · , · · · ΝΚΕΜΩϹΙΔΗΡΩ

Above the smoked recess. but below an upper niche, we find—

ΤΗΝΔΕ - ΕΑΝΑΝ ΕΘΗΚΕ
ΦΙΛΕΥΗΧΩΔΙΟ ΠΑΝΙ …
ΟΥΙΚΤΩΡΑΡΗΤΗΡΑΥϹΙ
· · · · · ΜΧΟΙΟΤΟΝΟϹ

Appendix. 459

In this inscription "the emperors" can mean no others than Vespasian and Titus, who had had one and the same Triumph in Rome on account of the conquest of Judæa; and this very title is used in Josephus, ("Wars," vii. xi. 4,) διὰ τὴν πράοτητα τῶν αὐτοκρατόρων·

It is peculiarly suitable to that place, inasmuch as Titus, previous to leaving the country, had celebrated there the birthday of his brother Domitian, with magnificent public spectacles—amid which, however, more than 2500 Jews were destroyed for popular amusement, by burning, fighting, and in combats with wild beasts.

Although these are copied with much painstaking, there may be errors unperceived in some of the letters; but at least one of the words is misspelt by the provincial artist, namely, ONIPΩ.

INDEX OF PLACES.

N B.—*Names with the asterisk are ancient and not modern.*

A.

Aaron's tomb, 306.
Abadiyeh, 80, 106.
Abasiyeh, 254.
Abdoon, 34.
Abeih, 392.
Abu Atabeh, 239.
Abu Dis, 1.
Abu Mus-hhaf, 47.
Abu'n Jaib, (Jaim,) 337.
Abu Sabâkh, 203.
Acre, 237.
Adâsa, 200.
Afeeri, 193.
Afooleh, 227.
Ahhsaniyeh, 183.
Ai, 204.
'Ainab, 391.
'Ain 'Anoob, 390, 391.
'Ain 'Aroos, 324.
'Ain Atha, 387.
'Ain Bedawiyeh, 240, 244.
'Ain Berweh, 241.
'Ain Besâba, 390.
'Ain Carem, 424.
'Ain Dirweh, 151, 194, 290.
'Ain Ghazal, 34.
'Ain Ghazal, 224.
'Ain Hhood, 224.
'Ain Jadoor, 41.
'Ain Jidi, 333.
'Ain Kaimoon, 230.
'Ain Kesoor, 392.
'Ain Mel'hh, 296.
'Ain Mellâhhah, 371.
'Ain Merubba', 48.
'Ain Merubba', 417, 419.
'Ain Nebel, 259, 266.
'Ain Noom, 270.
'Ain Saadeh, 235, 245, 250.
'Ain Shems, 156.
'Ain Sufsâfeh, 231, 250.
'Ain Taâsân, 321.
'Ain Weibeh, 302.
'Ain Yebrood, 89.
'Ain Zera'ab, 238.

Aita, 265.
Aitnrân, 387.
Ajjeh, 126, 219.
'Ajloon, 38, 56, 69, 79.
'Ajoor, 153.
'Akir, 157.
Alma, 108.
'Alman, 201.
'Almeet, 201.
'Ammân, 24-36.
Amoorîah, 156.
*Anâta, 200, 210.
'Aneen, 251.
Annâbeh, 127.
'Arabah, 301, 320, &c.
'Arâbeh, 217, &c., 251.
'Arâbet el Battoof, 241.
'Arâk el Ameer, 19.
'Arâk Hala, 183.
'Arâk Munshiyah, 177.
'Arârah, 248.
'Arkoob, 147.
'Arkoob Sahhâba, 336.
Arzoon, 254.
Ascalân, 163, 182.
Asdood, 164.
'Asfi, 234.
'Asker, 90.
Atârah, 126, 215.
Athleet, 224.
Atna, 162.
'Attar, 183.
Aujeh, 133, 134.
Awali, 348, 412.
'Azair, 244.
'Azoor, 355, 377.

B.

Bahhjah, 239.
Bait Ainoon, 290.
Bait Atâb, 147.
Bait Dajan, 163.
Bait Durâs, 162.
Bait Ezkâreh, 443.
Bait Hhaneena, 200.
Bait Hhanoon, 175.

Index of Places.

Bait Jala, 436.
Bait Jan, 271.
Bait Jirja, 166.
Bait Jibreen, 178, 443.
Bait Nateef, 147, 149, 196.
Bait Nejed, 176.
Bait Sahhoor in Nasâra, 428.
Bait Sahhoor el Wad, 428.
Bait Saweer, 447.
Bait Soor, (see Bezur.)
Bait Uksa, 140.
Bait Unah, 140.
Bait U'oon, 257.
Bait Uzan, 219.
Bait Ziz, (Jiz,) 157.
Baka, 247, 249.
Bakoosh, 435, &c.
*Balah, 297.
Banias, 364, 384, 385.
Barook, 354, 376, 407, 411.
*Bashan, 66.
Batteer, 195.
Battoof, 271.
Bayroot, 390.
Beerain, 291.
Beeri, 88.
Beer Eyoob, 418.
Beer El Kott, 433.
Beer Mustafa, 203.
Beer Nebâla, 200.
Beer es Seba, (Beersheba, 189, &c.
Beisan, 94, 96, &c.
Beka' el Bashà, 40, 46.
Balameh, 221.
Beled esh Shai'kh, 235, 245, 247, 250.
Belhhamiyeh, 80.
Belka, 19, 79.
*Belus, 239.
Beni Naim, 290, 291.
Beni Saheela, 171.
Berasheet, 257.
Berberah, 165.
Berga'an, 45.
Besheet, 160.
Buteadeen, 405, &c.
*Bethany, 1.
*Bethlehem, 436, 437, 440.
Beth Zacharias, 432.
Bezur, 151, 194, 430.
Bidias, 254.
Bint el Jebail, 114, 255, 257, 388.
Bisrah, 355, 376.
Boorj, (near Hebron,) 184, 187.
Boorj, (near Saida,) 253.
Brair, 176.
Burâk, 435.
Burka, 214, 219.
Bursa, 48.
Buttaa, 222.
Bursheen, 254.
Buwairdch, 321.

C.

Caiffa, 236.
*Carmel, 44, 67, 224.
*Cæsarea Philippi, 364.
Cocab el Hawa, 80, 82, 83, 103.
Cocaba, 360, 381.
Cuf'r Bera'am, 121, 388.
Cuf'r Cana, 126.
Cul'r Enji, 57.
Cuf'r Hhooneh, 358, 378.
Cuf r Ita, 247.
Cuf'r Kara, 222.
Cuf'r Menda, 244.
Cuf'r Natta, 398.
Cuf'r Rai, 126, 216.
Cuf'r Rumân, 127.
Cuf'r Saba, 132, &c.
Cuf'r Yuba, 58.
Cuferain, (beyond Jordan,) 9.
Cuferain, (near Carmel,) 251.
Curnub, 297.

D.

Dabook, 39.
Dahar el Hhumâr, 23, 80.
Dahar es Salahh, 441.
Daiket 'Arâr, 297.
Dair, 68.
Dair 'Ammâr, 137.
Dair el Belahh, 169.
Dair el Benât, 448.
Dair Dewân, 203, 204.
Dair ed Dubân, 177.
Dair Hhanna, 240, 272.
Dair el Kamar, 400, &c.
Dair el Mokhallis, 348, 374, 412.
Dair el Musha'al, 136.
Dair el Mushmushi, 377.
Dair en Nakhâz, 182.
Dair Thecla, 254.
Dair Yaseen, 427.
Daliet Carmel, 238.
Daliet er Rohha, 238, 1.
Damooneh, 241.
*Dan, 362.
Dar Joon, 349, 353.
Dar Kanoon, 254.
Dar Meemas, 254.
Dar Shems, 254.
Dar Zibneh, 254.
Dead Sea, 3, 4, 12, 326, &c.
Deâneh, 197.
Deheedeh, 378.
Dejâjeh, 157.
Desrah, 136.
Dibneh, 156.
Dilâthah, 107.
Dilbeh, 193.
Doherlyeh, 192, 193.
Doomeen, 238.

Index of Places. 463

Dothan, 127, 219, &c.
Duhheish'meh, 146.
Dûrtghayer, 254.

E.
Ebeleen, 242. 247.
Ed Dair, 169.
Edjâjeh, 157.
Eilaboon, 240.
Ekfairât, 17.
Ekwikât, 239.
Elah, 150, 151, 153, 196.
'Elealeh, 13, 17, 18.
El 'Areesh, 170.
El Hhabees, 425.
El Khait, 108.
El Kharjeh, 208.
El Khud'r, 146, 435.
El Mergab, 34.
El Muntar el Kassar, 34.
Er-Ram, (beyond Jordan,) 9.
Er-Ram, (near Jerusalem,) 87.
Er Rihha, 4, 414.
Esak, 194.
'Esfia, 235, 238.
Es-Salt, 12, 17, 33, 41.
Esh-Shemesâni, 33.
Esh-Shwaifiyeh, 33.
Etam, 444.

F.
Faghoor, 449, &c.
Fahh'mah, 216
Falooja, 176, 182.
Fârah, 108, 260.
Farra'ân, 127.
Fendecomia, 126, 219.
Ferdisia, 127.
Fooleh, 227.
Fort, 183.
Fountain of Apostles, 2.
Furadees, 224.

G.
*Gadara, 77.
*Gath, 157, 163, 183.
Ghawair, 324, 325.
Ghor, 3, 12, 301.
Ghoraniyeh 5.
Ghujar, 370.
Ghutt, 183.
Ghuzzeh, (Gaza,) 166. &c.
*Gilboa, 67, 102.
Gumrûn, 414, 416.

H.
Haddata, 257.
Hadeth, 390.
Hafeereh, 220.
Haita ez Zoot, 257.
Harakat, 252.

Herfaish, 270.
*Hermon, 67, 78, 264, 359, 364. 371.
Hhalhhool, 194, 291, 449.
Hhamâmeh, 163.
Hhaneen, 266.
Hhanooneh, 136.
Hbarrâsheh, 140, 141.
Hharatheeyeh, 234, 246.
Hhasbâni, 360, 380.
Hhasbeya, 360, 379, 381, &c.
Hhata, 176.
Hhatteen, 126, 240.
Hheker Zaboot, 13.
Hhesbân, 13, 16.
Hhizmeh, 201, 209, 210.
Hhooleh, (Lake), 361.
Hhooleh, 257, 386.
Hbubeen, 147.
Hhusân, 147.
*Hor, 301, &c.
*Hormab, 299.
Huneen, 386.
Hurbaj, 236, 247.

I.
Idsaid, 182.
Iksal, 228.
Ilmah, 183.
Ineer, 376.
Irtâhh, 127.
Izereiriyeh, 254.

J.
Ja'arah, 247.
Jadeerah, 200.
Jahhârah, 386.
Jaida, 246.
Jalood, 83.
Jâniah, 138.
Jarmuk, 117, 118, 262.
Jâwah, 17.
Jeba', 126, 219.
Jeba', (Gibeah of Saul,) 208.
Jeba', 147.
Jebel el Ghurb, 297.
Jebel Mâhas, 39.
Jebel esh Shaikh, (See Hermon.)
Jebel Sherreh, 305.
Jehâarah, 24.
Jelaad, 43, 48.
Jelboon, (Gilboa,) 96, 227.
Jelool, 17.
Jeneen, 84, 126, 226.
Jerash, 18, 48, &c.
*Jericho, (See Er-Rihha.)
*Jeshimon, 301.
Jezzeen, 357, 377.
Jifna, 88.
Jish, 114, 115, 121. 261.
Jis'r el Kâdi, 390.
Jit, 222.

464   *Index of Places.*

*Jokneam, 230.
*Joktheel, 337.
Joon, 348, 353, 373.
*Jordan, 5, 6, 77, 104, 105, 364, 380, 384.
Judaidah, 183.
Julis, 182
Jurah, 164.

K.

Kabâtieh, 219.
*Kadesh Barnea, 302.
Kadis, 107.
Kadita, 116.
Kaimoon, 230, 250.
Kala'at er Reehha, 414.
Kala'at Rubbâd, 44.
Kala'at Subeibeh, 365.
Kalinsâwa, 127.
Kalkeeleh, 127.
Kalôneh, 426.
Kanneer, 223.
Karatiya, 176.
Karaweesh, 446.
Kasimiyeh, 253.
Kassar Waijees, 33.
Kayaseer, 94.
Keelah, 152, 196.
Kelt, 3.
Kerak, 14, 18, 34.
Khalsah, 370.
Khan em Meshettah, 17.
Khan Yunas, 169, &c.
Kharâs, 151, 196.
Khash'm Usdum, 324, &c.
Khatroon 3, 202.
Khirbet el Kasees, 442.
Khirbet en Nasâra, 183.
Khirbet es Sar, 38.
Khirbet Saleekhi, 47.
Khirbet Sellim, 255.
Khuldah, (beyond Jordan,) 39.
Khuldah (on the Plain,) 157, 196.
Kifereh, 83.
Kobaibeh, 183.
Krishneh, 203.
Kubbet el Baul, 297.
Kubeibeh, 160.
Kubrus, 222.
Kuriet el 'Aneb, 179.
Kuriet es Sook, 17.
Kustul, (beyond Jordan,) 17.
Kustul, (near Jerusalem,) 426.

L.

Lahh'm, 183.
Laithma, 90.
Latroon, 427.
Lejjoon, 221, 229, 242, 250.
Lesed, 149.
Litâni, 359.

Lubbân, 90.
Lubieh, 126, 238.

M.

Ma'alool, 246.
Ma'an, 192, 301.
Main, 17.
Maisera, 44.
Ma' Kook, 206.
Ma'naeen, 195.
Manjah, 17.
Mar Saba, 418.
Marseea', 448.
Martosiyah, 183.
Mazaal, 224.
Medeba, 17.
Mejâma'a, 71, 104.
Mejdal, 163, 182.
Mejdal Yaba, 127, 128, &c.
Mekebleh, 228.
Menzel el Basha, 230.
Merash, 183.
Meroon, 117, &c.
Merj ibn Amer, 228, 249.
Merj ed Dôm, 187.
Merj Merka, 34.
Mesdar Aishah, 34.
Mesh-had, 126.
*Me-Yarkon, 158.
Mezer, 67.
Mezra'a, 19, 140.
Mezra'ah, 254.
Mobugghuk, 329.
Modzha, 224.
Mohrakah, 233, 237.
Mokatta', 233.
Mokhtârah, 407, &c.
*Molâdah, 296.
*Moreh, 90.
Mujaidel, 237, 245.
Mukhmâs, 207, 210.
Mukhneh, 90.
Munsoorah, 183.
Mushmusheh, 249.
Muzaikah, 297.
M'zeera'a, 136.

N.

Naaleea, 165.
Naamân, 239.
Na'ana, 157.
Na'oor, 18, 19.
Nabloos, 44, 90.
Nahhâleen, 147, 443, 448.
*Nazareth, 126.
Neâb, 241.
Nebn', 17.
Nebi Hhood, 56.
Nebi Moosa, 2.
Nebi Osha, 44.
Nebi Samwil, 44.

Index of Places. 465

Nebi Sari, 136.
Nebi Yunas, 290.
*Negeb, 145.
*Nimrin, 126.
Nooris, 83.
Nuba, 151, 196.

O.
Obeyah, 183.
*Olivet, 1, 16.

P.
*Paran, 212.
*Pelesheth, 144.
Petra, 311, &c.
Point Costigan, 332.
Point Molyneux, 332.

Q.
Quarantana, 202.

R.
Ra'ana, 157.
Rabbah, 34.
Raineh, 126.
Rama, 238, 272.
Ram Allah, 87, 143.
Rameen, 126.
Rami, 216.
Ramlah, 128, 197.
Ras el Ahhmar, 108, 114.
Ras el 'Ain, 131, 132.
Ras abu Ammâr, 147.
Ras Kerker, 135, 137, &c.
Rehhaniyeh, 251.
Remmoon, 203, 205, 206.
Resheef, 242.
Rubin, 158.
Rumaish, 264, 267.
Rumân, 48.
Rumâneh, 244.
Rummet er Room, 376.
Runtieh, 136.

S.
Safed, 107, 117, 262, 372.
Safoot, 47.
Sagheefah, 183.
Saida, 348, 412.
Saidoon, 197.
Salem, 90.
Salhhah, 108, 260.
Salhhi, 153.
Salim, 226.
Salt Mountain, 326.
Samakh, 76.
Samek, 17.
Samma, 71.
Samooniah, 246.
Samua', 187.
Sarheen, 254.

Sanoor, 126.
Sasa, 121.
Sattâf, 424.
Sawafeer Mesalkah, 182.
Sawafeer Odeh, 182.
Sawlyeh, 90.
*Scopus, 199.
Sebustieh, 15, 111, 215, 219.
Se'cer, 10.
Seeleh, 215, 219.
Seeleh, (on Esdraelon,' 226.
Sefooriyeh, 240.
*Seir, 305, 306.
*Selah, 337.
Selwân, 1.
Semsem, 176.
Semwân, 239.
Senâbrah, 182.
Setcher, (Setker,) 22.
Sha'afât, 86.
Shaikh Amân, 183
Shaikh el Bakkar, 63.
Shaikh Sâd, 231.
Shakrah, 257.
Sharon, 15, 127, &c.
Shefa 'Amer, (beyond Jordan,) 15.
Shefa 'Amer, (near Acre,) 240, 242, 243, 247.
Shelâleh, 238.
Shemuâta, 239.
Shemaniyeh, 183.
*Shephêlah, 145
Sheree'ah, (See Jordan.)
Shereeat el Menâdherah, 76.
Shibtain, 136.
Shukbeh, 136.
Shukeef, 254.
Shutta, 83.
Sh'waifât, 390.
Sh'weikeh, (Shocoh,) 150, 152, 196, 443.
Sibta, 193.
Sik, 313.
Sindiâneh, 247.
Sinjil, 90.
Siphla, 145.
Soba, 423, 425.
Solam, 227.
Sora'a, 156.
Santa Anna, 179, 183, 443.
Suâmeh, 224.
Subariyeh, 223.
Sufâh, 299.
Sufsâfeh, 231, 250.
Sukhneen, 241.
Sumkaniyeh, 407.

T
Ta'annuk, 221, 226.
Tahakra, 47.
*Tabor, 44, 67, 226.

2 G

Index of Places.

Taitaba, 107, 116.
Tallooz, 48.
Tantoorah, 224.
Tarsheehhah, 268.
Tayibeh, (beyond Jordan,) 68, 69.
Tayibeh, (near Jerusalem,) 205, 213.
Teereh, (on Sharon,) 136.
Teereh, (in Galilee), 266.
Teeri, 224, 238.
Tela'at ed Dum, 3.
Tell 'Arâd, 293.
Tell u'l 'Ejel, 169.
Tell el Hajjar, 204.
Tell el Kâdi, 362, 384.
Tell el Kasees, 233.
Tell es Sâfieh, 177.
Thekua', (Tekoa,) 337.
Terâbeh, 334, 422.
Thuggeret el Baider, 33.
*Thuggeret el Moghâfer, 48.
Tiberias, 78, 105.
Tibneen, 255, 264, 387.
Tibneh, 156.
Tibni, 68.
Timrah, 175.
Tool el Ker'm, 127.
Tubâs, 92.
Tuleh, 67.
Tura, 254.
Tura'âr, 126.

U.

Umm el 'Aamed, 17.
Umm Bugghek, 329.
Umm ed Damaneer, 47.
Umm el 'Egher, 47.
Umm el Fahh'm, 248, 249, 251.
Umm Kais, 62, 71, 72.
Umm el Kanâter, 77, 106.
Umm Malfoof, 33.
Umm er Rumâneh, 17.
Umm Saidet, 183.
Umm Sheggar, 17.
Umm es Swaiweeneh, 34.
Umm ez Zeenât, 251.
Ursaifah, 34.
Urtas, 435.

W.

Wadi Ahhmed, 195.
Wadi 'Arab, (or Shaikh,) 151, 196.
Wadi 'Arab, 248.
Wadi 'Aroob, 448.
Wadi Bait Hhaneena, 434.

Wadi Bedân, 91.
Wadi Berreh, 82.
Wadi Duhber, 417.
Wadi En-nab, 91.
Wadi Farah, 210.
Wadi Fara'ah, 91.
Wadi Fik'r, 301.
Wadi Fokeen, 147.
Wadi el Hharamiyeh, 94.
Wadi Hhuggereh, 325.
Wadi el Jaib, 301, 322.
Wadi el Kasab, 231.
Wadi Keereh, 232, 235.
Wadi el Kharnoob, 136.
Wadi Mel'hh, 230, 232.
Wadi Moosa, 316.
Wadi Musurr, 150.
Wadi Nemela, 318.
Wadi Netheeleh, 329.
Wadi Pharaôn, 316.
Wadi Soor, 151.
Wadi Sunt, 150, 154.
Wadi Surar, 158.
Wadi Suaineet, 207.
Wadi Tayibeh, 305.
Wadi Zahari, 72.
Weli Jedro, 247.
Weli Sardôni, 40.

Y.

Yaabad, 222.
Yabneh, 158, 159.
Yaero, 126.
Yafah, 245.
Yajoor, 245, 247, 250.
Yakook, 125.
Yarmuk, 75.
Yaroon, 260, 388.
Yehudiyeh, 257.

Z.

Zacariah, 154.
Zaid, 357, 377.
Zebdeh, 222.
Zeita, 182.
Zenâbeh, 127.
*Zephath, 299.
Zer'een, 67, 83, 226.
Zerka, 48, 49.
*Zin, 301.
Ziph, 152, 292.
Zoghal, 328.
Zubairah, 17.
Zumâreen, 223, 224.
Zuwîtah, 219.

Ballantyne Press
BALLANTYNE, HANSON AND CO.
EDINBURGH AND LONDON

www.ingramcontent.com/pod-product-compliance
Lightning Source LLC
Chambersburg PA
CBHW051857300426
44117CB00006B/429